GATHERED INTO A CHURCH

GATHERED INTO A CHURCH

INDIGENOUS-ENGLISH CONGREGATIONALISM IN WOODLAND NEW ENGLAND

Lori Rogers-Stokes

University of Massachusetts Press
AMHERST AND BOSTON

Copyright © 2025 by University of Massachusetts Press
All rights reserved

ISBN 978-1-62534-907-1 (paper); 908-8 (hardcover)

Designed by Jen Jackowitz
Set in Minion Pro
Printed and bound by Books International, Inc.

Cover design by adam b. bohannon
Cover art: detail from title page of the East Parrish Church *Precinct Records*, 1717–1801, Barnstable, Massachusetts. Courtesy of Sturgis Library Archives.

Library of Congress Cataloging-in-Publication Data

Names: Rogers-Stokes, Lori, 1965– author.
Title: Gathered into a church : Indigenous-English congregationalism in Woodland New England / Lori Rogers-Stokes.
Description: Amherst : University of Massachusetts Press, [2025] | Includes bibliographical references and index. |
Identifiers: LCCN 2025001964 (print) | LCCN 2025001965 (ebook) | ISBN 9781625349071 (paperback) | ISBN 9781625349088 (hardcover) | ISBN 9781685751883 (ebook) | ISBN 9781685751890 (epub)
Subjects: LCSH: Massachusetts Bay Company. | Congregational churches—New England—History. | Congregational churches—New England—Government. | Congregationalism. | Indians of North America—New England—Religion. | Christianity and culture—New England—History.
Classification: LCC BX7136 .R64 2025 (print) | LCC BX7136 (ebook)
LC record available at https://lccn.loc.gov/2025001964
LC ebook record available at https://lccn.loc.gov/2025001965

British Library Cataloguing-in-Publication Data
A catalog record for this book is available from the British Library.

The authorized representative in the EU
for product safety and compliance is Mare-Nostrum Group.
Email: gpsr @mare -nostrum .co .uk
Physical address: Mare-Nostrum Group B.V.,
Mauritskade 21D, 1091 GC Amsterdam, The Netherlands

For all who bring records to light

Contents

Illustrations ix

Preface xi

Acknowledgments xiii

A Note on Naming xv

INTRODUCTION
1

PART ONE
Church and Congregation in Woodland New England

CHAPTER ONE
Congregational Kinship
13

CHAPTER TWO
More
28

CHAPTER THREE
Questioning the Authenticity of Indigenous Conversion
38

PART TWO
Church Bodies at Work in Agawam/Rowley and N'ahteuk/Natick

CHAPTER FOUR
Thomas Miller's Tale
55

CHAPTER FIVE
Jacob Chalcom's Cases
76

PART THREE
Congregational Innovation on Noepe/Martha's Vineyard and in Hassanamesit/Grafton

CHAPTER SIX
"Give him a lift toward heaven"
89

CHAPTER SEVEN
The Note Writer of Hassanamesit/Grafton
99

CHAPTER EIGHT
Church Belonging and the Halfway Covenant in Hassanamesit/Grafton
105

PART FOUR
Mixed Church Bodies Sabotaged in Hassanamesit/Grafton and N'ahteuk/Natick

CHAPTER NINE
Finding Ezekiel Cole
129

CHAPTER TEN
The Note Writer of N'ahteuk/Natick
151

CHAPTER ELEVEN
Death of a Church Body
157

CONCLUSION
Haunted Houses
169

Notes 175

Index 203

Illustrations

FIGURE 1. Thomas Miller, from a letter, September 20, 1667.   67

FIGURE 2. From Thomas Miller's excommunication record, October 6, 1667.   68

FIGURE 3. From Jacob Chalcom's admonition, 1744.   83

FIGURE 4. From Jacob Chalcom's admonition, 1744.   85

FIGURE 5. Frontispiece, "Hassanamisco church book, 1731–1774."   100

FIGURE 6. Record of the Abraham family's Halfway Covenant, February 4, 1734.   111

FIGURE 7. Full communion record of George Muckamaug, January 5, 1736.   113

FIGURE 8. Full communion record of Elizabeth Abraham, July 13, 1740.   115

FIGURE 9. Solomon Prentice, note, March 28, 1746.   144

Preface

Congregationalism's close connection with the development and character of the Woodland New England colonies has been the focus of a large and long-established body of inquiry. If we include the first accounts of its practice as sent to England by Puritan practitioners and visiting detractors, Congregationalism's secondary canon is nearly as old as the denomination itself. Thomas Lechford was listing "what things I misliked in the Country" (that is, the Massachusetts Bay Colony) as early as 1641, and eight of his eleven complaints concerned the religious practice that so captured his attention. Commentators on both sides of the Atlantic and around the world have been having their say for nearly four centuries now. There is still more to be said, however, and this book offers new data and insights about the forces that shaped Congregationalism and, in turn, society in Woodland New England. In particular, it offers new ideas about the denomination's lived practice via the most important of the primary sources now available to scholars through digitization: Congregational church records.

I didn't set out to prove a preconceived theory. Instead, unbeknownst to me, I launched my work on this book eleven years ago, when I began my first transcriptions for New England's Hidden Histories (NEHH). This digital history project, which started at the Congregational Library and Archives in 2005, in partnership with the Jonathan Edwards Center at Yale University, had two purposes: to save invaluable church records from destruction and loss and to make the resource freely available via digitization and online publication. What began as a small-scale digitization project today includes 24,000 pages of records from 150 churches in Woodland New England as well as fifty collections of personal papers, generally from ministers, spanning the seventeenth through the nineteenth centuries. During the past eleven years, I have personally transcribed well over a thousand pages of church records and read at least a thousand more.

Given their sheer size and scope, Congregational church records may be our most important untapped, written, primary source from the American colonizing period. They provide detailed contemporary information about actual church practice, its depth and breadth, and its change over time. They also tell us a great deal about the tens of thousands of people who met together as congregations and churches over the course of more than two centuries, from 1630 through the mid-1800s. Tapping into this vast resource to tell a new story about Congregationalism is the focus of this book.

Of course, my study only begins to scratch the surface of what the church records have to offer, and I have by necessity limited my scope. First, to represent the depth of the archive, I have chosen to dive deeply rather than expand broadly. Thus, I concentrate on the records of three churches—in N'ahteuk/Natick, Agawam/Rowley, and Hassanamesit/Grafton—over years and decades in order to follow stories over time and offer a glimpse into the sheer scope of the records. Second, I focus on the Massachusetts Bay Colony: as the largest Puritan colony, it had the greatest number of churches with the largest number of records. Finally, I stay within the bounds of Woodland New England at the turn of the eighteenth century. Within these deliberately narrow bounds, I work to understand how Indigenous people helped to evolve Congregational practice in Woodland New England after the founding decades of the early to mid-1600s.

The church records offer a number of challenges to the existing canon, but this is not the fault of scholars, who had no way to access them until now. I see a new story emerging from this previously unavailable archive, and I'm excited to tell it. This book is just the start of a new conversation about the Puritans and their religion and about Indigenous participation in and contributions to it. I look forward to watching other scholars engage with this work, interrogating and extending it through their own exploration of the newly available archive of Congregational church records.

Acknowledgments

This work could not have been done without the support of my smart, kind, and funny family—Peter, Paul, and Juliette.

I received invaluable insights and generous help from Indigenous educators and scholars, including Rae Gould, a member of the Hassanamisco Nipmuc Band of Massachusetts as well as the executive director of Brown University's Native American and Indigenous Studies Initiative and an adjunct assistant professor of American Studies there; Cheryll Toney Holley, Sonksq of the Hassanamisco Nipmuc Band and First Nations American historian; and my friend Lance Young, EagleWolf, the chief sachem of the Nemasket Tribal Nation, Wamsley Wolf Clan, and the chair of the Nemasket Tribal Council, who read and commented on an early draft of chapter 1 and helped me sharpen my argument. He has taught me a great deal about what he would call *the Indigenous way*.

Thanks to Ross Beales Jr. for his interest in my work and the many files he shared, including curations of Ebenezer Parkman's diaries and a publication by Reverend David Hall. Our email conversations were invaluable. The enthusiastic support of Kyle Roberts, the executive director of the Congregational Library and Archives, was important and appreciated. My friend and colleague Sarah Stewart read an early chapter draft and offered constant support for this project. Finally, and as always, I thank Jeff Cooper for his mentorship, advice, tireless draft reading, and evergreen passion for this archive of church records and the transformation of our knowledge that it promises.

A Note on Naming

Colonization requires the colonized and their colonizers to live in opposing realities. A simple and pervasive example is naming. Colonizers rename most of the people, places, and things they claim as their own. The worst instance is the renaming of enslaved people, but the renaming of claimed land is also painful. When the September 6, 1639, records of the Massachusetts Bay Colony General Court reported in a single short line "Winacunnet shalbee called Hampton," another parallel universe was created in Woodland New England.[1]

The Eastern Woodlands is an English-language approximation of the Indigenous name for the southern part of the region that Puritan colonizers renamed New England and where they created the Massachusetts Bay Colony.[2] An outcome of colonization is that New England is presented as predating the arrival of the English, as having always existed as a space awaiting English people. *The Puritans set sail for New England. The Puritans landed in New England. The Puritans met the Native people living in New England*: each classic, familiar statement from our childhood history books is part of the colonizing narrative that Americans have inherited. That narrative has become so naturalized that any attempt to unmask the Eastern Woodlands universe that exists parallel to New England seems radical. Small language adjustments have an outsized impact in this situation. In the United States, the word *colonist* has long been equated to *patriot*, and our *colonial* period is often lauded as a time of heroism and independence. But when we instead describe the people of our *colonizing* period as *colonizers*, we are forced to step partway out of the familiar universe and live with one foot in the unfamiliar—one where we acknowledge colonization as the context for every part of our national story.[3]

Therefore, throughout this book I use double names for the places to which I refer, starting with Woodland New England. This is an imperfect invention of my own that's meant to illustrate the fact that while the colonization that created New England can't be undone, the reality that is the Eastern Woodlands has not been and will not be undone either. This includes double names for Indigenous places in which English towns were founded. The people I study in this book lived at the turn of the eighteenth century, when colonizers often relied on the original place names maintained by Indigenous people: Grafton, alias Hassanamesit; Natick, alias N'ahteuk; Boston, alias Shawmut. Restoring the name of a place shifts us into both worlds again while acknowledging that we can't go back in time. I use double names for towns where Indigenous villages were located, such as Hassanamesit/Grafton; and where there was no Indigenous village, I use broader regional names, such as Agawam/Rowley, which is better, I think, than trying to force all Indigenous places to become towns. In this small way I hope to contribute to long-established efforts to reverse, in Jean O'Brien's words, the "privileging of non-Indian stories to inscribe on the land" and the "claiming of Indian landscapes" by colonization.[4]

COMMON ABBREVIATIONS USED IN THE MANUSCRIPT RECORDS

C^{hh} = church

Ch^t = Christ

w^{ch} = which

w^n = when

w^r = where

w^t = what

w^{th} = with

y^r = your

y^s = this

y^t = that

y^y = they

X^t = Christ

X^{tian} = Christian

Introduction

> We have to be very careful when there's a silence in the records in assuming that something *didn't* happen.
>
> —Francis J. Bremer (2023)

Congregationalism was born in Woodland New England in the seventeenth century: conceived by the English colonizers known as Puritans, introduced to the Indigenous people of the region, and evolved by the churches and congregations they created, separately and together, ever since.[1] Congregational church records offer scholars new insights into the impact of sincere Indigenous believers on the development of this important denomination. In this book, I tell that story by examining the development and evolution of two of the foundational experiences of Congregationalism: finding assurance of sanctification (salvation) and gaining church membership through the Halfway Covenant. I concentrate on the decades at the turn of the eighteenth century, a period bookended by King Philip's War and the First Great Awakening; and, as I noted in the preface, my geographical focus is the Massachusetts Bay Colony.

Congregationalism as developed in Woodland New England in the seventeenth and eighteenth centuries was unique. It was defined by its origin and long practice in the region, and it was a crucial identity for Indigenous and English people alike for more than two centuries. As I'll demonstrate through excerpts from church records, its concept of the church body and church kinship was unparalleled in other Christian denominations.

What do I mean by *church records*? As the name indicates, Congregationalism was based on the primacy and autonomy of the individual congregation. There was no church hierarchy established by and living within the civil government—no archbishops, bishops, vicars, or rectors. There was no head of the church because there was no such thing as *the church* in the sense of an organization made up of hundreds or thousands of individual parishes governed by bishops, who reported to archbishops, who conferred with the monarch and carried out those orders. Congregationalism located all decision making within each individual group of believers, or congregation. No outside authority dictated their actions or made policy for them, and individual congregations were not incorporated into or governed by any larger organization or institution.

With responsibility for their own actions came the need to maintain a true record of those actions. Every congregation kept a record book, and that book was physically large because it was spiritually crucial, recording all decisions, deliberations, votes, discussions, debates, ordinations, births, admissions, dismissions, and deaths, as well as important correspondence. For Congregationalists, a church was a living body of believers, and they came to consider the record book that documented the life of that body as a living testament before God, a witness of God's work for both the church in that moment and in its later (re)generations. In Naumkeag/Stoneham, the record-book entry for October 23, 1794, states that "it was desired, by a number of the brethren, that other writings which have passed between the parties relative to the unhappy circumstances which have of late taken place in this Town between minister and people, may be recorded in the Church Book, as tending more fully to display the true state of the case, to any who may read the records of the C^{hh} for satisfaction."[2] In Pocumtuc/Granville, the church returned to an older record book in November 1769 to find information about an ongoing discipline case involving Luke Hitchcock: "The Church did then Search to See if there was ~~not any~~ any thing omitted or as yet unsettled in that old affair & they found by record that about three Years after that old Judgment ~~did~~ Deacon Hitchcock did own in a way of Discores that that Paper was transcribed."[3] In this case, the record they found was from 1762. But if it were physically large enough, a church record book might contain entries covering well over a century, with overlapping notations written by generations of ministers and lay church-meeting moderators.[4] Church actions from 1660 could be consulted in 1830 to help the church in its nineteenth-century embodiment remember what it had done in its seventeenth-century incarnation. Nor were the entries always in strict time order. Like many colonizing-era church record books, the Naumkeag/Danvers volume begins chronologically but then, after page 250, jumps back and forth in time as writers made successive fresh starts to record baptisms and other records. The effect is startling to the modern reader, as baptisms from 1773 to 1815 are immediately followed by baptisms beginning in 1755. After demographic records that reach into the nineteenth century, narratives of church and town meetings begin on page 273 with an entry from March 1672. This to-and-fro character was noted by an anonymous person in 1842, who wrote in the back of the book, "Now this old Book is out of Date & 'tis fill up at a quear rate."[5] But a church record book was never really outdated or obsolete, aged as its entries might be, just as the church body it represented was one eternal body of believers across time.

Congregationalism is not as well understood today as it might be, in part because many of the church record books that every congregation depended on to represent its eternal life, its actions, its people, and its way, have been lost. This sometimes happened through carelessness: as people's understanding of their importance faded, the books might be loaded into cardboard boxes and stacked on wet basement floors or stored behind Christmas ornaments in church closets. Loss might also be the result of reverent but misplaced attempts to preserve church history, when record books were hidden in safes whose combinations were subsequently forgotten or stored in ministers' homes and then accidentally auctioned off as part of their posthumous estates. In Whipsuppenicke/Marlboro in 1744, a church body's divisive breakup included the issue of which side would get to keep the church record books, which the minister, Peter Thacher, then deceased, had apparently included in his will as part of his personal estate. Outraged, the church body ensured that Peter's son "Thacher Jr and some deacons . . . [would commit] the church records to the new pastor, S. Conant."[6] An aged church officer in N'ahteuk/Natick recorded a cloak-and-dagger mission in 1885 to recover the church's colonizing-era records, written by the minister Oliver Peabody. An unidentified man had sent the officer a letter saying that "he knew where the Peabody Records were, & that he could procure them, if any one would pay his fare, giving me to under stand it was somewhere in the Cape, & the cash would be about five dollars." Luckily, this risky venture paid off in the return of the book, which I will cite later in this history.[7] Records were also frequently lost in one of the many catastrophic fires that destroyed wooden meetinghouses in Woodland New England and continue to pose a threat to those still standing.

The disappearance of Congregational church records from the historical archive has been devastating to our understanding of Woodland New England in the seventeenth and eighteenth centuries. We know this because those that are available have made a massive contribution to demographic records. Ministers were much more careful and accurate about recording the names in birth, marriage, and death records than town clerks were. In fact, for many decades, town clerks relied on ministers to record demographics for them, and in the church books ministers often noted that they had sent those lists to the town clerk to be recorded. Church records also carefully tracked which families had moved to other towns and often described the reasons for moving. But in their descriptions of church meetings, the books reveal, as no other source can, the unique conundrum that the English Puritans created in their colonies: a civil system that was incompatible with the Congregational ideal and reality they had worked so hard to create. On the surface, this disconnect is invisible, cloaked by Congregationalism's successes. The denomination's discipline developed in record time, with the first churches evolving practices in the 1630s and codifying them in the 1648 Cambridge Platform. The strength and reach of Congregationalism in Puritan colonies was foundational: the Puritans themselves defined their colonies as godly, while visitors and onlookers commented on the unusual importance, sincerity, and visibility of religion in the region. Every town had a meetinghouse, a minister, and a congregation. Congregationalism was supported by universal taxation and established as the state religion of the Massachusetts Bay Colony, and it dominated the mental and physical landscape of Woodland New England for more than two centuries, from the Shawmut landing to Transcendentalism.

All the same, it was incompatible with Puritan civil society, and this becomes visible in yet another set of double names: church/congregation and church/town. As I will show, every inhabitant of an English town was expected to attend worship services in the meetinghouse as part of the congregation of townspeople. But only those who could describe their experience of what modern Protestants would call salvation could be gathered into a church, a unique body called into being only by God. When Congregationalists used the word *church*, they referred to a body of people within a congregation who joined together to worship and were transformed by God when they met into one being. Over the course of this book, I will explain how different a church body was from a mere congregation, the similarities between the church body and Indigenous social organization, and how wildly incompatible the workings of church discipline were with the workings of English civil courts. In the church body, people relied on patient, long-term, multiparty mediation to come to full understanding of a problem and a satisfying, lasting resolution based on the restoration of all parties to mutual love and sympathy and healthy reunion. In the civil courts, however, the same people relied on rapid decisions made unilaterally by an unrelated authority figure who provided short-term resolutions that left one and sometimes both parties unsatisfied, nearly guaranteeing that they would return to the courtroom to argue the same case again, a zero-sum game played by individuals whose only goal was their own advancement.

Church records reveal how flexible and experimental Congregationalism was. For centuries in Woodland New England, it was an evolving, lived experience that mattered deeply to many generations of Indigenous, Black, and English people, a communally agreed-upon framework open to amendments, remarkably successful at making a spiritual ideal viable for real people living in the real world. Its records are a revelation of its co-created nature. Yet given the unavailability of these records for so many centuries, scholars have traditionally come to the reasonable conclusion that Congregationalism was 100 percent English and completely forced upon unwilling Indigenous and Black people. Now that so many church records are publicly available, it's time to deepen and extend their work and to come to a new understanding of Congregationalism's mixed nature.

A number of scholars are already engaged in this task. Richard Boles, for instance, has scoured church records in the late colonial period and beyond to document the reality of Black and Indigenous participation in and affiliation with congregations in Woodland New England. He writes, "Most Americans today usually think of northern colonial churches as being entirely 'white' institutions, but black and Indian peoples regularly affiliated with these churches. . . . [Scholarly] neglect [of church records] obscures the history of interracial churches where northerners typically worshipped in interracial but not integrated congregations from the 1730s to the 1820s." He argues that "most people experienced religion in interracial congregations" in Woodland New England and that "dynamic interracial interactions in northern churches were more common and persisted longer than has generally been acknowledged."[8] As I will demonstrate, such experiences within Congregationalism did not begin in the late colonial period but stretch back to the turn of the eighteenth century.⁹

As we uncover the participation of marginalized members of society in Congregationalism, we need to redefine *participation* itself. According to Francis Bremer, who has studied the deeply buried role of women as co-creators of Puritanism, women took part in the creation of Congregationalism—"[they took] part, as in *participants*." Like Boles, Bremer is not so much focused on discovering new Puritan primary sources but in reading old ones—in his case, breaking with centuries of scholarly tradition by including accounts in which women participated and voted in church meetings, spoke during worship services, and taught men. In this book, I do the same for Indigenous people's contributions to Congregationalism.

Reseeing existing primary sources is also key to Marie Balsley Taylor's *Indigenous Kinship, Colonial Texts, and the Contested Space of Early New England*, a powerful rereading of standard English colonizing texts that reveals the ways in which Indigenous contacts, conversations, and relationships shaped those documents. Margaret Newell's *Brethren by Nature: New England Indians, Colonists, and the Origins of American Slavery* describes Christianity as presented to Indigenous people in Woodland New England as "an ultimate form of colonization" but goes on to say that, "by participating in this society, Indians also recast it in ways that its English leaders did not always appreciate or intend. Together, English and Indians created a hybrid society in which Indian actions and goals sometimes determined the outcome."¹⁰ Again, these scholars are rethinking the word *participation*, which has become synonymous with minimal involvement or effort, in order to restore its power in the context of participating in a Congregational church body.

◇◇◇◇

In part 1 of this book, I define the Congregational church body in Woodland New England, shining a new light on a unique and powerful concept that was unparalleled in contemporaneous Protestantism and remains unmatched today. The church body stood in opposition to the political body of secular society, offering a divergent form of justice and government based on spiritual kinship and true resolution of disputes through loving kindness. It operated alongside secular civil forms in painful parallel until it was sidelined by colonizing's overpowering need for swift, surface-level law and order. As I will show, the Congregational church body that the English created had surprising commonalities with principles common to the Indigenous society of the Eastern Woodlands, and the colonizing forces that overcame them represent a lost opportunity that we live with to this day. This section also addresses the scholarly debate over Indigenous conversion and Christian faith or practice. Given the rapacity of English colonization in their homeland, how could any Indigenous person in Woodland New England willingly and *sincerely* convert to the colonizers' religion? Arguments that Indigenous Christianity was always a survivance measure or a misunderstood creole practice have been well established in the scholarly canon. For instance, Linford Fisher comments on "the perceived illegitimacy of the religious hybridization that resulted from the evangelical attempts" and the need for scholars to "redirect the focus away from normative measurement—away from quests to find out if the Indians were 'bona fide' Christians or not."[11] In fact, I believe it is important to reexamine both Indigenous and English Christian practice. Each side had a majority who clung to pagan folk beliefs, mixing them into Christian doctrine or honoring them in parallel with Christianity. Each side had innovators whose lived practice of Congregationalism advanced and evolved that discipline. We can never look into the souls of Indigenous Congregationalists at the turn of the eighteenth century. But by looking at their practices and reading the accounts they left, usually in English translation, of their spirituality and spiritual experiences, we can honor them and also resist the urge to overwrite their words with our own assertions about what was possible and real.

In part 2, I consider the difference between the established Congregational way that so many English and Indigenous people supported and the secular justice system they lived under. I do this by exploring adultery cases in the church bodies at Agawam/Rowley and N'ahteuk/Natick. First, I tell the story of Thomas Miller, an English Congregationalist from Agawam/Rowley, which illustrates the shocking difference between the resolution offered by the civil courts and the one made possible by a healthy church body. Then I turn to the story of Jacob Chalcom, an Indigenous Congregationalist of N'ahteuk/Natick, which took place seventy years later and illustrates how this Congregational ideal was still being practiced in a mixed church body.

In part 3, I focus on Indigenous contributions to Congregational evolution as made possible by generational religious belonging. I begin by considering Wampanoag Congregationalists on Noepe/Martha's Vineyard, whose practices, as documented in the missionary Experience Mayhew's 1727 report, *Indian Converts*, give us a glimpse into the evolution of the concept of assurance. While English Congregationalists relied on the mutual support and encouragement of friends and family to sustain them through the rigors of spiritual preparation, the moment of assurance of salvation they sought was something no one else could play any role in bringing about. English believers often testified to their reluctance to accept the positive judgments of their loved ones as hopeful proof of their own assurance. At first, Wampanoag converts adopted the English concept of an intensely solitary, internal, and private moment of realizing God's grace, or salvation, a moment that one would then struggle to express to others. But over generations of their own practice, they redefined assurance as social and kinship-based. They understood the support and encouragement of their loved ones as representing assurance: that is, human kinship on Earth mirrored and anticipated divine kinship in Heaven. This new understanding actually hewed closer to the Puritan requirement that no "human invention" be used in Congregationalism, and every part of its practice be derived from the Bible or the apostolic church, for English-style assurance was a very human invention found in neither source. Wampanoag assurance recovered the apostolic spirit of finding hope in the fellowship of believers and refocused church gathering on shared belief and spiritual kinship rather than individual proof of grace.

Later in the section we'll turn to the records of the second church gathered in Hassanamesit/Grafton, which will widen our conception of the forces that drove the adoption of the Halfway Covenant. This concept, introduced in 1662, allowed people who had not found assurance of salvation and thus could not become church members to participate in one and sometimes both of the only two sacraments that Congregationalists observed: baptism and communion. Thus, children who had been baptized by their full-member parents but had not found assurance by the time they had children of their own were able to baptize them. In addition, adults with no past connection to a church could also "own the covenant" and join a congregation. Scholars have already documented the long process that congregations and church bodies across Woodland New England went through in choosing or refusing to adopt the Halfway Covenant, but always through an English-only lens. Yet reading the church records shows how crucial it was for Indigenous people whose previous church bodies had been dismembered by King Philip's War. The people of Hassanamesit, for instance, had a Congregational heritage, as it had been a "praying town," but the devastating losses they suffered in the war meant they were unable to regather as a church and baptize their children after their place was redefined as an English town. In 1732, new English residents gathered their own church without any Nipmuc members, attempting to erase the history of Nipmuc Congregationalism in the new town they called Grafton. The Halfway Covenant allowed Nipmuc believers to join the new church without any existing connection, and this agency removed a potentially insurmountable barrier against reclaiming Indigenous church belonging.

This dual use of the Halfway Covenant helped to cement the practice in Hassanamesit/Grafton. The church records there contain no protests or skepticism from English members about Nipmuc halfway membership. In fact, many entries record that both Indigenous and English people owned the covenant at the same time. I suggest that English worshippers did not push back on Indigenous use of the Halfway Covenant because it helped to reinforce their own English use: that is, if completely unaffiliated Indigenous people could own the covenant and join Congregational churches, then certainly unaffiliated English people could do the same. In other words, Indigenous use of the Halfway Covenant helped establish it as a norm for English people. This was existentially important to Congregationalism at the turn of the eighteenth century, when a triple threat—increased non-Congregational immigrants after the loss of the Massachusetts Bay Charter in 1684, the imposition of the Dominion of New England in 1686–89, and the powerful separatist lure of the First Great Awakening in the 1730s and 1740s—rose up one after the other to threaten Congregational dominance and relevance. The Halfway Covenant gathered in outsiders from all populations, allowing near and far transfer of congregational belonging and church membership.

Finally, in part 4, we'll look at two very different examples of ministerial leadership in interracial congregations. First, the Hassanamesit/Grafton church records reveal how Reverend Solomon Prentice drove the church body almost to extinction by perverting its principles. A young Nipmuc church member named Ezekiel Cole played an important role in that crisis, which has never been described before. Thanks to newly available church records for Hassanamesit/Grafton, I can tell his story now. Then, in N'ahteuk/Natick, Reverend Oliver Peabody's commitment to the ideal of a mixed church body maintained by equal Indigenous and English collaboration was deliberately undermined by the English men who controlled his salary, leaving the church prey to secular forces of colonization and driving out both Indigenous members and those English members who protested.

Before proceeding, I must offer one caveat: record books from Indigenous Congregational churches, kept by Indigenous ministers in their own languages, are not currently included in the primary canon of transcribed church records. While the church records for mixed congregations give us insights into Indigenous practice, without the record books of Indigenous churches we can never know the whole story. Records kept by Wampanoag ministers on Noepe/Martha's Vineyard and by Nipmuc ministers in Hassanamesit/Grafton and N'ahteuk/Natick before King Philip's War would shed brilliant light on Congregationalism in Woodland New England during this period. Without them, for now, the record is still partial, even fractional, and forces me to extrapolate some meaning from English records. But I take heart from Marie Balsley Taylor's powerful readings of English colonizing documents that describe them as "co-authored" by Indigenous people: "the vision of leaders like Thomas Shepard, John Eliot, and John Winthrop Jr. was not as fixed as it often appears but was rather depending on the participation and ideas of its Indigenous participants."[12]

Congregationalism is fascinating. It successfully brought an untried, very ambitious religious ideal into real-world practice when that real world was, for both the colonizing Puritans and the Indigenous people who suffered colonization, unknown and dangerous and should have ruled out any spiritual experimentation. As this book will show, Congregationalism was an Indigenous-English collaboration, and the hobbling of the Congregational ideal was a tragic lost opportunity for the English to escape the mania of colonization, allow personal points of contact, develop reciprocal relationships between themselves and Indigenous people, and join those people in honoring the obligations of kinship, not only with each other but with the land, water, and living creatures of the Eastern Woodlands. Their complete failure to do any of this makes it seem as if such an opportunity could never have existed. Only by reading the church records can we see that the Congregational ideal, with its kinship and its obligations to building relationships, not fortunes, actually created positive outcomes that contrasted sharply with secular civil outcomes. As Taylor reminds us, church records are "unexpected archives [that] have been underutilized and unappreciated," remaining mostly unknown until the age of digitization.[13] They show us that a different path did exist. People traveled on it. The opportunity was there. We can learn something from the story of how that opportunity was lost, and perhaps our knowledge can move the needle even a fraction against the problems we are reaping now.

PART ONE

Church and Congregation in Woodland New England

CHAPTER ONE

Congregational Kinship

THE CHURCH BODY

> The records of the early New England churches . . . afford abundant evidence of the fidelity, at least, with which church "discipline" was enforced. Such contents on these records are fitly left where they are, perhaps in the interests of historical fidelity claiming a right to be preserved in manuscript, but with no warrant to be reproduced in print.
> —George E. Ellis (1881)

At the turn of the eighteenth century, every town in Woodland New England had one or more buildings that functioned, at least part time, as a meetinghouse, and each meetinghouse contained two entities: the congregation and the church.[1] My focus is on the church, or church body, a revolutionary spiritual entity created by Congregationalists—Indigenous, Black, and English.

A congregation was made up of everyone in the town. Attending Sunday worship was a civil mandate well into the eighteenth century in the Massachusetts Bay Colony, and in general most people freely chose to attend worship services as part of the congregation. A church, on the other hand, was made up only of those people within the congregation who possessed what the Congregationalists called *assurance*—what modern Protestant Christianity calls salvation. Congregationalists believed in predestination, which taught that eons before God created the Earth, he knew every human being who would ever live and decided whether or not to extend his redemption through loving kindness to each of them. Those whom God chose for salvation, or *grace*, as the Puritans would have expressed it, were the elect. Every person's fate, in heaven or hell, was decided before people were created, and no human action could ever alter that fate.

When Jesus accepted God's will and let himself be crucified, however (as Congregationalists believed he did), he took every condemned human's place, thus overcoming death itself. Because Jesus paid the price that humans were supposed to pay, he could consider a condemned person's sins as having been washed away by his own crucifixion, and he could choose to grant that person salvation out of his own loving kindness. The modern Christian idea that Jesus' death makes salvation available to any person who asks him to be their personal savior was not part of Congregationalism in the seventeenth and eighteenth centuries. Congregationalists believed so deeply in the election of the few that they crafted a complex piece of dogma to support it: while Jesus had died for all of humankind and therefore his death was "*sufficient* for all" to be saved, it was in fact *applied* to only a few—people who were predestined for hell whose fate he had reversed through his incomprehensible will.[2]

Given the question marks hanging over every person—were they elect? had they been granted saving grace?—Congregationalists' first duty and desire on reaching adulthood was to discover their own spiritual estate. This took place in a lengthy process the Puritans called spiritual preparation, and its means were, first and foremost, private Bible reading and then private prayer, listening to the sermons of a godly minister, and talking with other spiritual seekers. Such actions did not earn someone grace but prepared them to discover and understand what their fate was, and the process was idiosyncratic to each individual seeker. A Bible verse, read many times over the years, might suddenly send the message of assurance. During private prayer or meditation on a sermon, a person might suddenly feel an undeniable conviction of assurance. In other words, the process of spiritual preparation was not clear-cut, but the experience of true assurance was: a sudden, overwhelming, indescribably powerful moment of complete transport into joy that made people shriek, run, jump, and cry.[3]

Because the church was made up of people within a congregation who possessed assurance, the Congregationalists never referred to a church as being founded or established by an individual or a group. A town could be founded and built by people, and it could have a building that served as a meetinghouse that held a congregation, but this did not guarantee that a town had a church. Only God could gather a church out of that congregation.

People who experienced assurance shared verbal *relations* of that experience with the church, narrating the story of their preparation and their recognition of grace. A relation was a foundational moment in which a new person was joined to the church body and the integrity of that body was reaffirmed by its ability to assess the relation.[4] This reciprocity was crucial: in Congregationalism, only the church body united as one being could prove the integrity of an individual by allowing them to join the body, and only this addition of new members, new limbs, could prove the integrity and vitality of the body. In other words, a person's ability to join the church proved the person's integrity, and a church's ability to admit a new member proved the church's integrity. This reciprocal relationship is often lost on people who read about Congregationalism because, on the surface, people who were already members of the church appear to have gathered to sit in imperious judgment on individuals who were giving relations. The benefit seems to be one-sided, with the church conferring the benefit of full membership on select individuals who were declared worthy to join. But, in reality, when the church admitted an individual, this confirmed the worthiness of both the individual and the church. Only an authentic church body made up of people with assurance could accurately perceive the authenticity of a relation of faith and welcome new members, who, as the minister Ralph Partridge at Mattakeesett/Duxbury asserted, "giveth beinge to a particular visible church. . . . [T]he church covenant is that wch passeth, between the people of god amonge them selves, or one with an othere."[5]

To define a church as a body of people rather than a building was uniquely Congregational. People in Jesus' time had gathered in houses or open fields and squares to hear him preach wherever he went, so any place in which he stopped to speak became an impromptu, temporary, de facto place of worship. When he left a place, it reverted to its normal function. This was how Congregationalism was structured in Woodland New England. As Jesus would no longer appear on Earth, the united body of members, joined together to worship, became a church. The Congregational system was the reverse of the one we are more familiar with, in which places of worship are themselves sacred ground and people change upon entering them. For the Congregationalists, the gathering of people as a church was itself sacred and could happen anywhere; their presence did nothing to make the physical place where they gathered sacred. Thus, in the earliest years of a Woodland New England town, there was usually no dedicated meetinghouse: the church and the congregation met in whatever building was large enough to hold them, likely one that also served as town hall and commercial center. Once towns grew and their economy and politics became dominant, dedicated meetinghouses were built to physically separate religion from commerce and government and allow the town hall and merchants' offices to be furnished as places of individual business.

A healthy Congregational church body was made up of individual limbs with agency to act, think, and speak independently; but when they were gathered together to worship, they became one body, undifferentiated in the eyes of God. Each church was aware that it had to remain united as one body, authentic in its worship and the sacraments, or it would blaspheme God and come apart, sicken, and die. Therefore, the practice of the Congregational ideal meant constant, in-depth, personal attention to the spiritual, emotional, and mental state of every limb of the church body.

When a member displayed unusual or troubling behavior or made alarming statements, Congregational discipline outlined a series of steps for healing that individual. First, someone who knew the person well would speak with them privately to find out what was wrong. If this had no good effect, that friend would tell one or two church members—including elders—about the situation and invite them to speak with the troubled limb in private. The friend might attend this meeting as well. If one or two such meetings failed to uncover the problem or outline a way to work toward a solution, the elders and the friend would go to the minister, who would either join the friend and the elders in meeting with the person or meet with the person alone, depending on the recommendation of the friend and the elders. If this failed, then the male members of the church body would be called to meet, and the problem would be made public to them for the first time. The individual would be told beforehand about this church meeting and would be required to join it to speak for themselves. The participants would go through as many meetings as necessary to resolve the problem, with male and female witnesses being called as needed. With this system most problems could be worked out over the course of a few weeks. As we will see in the case of Agawam/Rowley, however, very angry, hurt, or dissatisfied church members sometimes involved the church in high-stakes, emotionally demanding meetings for years, even decades, before their issue could be resolved.

This Congregational kinship, as I call it, placed human relationships above all else and was deeply invested in maintaining them because they conferred identity. No matter how complex and exhausting the process might be—to fully realize a problem, hear all sides, and bring erring parties to repentance—healing the broken limb and restoring it to the church body were necessary steps to restoring the health of the body as a whole. Therefore, when the Congregational ideal was followed, this lengthy practice of maintaining kinship was observed. The pattern might be described as *rebuke-repent-restore*. The wayward individual had to be rebuked for their harmful actions in order to bring them to authentic repentance so that they—and the church—could be restored as a unified body.

There is a common perception of the Woodland New England Puritans as vindictive people obsessed with accusing others of sin and then excommunicating them. This was not the case. It was the exception that proved the rule when a Congregational church, acting on its ideal of kinship, could not complete the process of rebuke-repent-restore and heal itself. Even individuals who had profoundly and deliberately antagonized the church for years were often brought to real repentance and sincerely welcomed back into the church body. As the historian James Cooper points out, church records show that "even scandalous offenders were treated with concern and compassion."[6] Again, the reciprocity of this kinship is key: restoration was critically necessary for both the individual and the church body. An individual left outside their church was doomed, and a church with a diseased member was doomed. Excommunicating someone meant amputating a limb, which would leave the body permanently maimed. Therefore, excommunication for Congregationalists was a strategically employed, short-term, intensive form of rebuke designed to force someone to take repentance seriously so they could be restored. It was neither the first strike nor the triumphant final punishment that it is so often perceived to be.

What makes the process of rebuke-repent-restore especially fascinating is that it operated alongside the region's completely different English civil justice system. As I will detail in part 2, a crime tried in a civil court with the aim of closing the case as efficiently as possible could be retried within a church with a very different aim. The lengthy process of achieving the real restoration of all injured parties—identifying them, listening to them, working with them—was vital to the integrity of the church. This was the system that the Puritan leader John Winthrop championed in 1639 when he opposed the motion to create a code of civil law. He argued that simply consulting a civil law code to identify a crime and its punishment and move on as quickly as possible was the antithesis of restorative justice and the infant Congregational way: the laws that would be "fittest for us should arise *pro re nata*, upon occasions." That is, he believed a natural resolution would appear for each court case based on the unique situation and people it involved. Winthrop wanted the courts to continue using the same process as the churches, taking as much time as necessary to hear, honor, satisfy, and reconcile all parties through as many rounds of questioning, conversation, and counseling as necessary.[7] He was overruled, however, and courts began to operate according to a legal code that stood in fundamental opposition to the Congregational way.[8] As the historian David Hall states:

> Where change was also manifest was in social ethics and enforcement of the rules of Christian community. The burden of punishing premarital sex and the abuse of alcohol [eventually] passed from the churches to the magistrates and juries of the county courts. By the beginning of the eighteenth century, these courts were ceasing to require young men convicted of illicit sex to make a public confession. Instead, the courts used a simpler and, in some sense, secular system of fines.[9]

The kinship of "covenantal ideals" was under attack from the start of colonization in Woodland New England, but it did not completely disappear, even as the "privatization" of religion "diminished [the] relevance of corporate ties" within Congregationalism.[10] Church covenant and belonging could and did continue to work alongside the civil justice system.

CONGREGATIONAL CONNECTIONS WITH INDIGENOUS PRINCIPLES

In my work with the newly available Congregational church records, I did not immediately recognize a resemblance between the forms of English spiritual kinship that developed on the Indigenous land that the Puritans were colonizing with the forms of governance and kinship inherent to the Indigenous societies that were already inhabiting that land. Only while reading Lisa Brooks's descriptions of the role of the saunkskwa and sachem in *Our Beloved Kin: A New History of King Philip's War* did I begin to identify similarities between the roles of these leaders and the role of the Congregational minister. The conclusion I reached—that the Congregational ideal had much in common with Indigenous principles—seemed far-fetched at first, and even now I am sharply aware of and deeply cautious about two points.

First, there is no evidence that the English Congregationalists themselves identified, welcomed, or honored these similarities in any way. Congregationalism was originally created by the Puritans out of their own European and English experience as Christians and Protestants, with reference only to the Christian Bible and the writings of European Christians. Like Marie Balsley Taylor, "I am not aiming to portray a more sympathetic colonist."[11] Though Congregationalism was created in Woodland New England, its English founders neither consciously nor unconsciously adopted Indigenous social practice. Congregationalists wanted to create a world that was the opposite of the civil society in which they lived, and any resemblances to Indigenous practice were coincidental. Because Indigenous society was the opposite of English civil society, there are unplanned similarities between the Congregational way and Indigenous governance.

Second, Congregational practice did not make English people more like Indigenous people or more sympathetic to them. This statement is amply borne out by the history of English oppression of Indigenous people, often in the name of acquiring personal wealth. By privileging economic gain, English colonizers forfeited any ability to share an identity with Indigenous people; indeed, it often prevented them from sharing a unified identity with one another. As English colonization became entrenched in Woodland New England, it was quickly dominated by goals and practices that had no connection to Congregationalism.

This is the context in which I am examining the coincidental alignments of Congregationalism and Indigenous practice. Similarities are not choices. But they do matter, and noting them can help us, as Brooks writes, to "see a world we all inhabit with greater insight and clarity."[12] For instance, they can help us to understand some of the appeal that Congregationalism held for certain Indigenous people, particularly in the form of the church body, in which individuals were gathered into what the historian Daniel Mandell calls a "common character, . . . identity, . . . [social] intercourse, fellowship, and communion," a form that resonated with Indigenous society.[13] And it can make us painfully aware of a lost opportunity for connection with Indigenous people and for a possible moderation of European colonization in Woodland New England and beyond. Understanding the similarities helps us to see Congregationalism and the English and Indigenous people who practiced it in a new light and to make sense of both Indigenous adoption and advancement of Congregationalism and the failure of Congregational kinship to prevail against the cutthroat individualism on which colonization relies. In turn, such recognitions can help us make sense of our own world, in which cutthroat individualism has become even more pronounced in the nations that once sent their colonizers into the world and in the nations that those colonizers founded.

Let's start with the concept of belonging. As Brooks writes, in the Indigenous world of the Eastern Woodlands (as well as in the northern Dawnland), "one could not inhabit a place without belonging to a particular family, [and] this belonging could be cultivated."[14] This has some correlation to early seventeenth-century English colonizing in Woodland New England, where civil law forbade any individual to live alone.[15] Everyone had to be part of a family, whether by blood or cohabitation. But Congregational kinship was much more aligned with the Indigenous concept of belonging. Newcomers to a town were welcomed into the congregation, with the understanding that this adoption would bestow kinship obligations on both the newcomer and the congregation. Over years spent worshipping and living side by side, pitching in to support the minister and sharing each other's joys and concerns, once-strange individuals might be gathered into the church body. This intensified the reciprocity, validating both the new member and the existing body, with each conferring authenticity on the other.

In Indigenous society, Brooks writes, "every pronouncement of kinship invokes a bond."[16] In Congregationalism, church members who called each other sister and brother were acknowledging a bond that might include blood but went far beyond it; this was a spiritual bond that conferred the responsibility of keeping "mutual watch" over each other, and it committed church kin to playing active and constructive roles in each other's struggles and triumphs.[17] Belonging within Congregationalism required reciprocity in ways that paralleled Indigenous practice. No action taken by a church member was considered to affect only themselves or the other individuals who were immediately involved. Every action of every member influenced the whole, and the actions of the whole influenced each member. When this system was fully operational, as we'll see when I discuss cases from Agawam/Rowley and N'ahteuk/Natick, it was able to bring about great restoration for both individuals and church bodies.

Churches in different towns might also have kinship, operating as sister churches with obligations to support each other and maintain each other's well-being. The ecclesiastical council was a Congregational mechanism that allowed a church body that was struggling in vain with an internal crisis to invite delegates from sister churches to hear all sides of the argument and offer advice. The advice was nonbinding, and the church in question was free to act on it or not, as I will show later in the case of the church body at Hassanamesit/Grafton. But councils were generally successful in either resolving the issue via advice or driving the struggling church to try again to resolve it alone. Maintaining relationships from the ground up rather than from the top down, within and between groups of people, was key to both Indigenous and Congregational practice, though Congregationalism constrained this in a way that was non-Indigenous.

Orality was another Congregational concept that may have appealed to Indigenous people. Spontaneous, long-form prayer was central to Congregational practice. The Puritans fundamentally rejected the Catholic practice of reciting set prayers. Instead, they emphasized prayer as means for receiving information and opening their souls and minds to spiritual insight. As the historian Linford Fisher notes, this "praying as practice" seemed to speak to Indigenous converts, who were already accustomed to speaking and listening as a means of accessing the spiritual world.[18] Ministers who read from a sheaf of papers to deliver their sermons were considered subpar. Ideally, they would speak from notes, offering extemporaneous digressions based on spiritual inspiration in the moment. Along with regularly scheduled gatherings such as Sunday worship service, a Thursday lecture, and church meetings, Congregationalists expected to take part in many long informal gatherings where they could listen to people describe their seeking, hear laypeople exhort or prophesy, consider difficult questions, offer each other support, weep together over each other's troubles, and rejoice together when troubles were resolved. Joining with sisters and brothers, speaking and listening for however long was required to reach happy consensus or at least provide comfort to a suffering group or individual: these oral practices were intrinsic to Congregationalism in Woodland New England.

The first descriptions of Indigenous people interacting with John Eliot's 1646 mission in N'ahteuk show that they instantly understood and appreciated this aspect of Congregationalism. The Massachusetts who gathered to hear Eliot preach willingly listened to him and then sat in conversation with him for hours afterward. While the historian Craig White notes that "the Indians' attentiveness may [have] owe[d] more to custom than assent.... The

Massachusetts may [have] fatigue[d] their guests by design," he does emphasize the length of their engagement, writing that the "'ritualized exchange' continue[d] with the missionaries asking questions of the Indians, until 'after three hours time we asked if they were not weary, and they answered, No.'" White concludes, "Rather than rejecting that which was unknown, [the Massachusetts] welcomed it and sought to come to terms with it."[19] Eliot's records of his famously long Q&A sessions with the Massachusetts are evidence of a shared appreciation for extended, personal, extemporaneous sessions of counsel. White points out that the questions originally posed by the Massachusetts were not just the long lists of random questions that were later compiled for written presentation by and to the English but "events in narratives and dialogues that retain the 'gesture, ritual, and ceremony' of oral discourse. . . . Eliot's generous answer[s] to these new questions concerning natural origins open[ed] a way for the Massachusett to draw the missionaries further into reciprocity."[20]

The Congregational process of restorative communal justice—what I call rebuke-repent-restore—also shared similarities with Indigenous practice. Marie Balsley Taylor describes the case of Sarah and William Ahhaton in N'ahteuk/Natick in 1668, where members of the first Massachusetts Congregational church attempted to mediate the terrible situation between this couple to prevent it from going to civil trial: "Her father & mother with some other friends came downe with her to Packemit, & by their endevors a reconciliation was made between her and her husband."[21] This seemed to work at first, but after a few months it became clear that the resolution had only been partial. Still, we'll later see the same focus on resolving problems between church members within the church at Agawam/Rowley and in N'ahteuk/Natick, evolved by then into a very effective process after decades of Indigenous and English practice.

SAUNKSKWA, SACHEM, MINISTER

There are also similarities between the person and role of the Congregational minister and the Indigenous saunkskwa (female leader) or sachem (male leader). The saunkskwa or sachem was not the autocratic queen or king that English colonizers believed them to be. These leaders were primarily charged with maintaining existing kinship relations and inviting new ones so as to strengthen their communities and bring them into closer relationship, thus avoiding external war and internal conflict. Their skills as diplomats were honored and prioritized by the people who invited them to function as their representatives. Unlike contemporary European monarchs, whose personal good was presented as either superseding or representing the good of all, Indigenous leaders, as Brooks explains, "spoke on behalf of a community, a 'gathering' of extended families bound to each other through longstanding habitation, intermarriage, and interdependent relationships. . . . Effective leaders facilitated the renewal of relationships and amelioration of disputes through diplomatic councils and annual ceremonies, . . . negotiating rights and responsibilities among contiguous communities, thus enabling social and ecological sustainability."[22] The saunkskwa or sachem didn't seek their position in order to enrich themselves or exert their will. Their word was not law. They worked with councils and governed by consensus as much as possible, taking as much time as was needed to come to that consensus. An Indigenous leader foregrounded responsibility for community, not their individual power, because any power they held derived from their ability to represent, maintain, and expand their community.

In this way, Indigenous leaders resembled Congregational ministers—though one enormous difference proves that similarity is not connection: while there were female and male leaders in Indigenous society, there was no role for female political leaders (other than monarch) in English society and none at all for female religious leaders. Yet despite the fact that all Congregational ministers were male, they shared certain characteristics with the Indigenous leaders. Saunkskwas and sachems were supposed to "treat community visitors to hospitality, care for the poor and needy, host feasts, and arbitrate disputes."[23] Ministers, too, were supposed to do all of this, though they were usually too poor to host a feast. But as their diaries show, they offered what they had. There are frequent entries about visitors appearing without warning and staying for days, and many others about working with the congregation to provide care to the poor. A minister was also meant to be a careful arbitrator during church disputes, as we'll see later in the book when I present the example of Samuel Phillips at Agawam/Rowley.

The minister's role was also to represent a community, the church body, before God. Although he held the honorific title of *Master* (abbreviated as *Mr.*), which few other Englishmen held at the time had, he had no power of his own, no identity or purpose other than as a conduit between the church and God. He was called *Mr.* because of the importance of the role he inhabited rather than because of his own personal importance. For instance, in 1677, the minister Samuel Phillips reminded a correspondent who had described him as acting unilaterally to admit a new member that "he was not the Church."[24] An ecclesiastical council in the Ndakinna place that became Bennington, Vermont, went even further, saying, "We believe it is aggreable to the instructions of the bible as well as the dictates of common Sence, that Ministers are the property of the Churches, & are to be disposed of for the most effectual promotion of Christ's Cause."[25] The letters that men wrote to church bodies when they accepted their call as minister reveal how far the purpose of the minister stood from that of the proprietor and the seriousness with which ministers meant to carry out that role. Jonas Colburn's July 5, 1832, letter to the church in Naumkeag/Stoneham is representative of nearly two hundred years of such messages:

> You need not be apprised that the settlement of a Gospel Minister is a matter of no common magnitude. It involves the dearest interest of both Minister & people, the destiny of immortal souls.... The evils, which might result from a wrong decision on this subject, no human sagacity can foresee, no calculation can fully estimate.... [A]fter much deliberation & prayer, & anxiety of mind, I am prepared cordially to accept your invitation to settle with you in the Gospel Ministry—In coming to this decision, I adhere to what I conceive to be the plain dictates of Divine Providence— ... requesting an interest in your prayers, hoping that it will be our united prayer that if this endearing relation be consummated, it may be for our mutual good here, & for our joy & rejoicing, hereafter—I subscribe myself your unworthy friend & servant in the Lord.[26]

Ordination speeches recorded in church books reiterate that message. The minister Edward Payson recorded this charge in Agawam/Rowley in 1682: "at ye Desire of this c^{hh} & people I ordaine you a Minister of ye Gospel.... And I charge thee, before God & ye Ld J. X^t [Do] ye work of a Pastor unto this c^{hh} & people: Preach ye word, preach not yo^{r}selfe, [with] all Long Suffering, ... carefully tend ye Lambs of that flock, and Look well after every one both old & young, as a good Shepherd, y^t watches & must be accountable for their soules."[27]

The minister was not meant to amass riches or gifts. He didn't dress differently from the members of his church and congregation, for Congregationalists had deliberately and forcefully rejected the ornate gowns and robes of Catholic priests. Most ministers had to raise their own food or even sell produce as market farmers because their salaries, small to begin with, were precarious and often unpaid for months or years at a time (AR 293).²⁸ Men in town governments intent on secular growth and enrichment made it difficult for any minister who did not aggressively pursue regular payment and inflation adjustments to survive. Renowned and respected as he was, Samuel Phillips nevertheless recorded many battles over his pay, including this one from 1674: "the church also agreed that what they had foremerly voted viz an addition of 10 per annum to my maintenance should be presented[,] though [through] some neglect or mistake it was omitted the last yeer viz 1673. It was shown them what little cause y^r was to think 70 pounds of ye pay [to] be great incoragem^t[.] I had not bin all of 2 or 3 years in buyang cloathes for my self or mine or to make any pay wher I ought[.] I was faine to spend of my own legacy above 70 pound in a yeer or two" (AR 127).

There were many different payment schedules for ministers. In Agawam/Wenham, the new minister, Joseph Swain, was ordained on October 24, 1750. But his salary was "to begin ye first Day of July 1750 [and] ye one half thereof to be paid ye first Day of January following, & ye other half at ye Expiration of ye year, & so [during] his Continuance in ye Ministry in this Town." So he started his ministry in October and was paid on January 1 a retroactive salary from July 1 through December 31. From then on, Joseph would receive two payments each year, a setup that invited confusion and failure to pay. In Manchauge/Sutton, the minister David Hall recorded a long-term argument with his congregation over his salary because, as was often the case, the congregation had voted to reduce it during a tough economic time. On May 31, 1745, he recorded, "I was uneasy [at] my Brethren who came as a Committee and seemed to [argue] me down in my Sallery and [they were] there [again] at Night [and] informed [me that they] had really done it[,] upon [which] I chid some of them and spake hard to them and complain sadly of wrong doing." On June 18, he added, "My People have injuriously treated me & [lessened] my Sallery near a full [part]."²⁹ Often ministers were paid in goods such as firewood or services such as help with the harvest or household maintenance, but these debts also fell into arrears. The minister was expected to carry on in this situation, and almost always did, preaching and counseling and administering the sacraments, even if he were in negotiations with the town or a civil court for back pay at the same time. We'll see how devastating the consequences of this system could be when we look at the case of Oliver Peabody in N'ahteuk/Natick.

The minister's role and calling was to help keep the church healthy by overseeing normal operating procedures, preaching and teaching in an orthodox way that helped people with their spiritual preparation, conferring with church committees and moderating church meetings, and supporting the process of rebuke-repent-restore in any way he was asked to do so, from attending early meetings with a wayward individual to calling on the church to vote on the dreadful rebuke of excommunication—and then working with the church to find a way to lift that sentence by bringing someone to real repentance and restoration. Of course, a talented minister who was able to do all of this could become renowned and respected for it. But such a minister was exactly the type of person who would never seek such esteem, carrying on humbly as a "mediator, consensus builder, diplomat, and steward in the service of a community gathered by birth and by adoption, . . . carrying their community's deliberative decisions, communicat[ing] them effectively and persuasively with other leaders, and travel[ing] swiftly to return the wider deliberations home"—to borrow Brooks's description of a saunkskwa or sachem.[30] All of this leads us to the conclusion that the Congregational minister was so unlike any other English authority figure that he might be seen as more similar to an Indigenous leader in Woodland New England.[31]

The fundamental disconnect that the English maintained between the role of Congregational ministers and that of civil authority figures such as magistrates is key to why Congregationalism failed to remain the dominant motivating force for Puritan colonizers in the region. The minister was in service to others. He was not meant to become wealthy or individually powerful.[32] Given his low salary and its arrears, he often couldn't afford to build his own house. All of this made it very hard for a minister to leave wealth to his male relatives, a legacy that would have set them up for political and economic success and dominance. This led to marginalization. Yes, he was respected and honored for his unique and important spiritual role. A town wanted to have a minister it could be proud of. But if a man's labors were only valuable in a setting that did not generate income, this was an existential drawback in Woodland New England.

In short, the minister stood in sharp contrast to the proprietor, and there were many more proprietors than ministers in Woodland New England. To understand how this came to be, we need to look at the wider world that the English Congregationalists inhabited—the place they had come from and how it dictated their actions in the place to which they had arrived. The marginalization of the Congregational ideal and its kinship model in English colonizer society was the result of an extraordinary set of circumstances that did more than maintain an unsurprising difference between what people practiced and what they preached. The parallel universe began in the building that was both a meetinghouse and a counting house—but never both at the same time.

CHAPTER TWO

More

INFINITY INTO SCARCITY

English civil records in Woodland New England are stuffed to bursting with records of the seemingly endless, convoluted, multiparty, insistent, unstoppable land transactions—sales, inheritances, divisions, gifts, and grants—that made it possible for English colonizers to possess "empty land." Their inexorable, inexhaustible need to take land by law, hook, or crook has been consistently explained by the simple word *greed*. Jeremy Bangs's exhaustive documentation of land grabbing in Plymouth County speaks volumes: he requires 337 small-font, single-spaced pages to cover all of the transactions that took place during a seventy-one-year period. As he says, "we end up with the near tautology, that continued land acquisition was motivated by greed when there was no immediate agricultural use intended."[1] Often this greed is linked to racism by scholars, who say that the English didn't consider Indigenous people to be their equals and therefore felt justified in taking their land.

But English land greed did not begin in North America. It began in England. The English who arrived in the Eastern Woodlands in 1630 were the products of an economic, social, political, and religious upheaval that had been intensifying for more than a century. Since the 1400s, the general condition of England and its people had been exemplified by the actual growing scarcity of natural resources, which was compounded both the perception of scarcity and a deepening fear of scarcity, a lived reality that the historian Scott McDermott has ably described.[2] The beginnings of colonization in the fifteenth century had made all Europeans aware of the existence of a large and unknown world. As the historian John Lauritz Larson writes, they "struggled to absorb and contain the impact of new knowledge, new resources, new ideas, new foods, and new technologies that shook conventional realities to the core. This [was a] traumatic era [that] we benignly remember as the 'age of discovery."[3] We must always be aware, first and foremost, of the harm that Europeans did in the Americas, Africa, and Asia through these "discoveries." But to understand why that harm was so pronounced, we have to understand the effects of their discoveries on Europeans: they perceived these natural resources not just as an abundance but as an infinitude waiting to be seized.[4]

Scarcity of resources had characterized European society for centuries by the time Columbus made his first voyage west. Thus, England operated broadly on the basis of managed inequality. The wealthy few controlled the majority of resources, and Christianity served to justify this setup: *the poor will always be with us; give unto Caesar what is Caesar's; store up your treasure in Heaven and not in this world; blessed are the poor*. English people were steeped in the notion that it was God's will for the noble few to manage the kingdom's resources and that only the careful preservation of this unequal status quo could prevent total devastation and honor his mysterious plan. This precarious economic system was land-based. As Larson's description of material life in sixteenth-century England reveals, 80 percent of the land in the kingdom was unavailable to the market and permanently alienated from 90 percent of the country's inhabitants because the monarchy, the church, or the nobility possessed it via conquest, gift, or inheritance. Every part of England had been claimed since 1086, when the Domesday Book listed all of the assets in the kingdom and reassigned them to owners at the top of the great chain. Most of the remaining 20 percent of the land was not owned by the common people but leased to them by freeholders: yeoman farmers who either possessed large swaths of land themselves or leased it on terms that gave them many of the privileges of ownership.[5] Thus, the vast majority of English people were tenant farmers—a class that became known in America as sharecroppers—who were required or allowed to work a strip of a lord's or a freeholder's land (a practice known as the *open field system*), with the bulk of their harvest going to the lord and the market, leaving a remnant for them to live on. Their whole world was reduced to this small strip of land, and everything hung on their ability to make it pay.

For centuries, the creation and enforcement of this pattern of land use was the unnatural foundation of law and order in the kingdom. According to Larson, "safety and sustainability derived from the maintenance of order and the perpetuation of customary ways of administering scarce resources, [or of] resources not so much scarce as ill-distributed."[6] Thus, stability in English society was based on strict adherence to a system that created scarcity by ordaining personal greed among the few; this system then kept the destabilizing fear and anxiety of the many—their psychic distress—just under control by transferring the decision to God. As England's population grew through the fifteenth and sixteenth centuries, pressures on this system increased, but only the nascent capitalism that was born alongside colonization fundamentally changed how the landowning class profited from the land.

In the 1500s, international markets began to grow, and the concept that people other than merchants could make a living, even a fortune, from trade was introduced into Europe. Some landowners funded voyages to the Americas, Asia, or Africa, but many more began to act on both the supply and demand sides of the new proto-capitalist markets by dedicating a major portion of their land to market production. Larson writes, "The time had arrived when substantial profits could be made by raising surplus grain for distant markets," whether they were in Europe or in other parts of the globe.[7] In England, much of the land chosen for non-local market production was dedicated not to crops but to animals. As the historian Neal Salisbury explains, "increased international trade had transformed [regions] of self-sufficient farmers into specialists, capital-intensive centers of grain, beef, and dairy production."[8] Across the country landowners jumpstarted production by pulling their land out of collective farming and putting it into grazing. This was the beginning of a practice known as *enclosure*, a word that would resonate with the English colonizers of Woodland New England more than a century later. In the enclosure system, an individual landowner put up literal, physical barriers around once-communal farmland. Stone fences were erected and hedgerows planted, the latter supplanting the former as they grew into thick, permanent, immovable, maintenance-free walls that kept animals in and interloping humans out.

Beginning in the late sixteenth century, land that had been communally farmed for time immemorial was converted into an individual's grazing grounds in the relative blink of an eye. Families who had lived on that land for centuries were turned out and sent away. To prevent them from lingering or trying to obstruct their lord's new business venture, laws were created to punish "vagrancy" and "idleness." For centuries, England had required its people to have an official place of residence; now they were being forced out of their homes while still being required to belong somewhere—one of the numerous forms of psychic distress that characterized the English people who arrived in the Eastern Woodlands in 1630. The desperate search for work was so pronounced that the minister Thomas Shepard, who preached in Pequossette/

Cambridge in the Massachusetts Bay Colony between 1635 and 1649, could refer to it in a metaphor for salvation: "[T]hough Christ be not intended for all, he is offered to all.... Thou must venture and try, as many men amongst us now do, who, hearing of one good living fallen, twenty of them will go and seek for it, although they know only one shall have it."[9] As Salisbury writes, the "stable, predictable world of the self-contained village was a thing of the past in much of England by the late sixteenth century, and even though this stability and predictability had been predicated on fear of scarcity, it had functioned well enough so that most people had considered it to be successful, and could not imagine another reality than the one they had inherited."[10] Losing it was devastating.

The abandonment and freefall that most people experienced when enclosure barred them from their traditional farmland can hardly be called freedom. Yet a growing number of freehold farmers were enticed by the opportunities for wealth that the new markets represented. It was risky to get involved in the new ventures, but speculators were drawn by the potential rewards, which were unparalleled. For the first time, these people felt the pressure of competition; they wanted to be the first to get in on an opportunity—to discern, claim, and profit from a new path to riches. To move quickly in this way required the personal freedom to make choices, to travel and relocate, to take on risk, and to devote one's income to a chosen project. In this way, individual freedom was irretrievably linked with wealth. To make money, an individual had to be free to pursue any opportunity. To be free, then, was to be able to make money; and to make money was to be free. As the original wording of the Declaration of Independence emphasized, the fundamentals rights of the individual were life, liberty, and the pursuit of property.[11]

To survive, and potentially to thrive beyond all imagining, one had to compete, earn, invest, risk, predict, calculate, invent, and otherwise innovate at all times. One had to anticipate new demands, resources, and markets and capitalize on them ahead of everyone else. Competition became the basis of success, and natural resources were both the input and the output of wealth. Access to natural resources was key; and whether these resources were local or global, the race to find, control, and exploit them was fast and furious and left populations across the globe uprooted in its wake.

Enter the New World. Ironically, the psychic distress caused by scarcity, which the colonizers had known so well in England, was nothing compared to the psychic distress caused by the abundance they would discover in the

Eastern Woodlands. A paradox lies at the heart of the English reaction to that abundance: it appeared to them as scarcity. After centuries of conceptualizing the limitation of such resources as divinely ordered, the English mind was boggled by the region's apparently unending abundance for all. The ghost in this machine lay in that word *all*, for immediately the idea arose that potential riches would come only to those who claimed them first. The English saw the land through the gold-colored glasses of competition: that is, they saw not only what they might have but what they might lose if others had it.[12] As the historian James Cooper notes:

> Scholars have pointed to the gradual emergence in the seventeenth century of colonists who "were inclined to set their own advantage before the public good" [but] this individualistic spirit "is not to be identified simply with acquisitiveness," [for it] represented "a much broader attitude" that placed a heightened emphasis upon private goals, personal autonomy, and public reputation, "even at the expense of communal interests."[13]

We can see this process at work in the compulsive list making that characterizes early accounts of the Eastern Woodlands: long lists of material resources sent back to England with effusive descriptions of their fineness and, always, their endless proliferation. These exhaustive and obsessive lists convey the new arrivals' inability to make use of the windfall fast enough; their desperation to locate, name, and categorize it in order to profit from it. The emigrant Francis Higginson set the tone for these communications with *New-Englands Plantation*, a selection from a long letter he wrote to friends in England in 1629 to satisfy their desire to know what the new land was like. Higginson's listing begins on page 2 as he describes the "fat black earth" and continues with the enumeration of twenty kinds of vegetables and "pot-herbs," twelve kinds of fruits and nuts, fourteen species of trees, ten varieties of land animals, and eighteen different sea animals. In 1634, William Woods followed with his own report, *New Englands Prospect*, in which he devoted chapters to each type of natural resource, which he called "commodities"—things that were convenient, useful, ready to be put into human service.

Humans have always turned animals, plants, and trees into foods, building materials, medicines, and clothing. But in the Eastern Woodlands the English perception of their new trade wealth had disastrous consequences for the land, its creatures, and its people. First, the English were always thinking beyond their own subsistence toward the potential of global markets. This stripped away any awareness of ecology—that the land and its creatures made up something greater than the sum of their parts, that they were integral components of an ecosystem that could survive and thrive only when they were well understood, maintained, and protected. For the English colonizers, nature was a collection of parts that could be taken apart and sold separately. The impact of this mindset was visible two centuries later in the town histories written in Woodland New England, many of which revel in descriptions of pillaging the earth: "This quiet valley [still] bore up the ancient forest," declared Joseph White in his 1855 history of Pocumtuck/Charlemont, "but the time appointed for a wonderful change was at hand. The axe was to be laid at the root of giant trees." An 1856 oration celebrating the bicentennial of Miamogue/Bridgewater recounted that the land for the town had been purchased from Indigenous people for goods worth about $25 in 1656. Two hundred years later, the unnamed speaker proudly assessed the town's progress: "Such was the town valued [after] a long period of occupation by savage tribes [and it] was not destined to be increased in value by their mode of life.... Peopled by a civilized, Christian people, in the short space of two hundred years, the value of this same territory is more than five millions current money."[14]

All of those millions depended on taking action to claim land and make it pay. That's how abundance was transformed into scarcity in the Eastern Woodlands. Each Englishman was keenly aware that there was a fortune to be made; he knew that if he did not get to those resources first, someone else would, and that eventually even infinite resources might run out. The vast woods, the teeming waters, the fertile earth—all stood on the auction block, first come, first served, and any delay in claiming and commodifying as much as possible meant failure. After centuries of want, English hunger was insatiable. It was out of the question to leave anything untouched in the Eastern Woodlands.

Crucially, for the English, turning resources into commodities that could be bought and sold meant that those resources needed to be privately owned. Land had to become the personal property of an individual male, and it had to be purchased through legal transactions. Thus, the English relationship with the land and resources of the Eastern Woodlands was immediately economic and transactional rather than intrinsic. Land and creatures had no identity or purpose in themselves but were strictly valued as products that could be owned, traded, and sold.[15] In their relationship to natural resources, a person was an owner, a producer, a retailer, or a consumer, not a partner, a protector, or kin.

This meant that the English settlers behaved as if the natural world would always make its resources available in bulk. They indulged in magical thinking about the abundance of the Eastern Woodlands, describing the region as naturally infinite and fertile, as not requiring any human management or care. They disdained the idea that the thriving land they saw in the present moment was the result of centuries of careful cultivation, resource management, and, crucially, self-restraint on the part of Indigenous people—a notion that goes far beyond simply "respecting the land." As the historian David J. Silverman explains, for Indigenous people, "reciprocal relationships and associated responsibilities between indigenous peoples and their environments [were] the very foundation of indigenous traditional ecological knowledge (ITEK)." In other words, the land was kin. Rivers, lakes, mountains, marshes, swamps, and forests were living beings. All animals, including humans, were born into relationship with these landforms and had shared responsibility for them. According to the Indigenous view of the world, "humans formed a single symbiotic community" with the spirits "behind all the forms and elements" of the natural world: "They shape shifted into each other's likenesses, spoke one another's languages, married, made love, fought, and in every respect behaved like kin and neighbors.... Humans would find power and truth by collapsing the boundaries of their fleshy selves and entering a spirit world where human, plant, animal, and element were mutually dependent kin and ontologically the same."[16]

Indigenous people "sought to bring English settlers into this worldview [of] social and ecological reciprocity."[17] But to the English, the land was "untouched" and the Indigenous people too "rude"—that is, uneducated and uncivilized—to have thoughtfully prepared for future generations of humans and nonhumans. As Francis Higginson put it, they found it "sad to see so much good ground [lying] altogether unoccupied"; and when they took possession of that land, they did not "purpose to keep [it] unimployed."[18] As undeveloped land, it cried out for individual ownership, development, sale, and consumption, and the English set about consuming it with a passion that derived from their history of want, a fear of scarcity, the shock of plenty, and the fortuitous situation of being able to govern themselves in this rich and richly available new world. They would create a commonwealth that validated individual consumption, ownership, competition, and profit and then drive themselves relentlessly to consume every bit of land and resources before someone else did. One of the first results, ironically, would be the rapid depletion of forests, which led to firewood shortages.[19] The farmable land that those forests had been cleared to create also became scarce very early in the colonization process. With each individual head of household requiring multiple lots of land—farmland, woodland, saltmarsh, pasture, and meadow—and with the English population growing very quickly through migration and high birth rates, new towns rapidly found themselves running out of land to offer their residents. Among them was Cochichawick/Andover, founded in 1642, which experienced land shortages within two decades of settlement. The early 1660s, writes the historian Philip J. Greven Jr., was "the last period in which second-generation sons might have obtained abundant land from the town itself."[20] The town of Mattapan/Dorchester, founded in 1630, was in even tighter straits: it experienced its first outmigration due to "land scarcity" in 1635.[21]

This is what drove the heedless land grabbing that characterized colonization in Woodland New England, a hunger so insatiable that it became gluttony.[22] This mania for consumption drove the men who created the boundaries of the town of Cohannet/Taunton in 1639 to demand additional land grants later that same year. It also affected their relationship to Congregationalism. As James Cooper writes, "rising individualism and a declining commitment to the communitarian ideals of the church covenant clearly reinforced one another, as lay people began to place personal aspirations ahead of the corporate goals of the church." He rightly calls this "the painful expansion and division of New England towns."[23] Now that the Puritans could simply walk out their doors and take ownership of vast wealth, that intoxication overrode all other considerations, including their sincerely desired goal of creating a godly state in which spiritual seeking was the primary activity and purpose of the inhabitants. Instead, they built what Daniel Mandell calls a "strong government and aggressive culture," and they used it as a weapon to control members of their own society as well as Indigenous people and the land itself.[24] By politically empowering freeholders, they made land ownership—not spiritual seeking—the foundation of society, politics, and the economy.

Still, while it's tempting to debunk Puritan exceptionalism in every way, we must stop short at claiming that their religious goals were always a cover for economic gain.[25] Yes, the Puritans underwent a change of purpose; but in examining their religious motivations, we can't let the pendulum swing too far. The first Puritan colonizers did arrive with the intention of laboring only for a *competency*—their term for just enough to live on, without excess production or consumption—that would allow them to focus on their spirituality. The problem is that their new reality immediately overturned this intention. Scholarship tends to acknowledge Puritan psychic distress in England but then assume that it was relieved by emigration to the Eastern Woodlands, where land was plentiful and, to the newcomers, freely available. But the feverish land grab and the ensuing internal competition among colonizers and external aggression against Indigenous people prove that removal from England did nothing to relieve the generations-old psychic distress. As the historian Keith Pluymers notes, "the easy trajectory, in which colonial abundance cures European shortfalls, becomes problematic when examining England's early modern expansion."[26] The same holds true for New England: the relief of plenty was instantly translated into a compulsive, uncontrollable need for more.[27]

In a bitter paradox, this need was pursued through the old evil of enclosure. Enclosure in Woodland New England was one of the most important and powerfully destructive forces through which the Puritan commonwealth was built. The English freeholders quickly threw Indigenous people off the land, just as the nobility had done in Old England, using fences and ditches and bulwarking those vulnerable physical symbols with the power of their law. Once an Englishman was granted ownership of land by his colony or town, he set about enclosing it, and not just to keep Indigenous people away, though this was a strong motive.[28] Enclosure was equally meant to keep out other Englishmen. The courts of Woodland New England are filled with cases of land disputes among Englishmen. Controversies and even violence over property lines and fences were constant and involved every landowning man, from the highest in stature to the lowest. As I noted in chapter 1, even ministers such as Samuel Phillips of Agawam/Rowley were hauled into court by church members and had to defend themselves against charges of encroachment.[29] Once land was privately owned, its possessors guarded it against trespass as jealously as any nobleman might protect his grounds in Old England. Fear of enclosure did not teach the Puritans to abhor it. Rather, it taught them to ensure that the power of enclosure was in *their* hands, not someone else's.

In a nutshell, the Puritans who left England for North America had endured religious suppression and threats for decades, suffered increasing scarcity of natural resources, and struggled with increasing political and economic instability. In this agitated mental state, they "lacked," as the historian William Cronon explains, "the conceptual tools to accurately perceive and live in North America."[30] From the moment the members of the Winthrop fleet set foot on Shawmut, they were fundamentally, permanently affected by their perception of an infinite wealth of material resources, all of it up for grabs by whoever made the first move. Imagining Hernán Cortés's arrival in the New World, the poet John Keats wrote, "All his men / look'd at each other with a wild surmise." In this way, the Puritans and the Spanish conquistadors were one.[31]

CHAPTER THREE

Questioning the Authenticity of Indigenous Conversion

> This question could not be learned from the English, nor did it seem a coyned feigned thing, but a reall matter gathered from the experience of his own heart, and from an inward observation of himself.
>
> —John Eliot, on the conversion of the Massachusetts sachem Cutshamekin (1647)

> What the evidence also suggests is that the adoption of Christianity did not involve the erasure of Native spirituality, but rather its being symbolically interwoven into a hybrid cultural fabric [as] a dynamic interpretation of religious practice. We see this new spiritual reality as an Indigenous product rather than something developed out of resistance to English religious doctrine.
>
> —Stephen A. Mrozowski, Holly Herbster, David Brown, and Katherine L. Priddy (2009)

> Surely it were great uncharitableness, and derogatory from the glory of God, to think that none of these are truly changed.
>
> —John Eliot and Thomas Mayhew Jr. (1653)

In 1641, the English General Court in Boston granted Thomas Mayhew title to the island called Noepe. The Mayhews renamed it Martha's Vineyard, and by the late 1600s the men of the family had introduced the Wampanoags to Congregational Christianity.[1] For about a century, successive generations of Mayhews continued their mission to Christianize the Indigenous people on the island, and their efforts led to many conversions.

This narrative typifies traditional descriptions of Indigenous conversion to Christianity in Woodland New England, portraying it as a one-way process in which Indigenous people either accepted the religion offered to them or endured the religion forced on them. According to such narratives, history was an unstoppable force whose intrinsic teleology was Indigenous Christianity. Missionaries were simply the means by which history chose to effect that end, making the Indigenous converts mere objects of history. As the scholar Michael McNally points out, "native Christianity winds up being understood largely as an *outcome* of history rather than part and parcel of it, a derivative of missionary intentions rather than a complex process shaped both by missionary and native Christians."[2] This teleology has also been applied to Black converts: Richard Boles notes that "many scholars of church history have tended to dismiss early conversion and church participation of enslaved Africans as nothing more than forms of oppression."[3] Edward Andrews also argues against the assumption that Indigenous converts were mere "*recipients of the gospel.*" As his work proves, "indigenous peoples became vital *participants*" in their new religion, particularly as regards their extensive missionary work: "The very act of having an Indian preach the gospel meant that [he] became an active participant in the process of reinventing and translating the meaning of the gospel message."[4] The research of all of these scholars counters two common assumptions: first, that no Indigenous person would willingly choose to become Christian because this would require adopting the oppressive religion of the colonizer and abandoning their own people; and, second, no Indigenous person could ever understand Christianity well enough to practice it authentically. The habit of interrogating Indigenous converts—a practice that requires an unquestioned belief in the questioner's right to ask, judge, prove, approve, and disapprove—has created a realm of speculation in which interrogators are not only able to judge whether or not Indigenous people were truly Christian but in fact entitled and even required to do so—as if, in order to write about them, we must claim knowledge of their souls.[5]

As the Wampanoag faithful knew, a crucial component of Congregational belief was that no person could truly discern the state of another person's soul. One person's observations of another's "walk" and daily "conversation" were useful only insofar as they allowed the observer to draw limited human conclusions when the other person testified to discovering Christ's saving grace. When someone offered that testimony, those listening understood that their role was not to pass judgment on the person's actual spiritual estate—to decide for themselves whether or not that person had really received Christ's grace—but to give them the benefit of the doubt. If the person's relation seemed genuine, any lingering minor questions or doubts must be overruled by what Congregationalists called the judgment of charity—bowing to the impossibility of ever knowing the whole truth of someone's soul.[6] When we consider the Wampanoag Congregationalists on Noepe/Martha's Vineyard, then, we have to offer them the same judgment of charity. We can never know the full truth of their spiritual lives, and we must acknowledge that fact before we study Indigenous Christianity anywhere.

In this context, we benefit from turning to church records to expand our dataset. Before such records were available on a large scale, researchers were forced to rely too heavily on a small set of primary sources that, as a result, presented one moment in the story of Indigenous conversion as the whole story. The historian Richard A. Bailey illustrates a major drawback of relying, for instance, on the writings of English missionaries, including John Eliot, for insights into Indigenous and Black converts: "The degree to which white authors exercised [authority] over Native Americans and Africans troubles many scholars, who differ over whether one ought to read such accounts as the products of red and black intellects or of white minds."[7] Another issue is that most English missionary writings come from the first decades of outreach in the 1600s, forcing scholars to depend too much on the earliest descriptions of Indigenous conversion. By emphasizing the newness of Christianity to potential converts, they engendered the notion that the English religion remained new and alien to Indigenous people even generations later. In contrast, church records spanning the seventeenth through the nineteenth centuries reveal Indigenous responses to and evolutions of a Congregational practice they had internalized and made their own in the decades and generations after the initial missionary period. Without these records, writes Linford Fisher, "the sources upon which we are forced to rely usually come from the missionaries or their exemplary Native converts."[8]

Scholarly reactions to Indigenous conversion generally present two main sources of doubt. One is the purity argument: that any Indigenous person who sincerely converted was, in this context, no longer Indigenous because they had abandoned their own religion, culture, and people. The purity argument claims that, because Indigenous people knew they would be contributing to the disappearance of their own lifeways and identity by adopting the colonizing religion, few of them ever committed such betrayals. For instance, in his 1981 research, James P. Ronda presented the Quaker missionary George Fox's 1672 argument that "those who accepted the Christian god and became 'praying Indians' . . . lost their tribal identity" and that onlookers had witnessed the complete and irrevocable "cultural demise of the converts." At that time Ronda was likely correct in viewing this as "the standard gloss on the complex relationship between Indians and Christianity in colonial New England," writing that "modern scholarship has generally concurred" with Fox's stand that Indigenous people could not "live as both Christians and Indians."[9] This, in a nutshell, is the "degeneracy narrative" that Jean O'Brien describes as being created to describe Indigenous people, in contrast to the "progress narrative" of non-Indigenous people.[10]

The purity argument assumes that Indigenous Christianity was not sincere belief but an intelligent and effective survivance strategy—what the scholar Harold W. Van Lonkhuyzen calls a "protective coloration [that] helped preserve the Indians' 'crucial ethnic core' or their 'ethnic identity,'" a crafty front for maintaining "true" Indigeneity behind the scenes.[11] But the insistence that Indigenous culture and civilization cannot change after colonization, that only precolonization Indigeneity is real, is part of the trap that colonizers set to make it impossible for any Indigenous people to exist. According to this view, no one is Indigenous unless they are 100 percent blood- and culture-pure. Unless human populations are 100 percent isolated from every other influence, however, it's impossible for them to resist genetic and cultural sharing. Certainly white culture in Woodland New England resisted neither, and to demand this of Indigenous people is simply another way to erase them. As O'Brien writes, "going to 'cultural retentions' as evidence of Indianness . . . carries the danger of insisting on cultural stasis that is so centrally embedded in the New England project of modernity." Discounting Indigenous Christians as real Indians is yet another example of "the production of modernity through the purification of the landscape of Indians." That is, questioning the identity of Indigenous Christians becomes just another way to erase a category of Indigenous people.[12] The notion of *cultural purity*, defined as resisting and refusing all English goods, practices, or beliefs, supposedly disqualifies Indigenous people who adopt any of these from being "really Indian." Yet the irony is that non-Indigenous people who adopt the goods, practices, and beliefs of other cultures are not seen as being no longer members of their own culture. English colonizers who grew corn and used wampum and learned some Indigenous words and phrases are not described as failing to be culturally English. In fact, adoption of Indigenous practices reinforced their Englishness. The same should hold for Indigenous people.[13]

Unfortunately, well-intentioned scholars play into this extinction or disappearance myth with statements meant to protest anti-Indigenous policy. For Elise Brenner, for instance, any Indigenous conversion to Christianity was strictly a survivance or coping mechanism—what she calls "Mau Mauing." She describes "backsliding" or repeated sinning on the part of Indigenous Congregationalists as "recurrent and continuous 'nonobedient' behavior which may be classified as a coping mechanism of passive resistance. The praying Indians may well have been overtly following all colonial dictates, while covertly behaving in ways consistent with their traditional values as far as they could." A deeper understanding of Congregationalism could inform and adjust this point of view, given that white English Congregationalists expected and even hoped that they would backslide and sin both before and after assurance, seeing this as evidence that Christ was drawing them nearer and thereby making more sin visible to them. J. Patrick Cesarini also makes a purity argument, asserting that because "colonization 'tore at the native social fabric, leaving gaps in the web of kinship, political succession, technological expertise, and corporate memory,'" conversion was effective primarily with "groups that were relatively weak (such as the Massachusetts bands first approached by Eliot) or those that remained outside the direct control of the powerful over-sachems. . . . Conversion to Christianity clearly offered such natives a number of benefits." He promotes the purity argument that conversion meant that Indigenous Christians had rejected their culture, quoting Charles L. Cohen's position that "accepting the Redeemer by faith provided Amerinidans a far stronger medicine than the powwows could procure."[14]

Some scholars have disassociated themselves from the purity argument. Among them, Hilary Wyss makes particular reference to Noepe/Martha's Vineyard: "As the Natives on Martha's Vineyard determined for themselves the boundaries of 'ethnicity and acculturation,' the result was often a 'strengthening or reaffirmation of traditional identities, redefined in new institutions and symbolic forms.' . . . Rather than eradicating their own traditions, Natives incorporated new elements into those traditions."[15] In this way, according to Glenda Goodman, seventeenth-century Indigenous Christians in Woodland New England can be understood as "incorporating Christian ideas and practices into their own cosmology [to] rebuild their strength."[16] If scholars abandon their own role in "the project of erasing kinship" by identifying "the Indigenous convert [as] so eager to join the English community that he or she willingly abandons his or her Indigenous one, [which] effectively mask[s] a convert's network of relations," as Marie Balsley Taylor describes it, the purity argument can be discarded when considering early Indigenous Congregationalists.[17]

The missionary Experience Mayhew (1673–1758), whom I'll discuss at length in chapter 6, documented specific acts of Wampanoag kinship that crossed any boundary that might have existed between Christian and non-Christian people, particularly those involving women. For instance, Hannah Ahhunnut of Nashouohkamuk/Chilmark, was a Christian Wampanoag who attended Wampanoag women through childbirth and used her Indigenous medical knowledge "in difficult Cases, [and] it has been reported, that she had sometimes very remarkable Answers," or successes, in them. Hannah Nohnosoo of Takemmy/Tisbury was another skilled Indigenous midwife "having very considerable Skill in some of the Distempers to which human Bodies are subject, and in the Nature of many of those Herbs and Plants which were proper Remedies against them." She served both her Indigenous and English neighbors. Mayhew also described Sarah Hannit, the wife of the Wampanoag Congregational minister Japheth Hannit:

> [She] was one of those wise Women that builded the House, [for] the fair and large Wigwam wherein she and her Husband lived, was a great part of it her own Work; the Mats or platted Straw, Flags and Rushes with which it was covered being wrought by her own Hands, and those of them that appeared within side the House, were neatly embroidered with the inner Barks of Walnut-Trees artificially softned, and dyed of several Colours for that end; so that the generality of Indian Houses were not so handsome as this was, neither was it inferior to those the chief Sachims lived in.[18]

Overall, then, there is evidence, as Van Lonkhuyzen writes, that "the conversion of most praying Indians [cannot] really be seen as a sudden wholesale transformation and adoption of English values."[19]

The other common scholarly reaction to Indigenous Christianity is the incompatibility argument. As contemporaneous English colonizers would have said, Christianity was so much a part of European society and culture that it was almost impossible for anyone who did not inherit that culture to ever completely understand it. How could any Indigenous person understand a religion whose concepts were so different from anything they had ever known, presented in a language they didn't fully understand? The historian Henry Knapp's claim that Puritan missions to Indigenous people were "surprisingly visionary attempts to spread the Christian religion to a particularly foreign people" is a concise representation of the incompatibility argument—and one that most Puritans would have agreed with.[20] Those who support this view assume that Indigenous Christianity was sincere but incomplete and therefore inauthentic—in short, a creole.[21] The scholar Alfred Cave shares a good example of the incompatibility argument as expressed by English colonizers such as Daniel Gookin and Cotton Mather and thoughtfully described by himself: "There [was] no Algonquian counterpart to the Puritan conversion experience. . . . New England's Indians possessed no holy books, nor any other form of scripture, had no formal theology, and had great difficulty in comprehending the logic underlying the Puritan insistence that belief in certain abstract doctrines is essential to one's well-being in the afterlife."[22] The overall effect of such claims is to establish Christianity as so foreign to Indigenous culture and intellect that conversion could never be authentic because it could never be complete. This leaves researchers in the double bind of rejecting both the goal and the efficacy of Indigenous Christianity. As Neal Salisbury puts it, critical evaluations of Indigenous conversion "suggest that Natives were forced against their will to convert [or] that Indians turned to Christianity as a means of surviving and rebuilding their society in the face of [English colonization]"—in other words, survivance.[23]

People on both sides of this argument have spilled an ocean of ink to make their cases. From Eliot's first mission in 1646 to history conferences in the twenty-first century, people have asked existential questions about Indigenous Christians and vested their answers with considerable importance.[24] The problem is that those questions have come to be increasingly rhetorical because they present the Puritan missions as a zero-sum game in which "Christianity's gains were unequivocally the losses of traditional religions." Robert James Naeher argues, "Scholars holding this view have universally assumed that although the 'imposed religion' was invested with traditional Indian meaning wherever possible, it was at best a poor substitute for that which was lost. Indian volition has not been adequately taken into account, however, and therefore what Puritan Christianity may have offered and meant to the Indians has not been measured."[25] This "religious all-or-nothingism" contributes to a narrative wherein "the epic struggles of missionaries" lead inevitably to "the triumph of Christianity" and the alleged destruction of Indigenous religion and culture or the continued resistance of Indigenous people against the colonizing religion they can never authentically practice.[26] In the end, scholars who reject the possibility of authentic Indigenous conversion on either basis, whether it be purity or incompatibility, are reinforcing a view as old as William Hubbard's 1677 history of King Philip's War, in which he rejected authentic Indigenous Christianity, "not only point[ing] to the inherent contradiction of a Christian Indian, but also critique[ing] anyone who defends them."[27] Yes, some Indigenous people converted as a survivance measure, whether to gain the protective coloring of a Christian or to access education and financial opportunities. But others converted sincerely because the new religion spoke to them. Both reasons existed. It is inaccurate to focus on survivance to the extent that authentic conversion is dismissed out of hand. Salisbury emphasizes, "Scholars must find ways to reconcile the realities of imperial power and of Native agency before they can comprehend the totality of Indian experiences with Puritan Christianity."[28]

We can learn a great deal from the new generation of archaeologists, Indigenous and non-Indigenous, who have deliberately set out to interpret Indigenous historical sites in Woodland New England without prejudging what is authentically Indigenous. Stephen Silliman's work with the Eastern Pequot nation to uncover and listen to eighteenth-century homestead sites is one excellent example.[29] Rae Gould, Stephen Mrozowski, and Heather Law Pezzarossi's work with Nipmuc sites in Hassanamesit/Grafton is another. Christina Hodge's account of the eighteenth-century Waldo Farm Wampanoag Congregational burial ground rejects the purity test that would see it as a site of "mimicry and appropriation" because the burials there seem "indistinguishable from local Anglo-American practices."[30] Hodge's conclusion is that Wampanoag Christians who buried their dead at Waldo Farm did so in the way they had been taught—first from missionaries, then from their own Christian ancestors: "Identity is recognized as multiply constituted and experienced; colonialism existed not as an 'abstract force' but through daily, lived practice in the material world." This lived practice was Wampanoag lived experience.[31]

These approaches present Indigenous Christianity as something that became truly Indigenous through generations of sincere practice. We must never downplay the harm on which colonization depends for its success or forget the English colonizers' intent to erase Indigenous civilization and culture in Woodland New England. In their study of the region, Floris W. M. Keehnen, Corinne L. Hofman, and Andrzej T. Antczak remind us that "European colonialism was an unmistakably painful process, the effects of which—many still felt today—cannot and should not be minimized. Many groups were severely restricted in her self-determination, some of whom never were able to stand up to their oppressor or make choices for themselves."[32] But as Gould and her colleagues write, we must "attempt to move beyond the notion of indigenous resistance to a new understanding of the role innovation played and continues to play in the production of contemporary indigenous society, particularly in New England."[33]

In short, we can reject both the purity argument and the incompatibility argument, not because colonizers did no damage to Indigenous societies but because Indigenous people were able to meet those attacks and overcome them. If we accept the idea that "all 'pure' Indigenous achievement can only happen pre-colonization, then any further 'advancement" or 'innovation' is deemed evidence of cultural breakdown and illegitimacy," as Mrozowski, Gould, and Pezzarossi explain: "After that moment of contact, change is equal to loss, and stagnation is equal to continuity and legitimacy [and] the result is a view of the Native American past as a deep, slowly changing prehistory truncated by European colonization." Rejecting that view helps upend the idea that Indigenous Christian practice was always external to Indigenous identity and that all Indigenous converts were unusual specimens to be assessed and categorized.[34] It also allows for a different reading of primary sources surrounding Indigenous Christianity, which Balsley Taylor believes may help undo "narratives of erasure" through conversion that "predetermine our understanding of Native people," narratives implying that the weight of their cultural past made it impossible for them to authentically convert to Christianity even as the onslaught of single-minded English colonizing missionaries made their false conversion inevitable.[35] Edward Andrews hones this point in his fascinating research into the many Indigenous preachers and missionaries in Woodland New England—275 documented so far—who were by far the primary conveyors of Christianity to Indigenous people between the mid-seventeenth and mid-eighteenth centuries. These Indigenous missionaries outnumbered English missionaries in general and completely supplanted them in most cases, but to this point they have been almost entirely missing from the scholarly record of Congregationalism.[36] Andrews makes it clear that English missionaries were "forced to rely upon non-English people for the creation and development of Christian missions." So why did so many of Indigenous people take up that work rather than let Christian evangelicalism wither and die? Why did Indigenous missionaries regroup after King Philip's War? That conflict "devastated evangelical efforts among Indians, but it did not annihilate them, for native peoples were the ones to reenergize, restructure, and reinvigorate Christian missions after the war."[37] Across Woodland New England, Indigenous preachers counseled new congregations and ordained their own ministers within them in the decades after 1676, a period when English ministers drifted away from the hard work, itinerancy, and low pay of the missions. Far from being the "instruments" or "creatures" of the English, most Indigenous people were converted and ministered to by their kin. Far from abandoning their culture, heritage, and kinship ties, the majority of Indigenous missionaries and ministers used their position and skills to fight English land grabbing. Congregationalism was part of their Indigenous identity, syncretic as it might be.

Awareness of syncretism is essential, and not just when we look at Indigenous Christianity. The authenticity and purity of English Christians are equally worthy of examination and interrogation. One might argue that such interrogation is already common: the "dubious" conversions of English Congregationalists have occasioned considerable scholarly hand wringing over the emotional tarpit that allegedly characterized Puritanism.[38] But the scrutiny of English souls never questions whether their continued practice of folk culture, most often in the forms of fortune telling, good-luck charms, ghost stories, and omens, meant they were not really Christian. In contrast, all of the above happens whenever Indigenous Congregationalists are studied because the roomy definition of "Christian identity" offered to English Congregationalists—what Charles Cohen calls a "persistent, durable commitment to and engagement with a panoply of beliefs and behavior"—is not extended to Indigenous Congregationalists. Yet if Linford Fisher is able to introduce his work on Indigenous Christianity via the subtitle "Bear Paws and Bible Pages," we need to accept that any work on English Christianity in Woodland New England could well be introduced as "Brownie Shoes and Bible Pages." Just as they had in England, English Congregationalists in the Massachusetts Bay Colony carved hexes and good-luck charms into their mantelpieces and house framing, read fortunes, and heard voices in the air. What we call *popular piety* existed on both sides.[39]

English ministers paid close attention to what they perceived as unnatural phenomena and clearly believed that supernatural forces that did not represent the hand of God were at work in the world. On September 20, 1719, the minister Samuel Niles of Neponset/Braintree wrote in his diary that he was in the outhouse when he

> Heard a very Unusual Sound Something like a persons blowing thro Some a Large pipe made for such a purpose—which sound I heard four or five times att the South End of the house as I thought—I went out of the house, to See If I could make any discovery, what occationed the sound but saw nothing—when I was at the South End of the house the Noise seemed to be at the North End then I went to the North end and the Noise seem^d at the South End.

Niles circled the house again but never located the sound. It "gradually removed (as it seem^d to me) to a greater distance and as it removed the sound was smaller still—till I heard it no more."[40] Reverend William Homes of Nashouohkamuk/Chilmark wrote in a 1733 diary entry that "one Gold in the south end of Boston . . . sitting in his chair in a room where there was no fire either on the hearth or else where to any bodies knowledge did unaccountably catch fire and was miserably burnt." In 1736 he relayed a chilling mystery surrounding a man who had been killed by lightning: "when they came to search his body they found no hurt upon any part of it only upon his breast there was the lively resemblance of a pine tree imprinted on it. . . . [T]here grew a pine tree before the man's door, and near the place he was killed."[41] Both English and Indigenous Congregationalists had a minority of truly orthodox practitioners who vehemently rejected such notions but a majority who relied on them as needed to supplement their Congregational practice. Yet in general only Indigenous Congregationalists have been described for this reason as "half Christian—eclectic spiritual cobblers who were actively engaged in assembling a coherent worldview from diverse cultural resources," as Douglas Winiarksy puts it.[42]

As I have demonstrated, there is a large body of scholarship on Christian missions, Indigenous Christians, and Christianity as well on the question of whether people who convert under colonization are simply practicing a wise survivance measure and whether authentic conversion inevitably dilutes Indigenous culture.[43] Later in the book I will look narrowly at Wampanoag Congregationalism on Noepe/Martha's Vineyard during the seventeenth and eighteenth centuries to demonstrate that Indigenous Congregationalists were indeed sincere, that they adopted Congregationalism into their culture, and that they helped to redefine the concept of assurance as a prerequisite for full church membership. Wampanoag Congregationalist practice evolved the English concept of assurance from an intensely personal, individual experience into a communal experience of kinship.

It is unusual to study Indigenous and English Congregationalists as people united in their practice and experience of the religion. The two fields are effectively siloed. Yet as Daniel Mandell points out, while it's true that "key distinctions set native congregations apart from their English neighbors [and] reinforced the Indians' sense of a common, separate identity," this differentiation didn't completely outweigh the "similar stress in their rituals on sermons, prayer, and Biblical verses."[44] Among scholars, however, the belief that differences did outweigh similarities has allowed a strange parallel to develop, in which experiences shared by Indigenous and English Congregationalists are described as unique to one or the other. For example, scholars who study Indigenous conversion in isolation tend to describe it as a very negative influence, one specifically designed to break down Indigenous people and destroy their identity and sense of self. In these accounts, Indigenous people were forced to denounce their family and their upbringing as sinful, to bewail their terrible sinfulness and hopelessly sinful natures. They were told to humiliate themselves before God, their own people, and the church. All this, we are told, was part of the English drive to destroy Indigeneity through religion. At the same time, in a separate universe where English Congregationalism—that is, Puritanism—is studied in isolation, English conversion is described in exactly the same way: renouncing family, bewailing sinfulness, and humiliating oneself before God and man so as to break down the individual's identity and sense of self.

The primary sources are filled with lines such as "[I] followed w^t Satan & afrayd he would have me away"; "I was much troubled & then the L^d lay^d a sad affliction upon me where I saw all my sins in order & apprehended noth but death and wrath"; "I could not speake to any . . . & [so] I went sadly loathinge my s[elf]." Yet these particular dark statements were made not by Indigenous converts but by English women living in Pequossette/Cambridge in the 1630s and 1640s.[45] As Edward Andrews points out, the "intense focus on spiritual depravity and sinfulness" were "classic Puritan tropes," not specially reserved for Indigenous converts.[46] While crucial to jumpstarting spiritual seeking, this despair was not the end goal: it would be eventually replaced by joy through continued spiritual preparation, and the same process was expected of Indigenous converts. Fisher explains that the "extreme yet routine expressions of contrition expected in the normal rhythm of Puritan spirituality, as evidenced in the conversion narratives of English men and women *and* in the Indian conversion narratives, [merely] confirm the depth of internalization and appropriation of [Puritan] practices by some of the Native proselytes."[47]

Characterizations presented as unique to Indigenous or English Congregationalists almost always apply to both because there was not a complete divide between their experiences. The most important differences were that English people had been born into a centuries-old Christian identity and had invented Congregationalism in Woodland New England. They had original ownership of Congregational practice and principles, and they felt a fundamental cultural separation from the pagans whom they converted. For their part, Indigenous people had to accept a new religion, learn its concepts, integrate them into their own culture, build new connections and strengthen existing bonds with their non-Christian kin, and find a way to separate the English religion they valued from the English secular attack on their civilization that they resisted. These are important differences. But they don't erase the important similarities between the Indigenous and English experiences of Congregationalism. Both groups were told to deny their upbringing in their traditional culture and to leave behind unconverted family and friends who would hamper their spiritual progress.[48] Both were told that their inherited religious practices were satanic and angered God and that their sin endangered them to the point that it hampered their spiritual seeking.

It's important to remember how new Congregationalism was in the colonizing period, for both Indigenous and English people. In England, the Puritans had imagined what it might look like to worship God properly, but that had been the extent of their actions: according to Richard Bailey, they "did not attempt to establish the formal, theological plan for their venture [because] no such uniform paradigm existed for puritan society."[49] They didn't create their paradigm until they relocated to the Eastern Woodlands, a change in circumstance that prompted a lightning-fast development of Congregational discipline and the constant process of experimentation, definition, and redefinition of Congregational orthodoxy.[50] Congregationalism was new, plastic, and necessarily dynamic for the first two generations of Congregationalism, and it retained its elasticity even after it was the identity-conferring settled inheritance of many later generations. In short, Congregationalism was not a monolithic, unchanging rock of ages with rules set in stone when it was offered to the Indigenous people of the Eastern Woodlands but a hybrid that was still evolving for the English themselves. Congregational churches were "a fascinating amalgam of English and aboriginal customs," as Mandell writes.[51]

Thus, we can consider the ways in which Indigenous Congregationalism was different from English Congregationalism outside of the restrictive framework that sets up the English as naturally orthodox by inheritance and the Indigenous as unnaturally creole by colonization. We can validate differences in Indigenous practice as evolutions in orthodox practice that fully honor and represent the nature of Congregationalism itself. This helps us to avoid the skewed perception of an "imagined static orthodoxy professed by Anglo-Americans" from which Indigenous Congregationalists departed. As Fisher points out, "'syncretism,' 'hybridity,' 'dimorphism' . . . arguably these potentially pejorative words apply equally to European and Indian Christianity in this time period. [There was] diversity of belief, practice, and meaning-making among Indians and their Anglo-American counterparts."[52] An important part of that belief, practice, and meaning making for Indigenous and English Congregationalists was maintaining the Congregational way and the structure and purpose of church discipline at its heart. As we'll see in chapter 4, this was a world within, and opposite to, the world of English colonizing society in the Eastern Woodlands.

PART TWO

Church Bodies at Work in Agawam/Rowley and N'ahteuk/Natick

CHAPTER FOUR

Thomas Miller's Tale

> Soveraign & Relative justice, is enough to silence us;—not enough to content us. The Damned are under it.
>
> —Cotton Mather (1695)

If anyone in the twenty-first century has heard of the colonizer Thomas Miller of Mattabeseck/Middletown in the Connecticut Colony, that's probably because they happened across the brief 1661 court records for his crime of adultery.[1] Miller appears three times in the Hartford County court records for this crime, three short entries that constitute his entire story arc: first judgment, second judgment, final satisfaction. Justice was swift and seems to have achieved its ends: to satisfy those who were wronged by Miller's crime and to prevent him from ever offending again.

His court record begins on March 1, 1666, with an entry identifying Thomas Miller, his crime, his immediate punishment, and his future, final punishment. The entry also describes the one-time punishment for his victim/co-defendant Sarah Nettleton:

> At the County Court held at Hartford March: 1. 65:66
> ... This Court doth adjudge Thomas Miller for his notorious wickedness in committinge uncleanes with Sarah Nettleton his servant who saith (to wch he ascenteth) she is with child by him. To be kept in safe Custody in the Gaole until the next Lecture day at Hartford and then to be brought forth and to suffer Corporall punishment by whipping upon his naked body to ye number of twenty stripes at least. And further the said Miller is either to pay five pounds as a fine to ye Publ: Treasury or

to suffer corporall punishment by whipping on the naked body three months hence. And he is disenfranchised according to Law.

Sarah Nettleton for her actuall uncleaness with Thomas Miller is sentenced by this Court to suffer corporal punishment by whipping on her naked body after she is delivered of her Child or she to pay a fine of 10ˡˡ: to yᵉ publ: Treasury.²

In short, for committing the crime of adultery and for impregnating a woman who was not his wife, Miller paid with his body, his money, and his prized political liberty: he was disenfranchised, which means he had held the status of a freeman, which also means he had been a full member of his church. Although the disenfranchisement was probably temporary, losing it would have been a blow, and both the whipping and his loss of legal freeman status would have been humiliatingly public. As a party to the crime, Nettleton was given the option of either paying a fine or being publicly whipped after delivering the baby. She may have had male relatives who could scrape together £10 to spare her the whipping. Or it's possible that Miller was expected to pay her fine: because he had publicly admitted that she was carrying his child, he would have been legally bound to support her and the baby for as long as she remained unmarried.

Complete as this punishment seems, however, it was only phase 1 of Miller's and Nettleton's legal journey. Shortly after the March 1 judgment another entry appeared in the record book: "Upon yᵉ request of some of yᵉ Inhabitants of MiddleTown to yᵉ end that yᵉ wife of Thomas Miller and Sarah Nettleton may be provided for This Court doth order The Constable and Nathˡˡ Bacon of MiddleTown to secure Millers estate until further order be taken by this Court."³

Why were the unidentified inhabitants of Mattabeseck/Middletown concerned about whether or not "the wife of Thomas Miller and Sarah Nettleton" would get a fair share of Miller's wealth? Who was Nathaniel Bacon? Why was he authorized to freeze Miller's accounts, as it were, and prevent him from buying or selling anything until an inventory could be taken? The final court record for Thomas Miller, after noting that this inventory was completed by May 9, 1666, explains all:

> This Court considering the estate of Thomas Miller Inventoried and the desire of his wife lately deceased in reference to yᵉ wrongs done to her by his notorious uncleanes That yᵉ Court would settle some considerible part of yᵉ estate of the said Miller upon her Child the wife of Nathaniel

Bacon Doe therfore see just cause to allow to Nathaniel Bacon husband to Anna Bacon daughter to the said Thomas & Isbel Miller All ye wearing Apparel linnen and Woolen with those other smal things mentioned in the Inventory [and] out of ye Estate Thirty pounds more to be pay^d unto ye said Nathaneel Bacon. . . . This being discharged by Thomas Miller it is to be a final issue of all demands that Nathaneel Bacon may make for charge in Keeping Isabel Miller or for her Buriall or upon Any Account for things past. The Land of Thomas Miller stands as security for payment of ye said summ.[4]

In other words, as Miller's wife Isabel (or Isbel) Miller lay dying, she asked the court to ensure that her adult child, Anne Miller, by then married to Nathaniel Bacon, would receive the goods and money she was due from her father's estate before Miller had a chance to write her out of his will in favor of his new child with Sarah Nettleton. Isabel Miller saw this demand as a way to right one of the "wrongs done to her" by her husband's adultery. She had, in her own way, also been publicly shamed, humiliated, and punished by his crime; and as the fines he had paid had gone to the court, not to the injured parties (that is, to Isabel and Anne), she wanted to make sure that her daughter received what she was due from her untrustworthy father. The court granted Isabel Miller's dying appeal, appointing Anne's husband, Nathaniel Bacon, to join the constable in sorting through Miller's estate to select items—first for himself, then for his wife, and then for their daughter, also named Anne Bacon. Physical items would be seized immediately, and another fine would be paid during the following March to cover the Bacons' expenses in housing and caring for Isabel as she lay dying. Once this fine was paid, Bacon's right to a portion of his father-in-law's estate would be permanently satisfied. Thomas Miller's most precious possession, his land, would be held as a security until his final payment was made. Once he had officially provided for his daughter and her household, he could turn to providing for Sarah Nettleton and their child without any danger of robbing Anne Miller Bacon of her rightful inheritance.

What do we know about Thomas Miller? He committed adultery with Sarah Nettleton, got her pregnant, and was punished for it by the court; and before her death his wife, Isabel Miller, forced him to give over part of his estate to his daughter. We can guess that he lived peacefully and lawfully after this brief run-in with the legal system, which lasted for only a little more than two months in 1666. Miller died in Mattabeseck/Middletown in 1680, and on

December 2 of that year he made his final appearance in the court records, which documented that his will had been read and proved by the court. What does this tell us about the colonizers' legal system in the mid-1600s? It seems to have administered swift justice according to well-known and accepted rules of behavior, and it took forceful, immediate steps to ensure the just treatment of Anne Miller Bacon after hearing from her mother and some unidentified concerned citizens.

But the legal records don't tell the full story of Thomas Miller and his crime or how its resolution spanned eight long years and immersed two churches in two colonies in a passionate magnum opus of rebuke, repentance, and restoration that did not end until all of the living parties were reunited and reconciled to their churches, their families, and themselves. This larger story lies within the records of the Congregational church in Agawam/Rowley in the Massachusetts Bay Colony, where Miller had become a member before moving to Mattabeseck/Middletown. The town of Agawam/Rowley's civil records give us no further insights into the man; the longest entry for Miller is a note under the heading "A list of those who had house lots in the first division is here given with a brief account of each," which reads, "Thomas Miller. Had wife Isabel, and was a carpenter. About 1652 he removed to Middletown, Conn., where he died 14 Aug. 1683, aged above 70 years."[5] The other nineteen entries for Miller are all records of his land transactions. It is the ecclesiastical records that provide us with an epic account of spiritual failure and redemption.

Occasionally, the Agawam/Rowley church records of the Thomas Miller story seem to operate as a ghost in the machine in secular annals. George Blodgett's 1887 history of the town includes an inside-story twist that clearly does not come from the court records:

> In 1666, although living in Middletown, he was placed on trial before the church in Agawam/Rowley, wherein he still retained membership, for an offence committed in Middletown. The church adjudged him guilty and ordered him ex-communicated, which order was publicly read, 6 Oct. 1667. "Afterward pray' was made the God would ratify the sentence & let loose Satan on Him" (Ch[urch] R[ecord]).[6]

This mention of a "church trial" hints that Miller's offence was not restricted to his public, civil life, but it explains nothing about what that really meant. Blodgett simply cherrypicked a line from a church record that, in his opinion, succinctly represented and summed up the difference between the beneficial logic of jurisprudence and the benighted illogic of religious belief. He misinterpreted the Agawam/Rowley church records to support the stereotype of an unforgiving and irrational Puritan religion.

Yet the truth runs contrary to the popular vision of Puritans who were eager to punish, excommunicate, and ruin an adulterer. The Agawam/Rowley church records show us the extreme lengths to which two churches went to carry out the Congregational process of *rebuking* a sinner and then helping them to authentic repentance in order to restore them to the church without lingering resentment or shame. These records even help us to understand, and approve of, the church's stated desire that Satan be let loose on Thomas Miller after his excommunication.

Following is a much-reduced summary of the Thomas Miller records, which ran into dozens of entries and filled more than a hundred pages in the Agawam/Rowley church record book between November 1666 and September 1674.[7] For clarity, I've removed crossed-out words and lines and expanded some abbreviated words.

REBUKE

In November 1666, Agawam/Rowley's minister, Samuel Phillips, made the first of many entries in the church records regarding Thomas Miller's adultery. In keeping with his goal to create records that would be easily understood for all eternity, Phillips referred to himself in the third person.

> November 4, 1666
>
> Br. Thomas Miller living now at Middleton in Connecticut guilty of Adultery wth his mayd. as was prooved by a Letter formerly from B^{r}. Harris, [&] an extract out of ye Court Records there . . . [m^{r}. phillips] propounded [to] ye Church & say^{d} in order to doe someth: farther Sc: Excommunication next Sabbath *mentioned it as needlesse to send to Him or for Him* . . . yet at ye Urgency of Some Brethren it was agreed, to send to Him to Come if he could. (AR 68)

Phillips had received a letter bearing the news of Thomas Miller's crime and punishments from a church member (the title "Brother" alerts us to his status) whom the minister would later identify as Daniel Harris of Mattabeseck/Middletown. Both Phillips and Harris call Miller "brother" because a brother in one church was considered to be a brother in any other church as they were all brethren in Christ. (The same was true for sisters.) Miller was "living at" Mattabeseck/Middletown—that is, it was the site of his house and business. But he was still a member of and a brother to the body of believers at Agawam/Rowley, even though he hadn't lived there for fourteen years, because the people worshipping at Mattabeseck/Middletown had not yet been gathered into a church. They were only a congregation without a minister; a church would not be gathered until November 4, 1668.[8] So when Miller's story began in 1666, the Mattabeseck/Middletown faithful had to turn to the church at Agawam/Rowley and to Samuel Phillips to begin the process of church discipline and to call Miller into it.

In this entry, Phillips wrote that he "propounded" to the church that it was *"needlesse to send to Him or for Him"*—that is, to write to Miller and ask him to come to Agawam/Rowley to meet with church members in person. It's odd and out of character for Phillips to have made such an unorthodox suggestion, given that the process of rebuke-repent-restore always took place in person. Thus, the brethren urgently dissented, and Phillips agreed to "send to Him [Miller] to Come if he could." The minister did so the next day in the name of the church. "We did send a Letter unsealed," he noted, using the plural to show that the letter came from those who embodied the church, not just from him as their leader. The fact that the letter was unsealed emphasizes that it was not a private communication but a public one from the body of the church to one of its own limbs.

> The Church of X^t here at Rowley, of wch you yet remayne a member, having some time since heard sad tidings concerning your fall into scandalous Evill of Uncleannesse, we were not a little grieved for it, for much as you have hereby wounded your own soule . . . & the profession wch you have made; And especially, we are grieved that we heare nothing, neyther from your Self, nor none else touching any Sound Repentance. (AR 68)

In the letter Phillips made it clear that Miller's crime had harmed his soul, marring it with sin and thus damaging his profession of faith. He also noted that, in the eight months since Miller's civil sentencing, he had never reached out to the church for help or to express remorse. This was a very bad sign, an indication that Miller was unrepentant, which is why the church's next suggestion, voiced by Phillips, was so important: "oh Brother! Sit down & aske your Self, what have you done; Did you not hasten ye Death of your deare wife now at Rest[?] judge your self now, that you be not judged of ye Lord another day when every secret thing shall be brought to judgment" (AR 68).

Here began the rebuke. In the eyes of the church, Miller's crime of adultery directly contributed to the untimely death of his wife, Isabel Miller, who could not bear the sorrow of seeing him commit adultery with someone in their own household. Nowhere in the stentorian and concise civil court records do we see any mention of this idea. They required only that "the wife of Thomas Miller may be provided for," and that provision was strictly material—the household goods and money due to the Millers' daughter. Isabel had been wronged, so the court swiftly rectified that wrong via payment and goods.

The church records present a completely different picture. Isabel Miller had been wronged because her husband had broken faith with her, causing heartbreak that contributed to her early death. Erasing those crimes required Thomas Miller's true repentance—his open acknowledgment that his guilt had not been at all expiated by the court's sentence, that handing over a warming pan and some corned beef to his daughter had not washed away his crimes. He needed to take responsibility for the harm he had done to his wife before he could begin to address the harm he had done to his own soul.[9]

But rebuke, even at this level, could be swiftly followed by hope of restoration, if Miller were able to truly repent of his sins:

> Yet y^r is Hope in Israel, if ye Lord help you to take shame unto your self: ... But we have not time to speak to you at this Distance as we would if you were with us. The Church hath Desired [to] signify to you that they^r desire is [that] you would make a journey to Agawam/Rowley as soon as possibly you can, & send us word when that will be: We have not proceeded to censure tho: your sin deserve, because we are willing to wayt a while for your Repentance coming to us, Hoping that ye meanes y^t may be used for your reforming may be more effectuall by your being present then if you were absent, & you know not but some thing may be spoken by your Brethren, & old Neighbours that may have some Impression on your heart.... Thus desiring ye Lord to grant you Repentance & Remission of Sins. We rest Your Loving friends Rowley. 5 (9) 1666 (AR 68)

Miller's first step in getting to real repentance would be to take the time to make the long journey to Agawam/Rowley and allow painful but "more effectuall" conversations to take place between himself and his "Brethren, & old

Neighbours." This work would begin to restore both him and the church body that he had maimed. The church did not blink at asking Miller to undertake a long and expensive journey that would require him to leave his occupation and his new wife and infant for many weeks. What could be more important than redeeming his soul to God and rejoining the church body to make it whole? The danger was that his crime could result in excommunication from the church body of Agawam/Rowley, which would expose him to the full force of Satan's wiles. A whole and healthy living church body had a strong immune system to help protect it from Satan's overtures. If this immune system were weakened, not only Miller but the entire church body would be exposed to danger, for it would no longer be whole. Excommunication would not heal the church's wound, nor was it meant to be a final, irrevocable action. On the contrary, it was an extreme form of rebuke—an emetic used only when necessary to expel a poisonous member. The goal was always to lead even the most egregious, damaging, and recalcitrant sinners to repentance and restore the church body. That's why the church, through Phillips, closed the letter by asking God to "grant you Repentance & Remission of sins." This was the goal.

Miller's reply to Phillips's letter of November 5, 1666 arrived in Agawam/Rowley six months later, on May 25, 1667. It was dated April 30, and Phillips noted that it had been "sent in his [Miller's] behalf," which likely means that a member of Miller's church in Mattabeseck/Middletown had written it for him. While most Congregationalists could read, not all could write, and in this difficult situation Miller may have found it easier to speak aloud and have someone else record his words. A close reading reveals just how negative his message was and how badly his church at Agawam/Rowley received it:

> Loveing and Deare Brethren
>
> I that am now unworthy to be called a Brother have received your carefull Letter wch I finde was written Nov: 5th last but nothing thereof was communicated to me till 28th instant upon ye Evening. (AR 69)

In other words, Miller unwisely began his letter by accusing Brother Harris of Mattabeseck/Middletown, who had been entrusted to carry the letter to Miller from Agawam/Rowley, of concealing it from him for six months. He went on to grieve that

> ye satisfaction of so base a Lust should be more precious to my vile Heart, then ye will of God, his glory, the honour of his [glorious] Gospell, the

credit of his Churches, the comfort of my Deare wife, Relations, neighbours, [and] my own Spirituall interest. . . . [T]o be sure, I doe wonder greatly at yᵉ kindenesse of God to such an one as I, that *he Should provide yᵗ Such as are Spirituall should indeavour to Restore such an one.* (AR 70)

Though Miller offered a laundry list of all the entities and individuals, his "Deare wife" included, that he had harmed by his actions, his hasty apology for failing to take their "comfort" into account was weak repentance. Rather than moving on quickly to speak of his gratitude for the efforts of the saints at Agawam/Rowley to restore him, he should have focused on fully stating his repentance. The falsity of his remorse and gratitude was made concrete in his claim that he was too busy to go to Agawam/Rowley, as he had "many [engagements] of work for my Necessity, wᶜʰ I think I cannot Lawfully neglect to performe" (AR 70). That statement made it clear that Miller believed it was unreasonable for the Agawam/Rowley church to ask him to forget his professional responsibilities.

Then Miller admitted his real reason for taking so long to respond to Agawam/Rowley's letter. It wasn't that Brother Harris had concealed it from him; rather, Miller assumed that the church had already heard about his public confession and wouldn't require him to do anything more:

> I ought to have confesst my sins to you that I might have bin holpen by your prayers, but yᵉ ground of that Silence was yᵗ I [had] on yᵉ Lord's day made a publicke Confession to justify yᵉ Lord & Shame & Condemne my selfe & warne others[.] I did think yᵗ this being Known in all yᵉ parts where I had done this dishonʳ to God & set the Evil Example to others was as much as I was to attend [to]. (AR 70)

Given that his public confession of sin must have been "Known in all yᵉ parts where I had done this dishonʳ," he claimed to believe that this "was as much as I was to attend [to]"—in other words, that he had completed his work of repentance. He then added a version of this confession to the letter and closed with a clear expression of the concept of rebuke-repent-restore: "*Repentance is Commanded & required of all men [& that] in ordʳ to Remission.* . . . I desier to Heare from you to have farther Directions & *that you would not reject me*" (AR 71).

Thomas Miller's letter demonstrates that he believed that he had done all that was required of him to put his sin behind him. He had made a voluntary public confession of his sin and the crime to which it had led, emphasizing his foulness and the endangerment of his soul. He had begged the forgiveness of those in Mattabeseck/Middletown who had been forced to witness his sin and had warned all hearers to avoid his fate and learn from his terrible example. Now he had shared this confession with the Agawam/Rowley church in writing, and he was asking it to deliver the restoration that his repentance had earned him.

Miller's letter arrived in Agawam/Rowley along with a short but profoundly effective message from the brethren at Mattabeseck/Middletown, which Samuel Phillips duly recorded in the church record book: "These are to certify [that] about an hour or rather lesse, before ye death of Izbell Miller, her husband desiring of her forgivenesse, she made that Returne y^t she forgave him wth all her heart, as God for X^t his sake forgave her" (AR 73). Miller wanted the church at Agawam/Rowley to know this fact. If his wife could forgive him, then the church, which in his view hadn't been injured by him, should certainly have been able to do the same.

This was not, however, how the church understood the situation, and one member's reaction to Miller's letter was immediate and clear: "Upon the reading of this, Br. John Pierson stood up and told us that [it spoke] not so much in favour of Miller's Repentance, [saying] that indeed while he was in Prison at Hartford and fared Extreme hardly in Irons, etc., *then* he was willing to hear, but his carriage *after* that was that for which he could not give any such testimony as arguing Repentance." But the rest of the church members were doubtful and resolved to wait to vote on Miller's case, "eyther to absolve or Censure," until two more of their body returned from a trip to Boston. More conversation, prayer, and debate were needed (AR 73–74).

Three weeks later, on June 15, 1667, that "farther discourse" took place, and Brother Swan confirmed Brother Pierson's story about Miller's seemingly inauthentic repentance. Still, it wasn't this or even the tacked-on note about Isabel's forgiveness that rankled the church body most. Members remained focused on the heart of the matter: "*he had spoken little or noth: to y^t matter of his Cruell carriage to his wife*" (AR 74). Though he had included his wife in the long list of people whom he had harmed by his crime, Miller hadn't differentiated between the harm he had done to her from the harm he had done to his neighbors and to other uninvolved onlookers. His public confession had been all about himself: his sin, his fear and trembling before God and man, his shame, his sorrow, his stated repentance. Miller's attitude was that he had endangered himself through his sin but now, through his repentance, was back on the straight and narrow. He was once again safe, and to him that was the most important thing.

But the church at Agawam/Rowley knew that Miller was not safe. For as long as he avoided acknowledging that the worst part of his crime was not the harm it had done to him but the harm it had done to his wife, he was still in peril. Because he had not acknowledged the real extent of his sin, he could not make the true repentance that would restore him to his church and move him closer to Christ. Miller seemed to think that Isabel's forgiveness meant that she had not been badly harmed by his sin. But the church at Agawam/Rowley demanded that he repent for sinning against her first and foremost because that was the most serious of his sins, a betrayal of the deep bond between husband and wife. Agawam/Rowley's insistence on this was important. For Congregationalists, betraying one's partner in marriage was a serious offence against the sanctity of kinship, one that revealed deep sinfulness within the guilty party. Thomas Miller had shown an inhuman lack of love and loving kindness for his wife during her life and even after her death. Until he admitted this, his repentance would not be authentic and could not open the way to restoration.

REBUKE ... REPENT?

On May 25, 1667, the church at Agawam/Rowley sent a letter again asking Thomas Miller to travel to meet with its members. While waiting to hear back, it dealt with other matters of church discipline, read letters to and from other churches, and conducted other business. Four months later, on September 22, 1667, his reply finally arrived. It was again accompanied by a message "from some Brethren in Middleton," who stated, "We cannot but wth much thankfullnesse take notice of ye faithfullnesse & Love towards Him as we wish his welfare; & your truely X^{tian} tendernesse towards us y^r in, Wherein your selves are (thro: Gods grace) pleased to contrive for [our] future peace, with truth & holynesse" (AR 80). The brethren understood that Miller's unrepented sin was not only harming the church at Agawam/Rowley but preventing the faithful at Mattabeseck/Middletown from becoming a church, again harming Agawam/Rowley, which longed to welcome a new church body into reciprocal relation.

The outlook was grim. Speaking of Miller, the brethren reported that "we wish we could say we find Him truly broken under sight & sense of his sin [but instead he is] *rather blaming his former Yokefellow then Himselfe*: we dare not say we judge him fit agayn to be received into ye boosome of Church–:fellowship as one to our charity absolved in heaven" (AR 80). This time, instead of using Isabel's forgiveness to pave the way for his restoration, Miller had contorted it into a claim that his infidelity had been her fault. The implication was that she had readily forgiven him not out of Christian loving kindness but because she had felt guilt over having driven him to betrayal. For the brethren who had gathered to speak to Miller in his home, this attitude was shocking and repellent and absolutely precluded his restoration "into the boosome" of the church. Yet it did not mean that Miller would be abandoned to his sin: "Through grace we shall not faile to discharge any duty of Love towards Him; as his Spirituall need Shal require" (AR 80–81). He needed to be brought to repentance so that he and the Agawam/Rowley church could be restored to health and the Mattabeseck/Middletown church could be gathered. This would require a big effort on the part of the Agawam/Rowley church body; but as Lisa Brooks writes, "when the network falls out of balance, everything else must shift into action to create a new equilibrium."[10]

Shocked as they likely were by this note, church members in Agawam/Rowley were in for even more grief and disappointment when they read aloud Miller's own letter, dated September 20, 1667:

> [Y]ou are pleased to charge me wth mercyles & Cruel carriage to my wife while she lived, whereof I cannot charge myS. in ye full extent of it, yet thus farre I doe own & bewayle my breach of covenant wth Her, wch did [justly] cause sore griefe of heart to her to see me sin so heynously agaynst God & to violate those bonds wch I ought to have maintayned wth her self & [while] I cannot but conclude it was matter of bodily weaknesse to her, *God alone knows whither it did hasten her end yea or no*. (AR 81–82)

Miller plainly stated that he could not accept the church's accusation that he had been cruel to Isabel. Yes, he had broken covenant with his life partner, and, yes, this had grieved her deeply, and, yes, this probably had affected her health to some extent, but no one, he claimed, could jump to the conclusion that it had "hasten[ed] her end." In his letter, he did not ask the church at Agawam/Rowley to let him know if they agreed with his view; he simply stated it as fact. Then, washing his hands of the issue, he went on to reiterate that he himself had been more harmed and burdened by his sin: "I begge y^e Lords

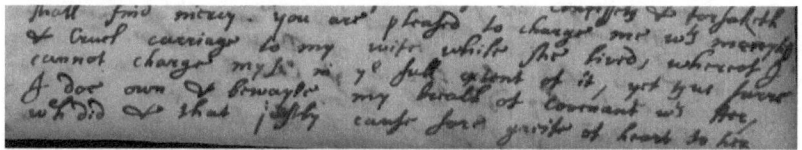

FIGURE 1. Excerpt from Thomas Miller letter, September 20, 1667, in "The Phillips Diary (church records), 1664–1784," in the Rowley, Massachusetts, First Congregational Church records, RG 4836, Congregational Library and Archives, Boston.

pardon for my sin therein [and] doe humbly begge [your] pray^{r}s dayly for me at ye throne of grace, [that] I may show forth my true Repentance in an humble holy watchfull walking before Him & that all ye dayes of my Life" (AR 82). That is, over time, perhaps, with God's help, he would "show forth true Repentance," not by acknowledging that he had broken faith with his wife but by living out the rest of his days in a respectable manner. Miller managed to shrink his infidelity from one of the worst sins he could commit to one of many sins in general. All he needed to do to be restored to God's grace, he implied, was to put time and distance between himself and that act. Thus, there was no real urgency, and he again refused to travel to Agawam/Rowley, which, he said, would leave "my family remote without help" and affect his "public employment" (AR 82).

It seemed clear that stronger rebuke was needed. On September 29, 1667, the church revisited the letters they had received and considered again the report of Nathaniel Collins, the ministerial candidate helping the congregation deal with this matter, that "in ye Eyes of Brethren [in Mattabeseck/Middletown] he was such an one as [that] ye Church [in Agawam/Rowley] would give offence if they did not Excommunicate Him. And it was then Voted y^t ye sentence should be pronounced next Sabbath" (AR 82). And so, at last, on October 6, 1667, the Agawam/Rowley church voted to do so:

> Mr Phillips after his sermon [spoke] to the Congregation & related the sin, & lay^d before y^m ye Comdmt broken & aggravations[;] and then craving the Churches consent by y^r
> Vote agayn past & then was the sentence pronounced-----
> We doe in ye name & authority & by y^e powr of y^e Ld Jesus y^e great King & Law-giver of y^e Church, & by y^e Consent of this Church, cutt of the say^d Thom: Miller–Afterward pray^r was made that God would ratify the sentence, & let loose Satan on Him---(AR 83)

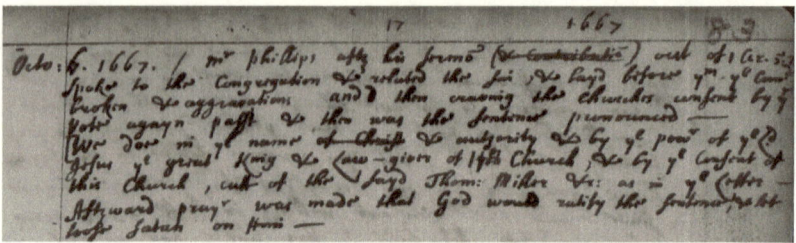

FIGURE 2. From Thomas Miller's excommunication record, October 6, 1667, in "The Phillips Diary (church records), 1664–1784," in the Rowley, Massachusetts, First Congregational Church records, RG 4836, Congregational Library and Archives, Boston.

At the end of this section appears the short line that Blodgett's 1887 history reads as damningly vindictive: "pray^r was made that God would ratify the sentence, & let loose Satan on Him." Yet as I have shown, this statement was not vindictiveness but the necessary condition of excommunication. The church at Agawam/Rowley wanted Miller to feel his alienation and endangerment, hoping that that they would bring him to his senses and, as soon as possible, make him fully aware of how far he had strayed from God. The rebuke of the church had not been enough; therefore, Satan must be set upon him. Still, even in the worst of circumstances, the hope of and for restoration remained. The church made this clear by again offering Miller a path toward restoration, including it in the same letter that informed him of his excommunication, though not before emphasizing how deeply he had sinned:

> That your repentance is not thorough appears [in] that you judge not your self for blood-guiltynesse in respect of your carriage to your former wife but rather lay blame upon her then your self. . . . [Y]ou are und^r great guilt as to Shortning of y^r wives Life and thereby breaking ye 6th Command. . . . It will be not easy to undoe by Repentance what you have done by sin. but Xt can give it. . . . Consid^r how much you have done to undoe not only your self, but ye soul of her y^t is now y^r wife. when you inticed her how knew you that God would ever give her Repentance, wch God give you both that you perish not. . . . Consid^r whither you have not cause to question whither ever you had any true work of grace wrought in you. (AR 84, 85)

Notably, for the first time, the church identified Sarah Nettleton as another person whom Miller's sin had harmed. Not only had he caused the untimely death of Isabel, but he then put "her y^t is now y^r wife" in grave danger by leading her into sin. The writer unblinkingly described the reckless selfishness of that act: "when you inticed her how knew you that God would ever give her Repentance"? Miller remorselessly endangered another soul, and now he needed to consider if he had ever really possessed God's saving grace. This was the low point he must reach in order to make any progress toward true repentance and restoration. Yet his grieved friends in Agawam/Rowley held out that hope in the conclusion of their letter: "God of all grace effectually convince you of & humble you for, & turne from your sin that so you may find Mercy" (AR 85).

In composing this letter, the church at Agawam/Rowley did not triumph over Miller or take glee in setting Satan loose on him. Instead, the body wanted to make it clear that he had passed through a gate into what might be a land of no return, if he did not take his expulsion seriously. But the church received no reply for five long years. During that interval, the church at Mattabesecck/Middletown was gathered at last, and Nathaniel Collins was ordained as its minister on November 4, 1668. Then, in late May 1672, Samuel Phillips sent Thomas Miller a short personal letter:

> I could not but put you in mind how much it is to my greif & to ye greif of this Church (of wch sometimes you were a member) that soe many years have past since that dreadfull ordinance passed upon you, & yet we hear nothing of any good Effect that ordinance has had upon you: ... you have not onely refused to come to us, but have had noe heart soe much as to write to us how it is wth you since your cutting off: ... [I]t were better to hear y^t you are troubled that your heart is noe more affected nor afflicted for ye dishonour you have cast upon ye house of God, then to hear y^t you look upon your self as haveing repented already.... [D]oe not be senceless of your separation from Gods people.... [M]y desire to God is that your repentance may be as deep & evident as your sin was great & aggravated.... I Rest your greaved friend S. P. Rowley 29 May 1672 (AR 92)

In other words, Phillips would rather hear that Miller was concerned about feeling no repentance than to learn that he believed he had already repented.

More months passed. Then, when even Phillips may have lost hope, a letter came from Thomas Miller. Read to the church on November 3, 1672, it began with his usual excuses for being unable to travel to Agawam/Rowley "wthout indangering the comfort of myself and family" (AR 102). Miller went on to say that God had helped him to actively seek out the work of confronting ("seeing") and assessing his own sin; despite his own sense of deep unworthiness, he felt able to once again hope that God might pardon him. Then he wrote: "[Y]ᵉ lord was pleased to shew me that ther was yet hope of pardon for yˢ my great transgression, & to convince me *yᵗ yʳ was no other way to it but by my returning to yᵉ lord my God & by acknowledging my iniquity before him*, yᵗ I have transgressed" (AR 102). He had cut out the middlemen, deciding that he no longer needed to listen to his brothers and sisters or be in conversation with them. He told the church that he was aware of *"my horrid sin that I am not onely guilty of my self, but the instrumental cause of drawing her that is now my wife to alsoe; likewise the heart sorrow it brought to my wife deceas'd* wᶜʰ Covenant I ought alsoe to have kept pure" (AR 103). Via these words, Miller edged closer to acknowledging the full extent of his sin, but he steadfastly refused to admit that this had contributed to Isabel's untimely death. Then he asked the church to let him know if they were satisfied with his explanations and ready to lift the ban of excommunication: "That if it be the good will of the lord that you may receive soe farr incorragement from what you hear from me, or may hear from others, that you may see cause to reinstate me into those libertyes of the house of God which I have though unworthy sometime injoyed, that I may partake of the good things therof which I doe in some poor measure pant & breathe after" (AR 103).

The letter was a major red flag. In essence, Miller was suggesting that the church rely on any information other than his own. He refused to appear before them and engage in a two-way conversation, clearly revealing his fear that such questioning would expose the falsity of his set pieces. Equally important, his refusal to go to the church at Agawam/Rowley made it impossible to heal the injuries done to the sisters and brothers there. He was asking them to focus only on his restoration and to ignore their own. Members of the church, still anguished by his crime, had no way to recover because Miller would not talk with them, listen to them, and offer healing to them. Once again, his alleged repentance had made no dent in his selfishness.

The Mattabeseck/Middletown church was aware of Miller's faults and understood how his letter would affect the church at Agawam/Rowley; so, via their minister Nathaniel Collins, they sent along a contextualizing letter. In it, they expressed cautious optimism and suggested a solution to Miller's stubborn refusal to allow the church at Agawam/Rowley to question and counsel him:

[T]he substance of what ye brethren say, (& I dare not therin contradict them but joyne my hopes wth them) is that he is on the coming hand, [and that] the most Expedient way for ample satisfaction would be to draw out the substance of what he sayth [with] sutable understanding & penitance, [and] *to owne the same [in] the congregation in our Towne, & y^t it be returned attested by some of us in order to his acceptance*: We are very willing to incorrage his return, & afrayd to heal him slightly. (AR 103)

In short, the church at Mattabeseck/Middletown would work with Miller to draw him firmly but lovingly toward the full understanding of his sin that was vital to true repentance and restoration, continuing those efforts until he was willing and able to "*owne the same*" in the presence of church and congregation. Proof of an authentic repentance, as witnessed by the church at Mattabeseck/Middletown, would then be conveyed to the church at Agawam/Rowley. Collins closed by asking the church at Agawam/Rowley to respond to Miller's message and grant permission for him to work with the church in Mattabeseck/Middletown "before winter" (AR 103).

The church at Agawam/Rowley duly wrote to Miller: "The church [do] by thes give you to understand that *as they were not hasty to cast you out if it could according to Rule have bin prevented, soe neither dare they be ovre hasty to loose you till they may have farther* [understanding] *that your repentance is soe thorow as that you shall alsoe be loosed in heaven, without which looseing on Earth will avail nothing Except to your hurt*" (AR 104–5). The church emphasized that it could not restore Miller on Earth if he had not truly been restored by God. Each step of the process had to be authentic: serious rebuke for a serious crime, real repentance before God and man, and true restoration of the church body on Earth and in heaven. Otherwise, many souls besides his would be in danger. The church then turned once more to the core of the problem with Miller's alleged repentance: his refusal to admit that his adultery had been a crime against his wife and had directly contributed to her early death. The vivid emotional language in this passage is striking:

[T]hough the Church has told you foremerly that they judged you were guilty [of] shortning your formar wives life [through] greif at your unclean doings, *yet you past it by in your last lettre with a very short mention as not much convinced or sencible of your Evill carriage towards her*.... To greev & vex a neighbour to ye shortning of his life is not soe bad as to greeve & vex a wife [to] ye shortning of her life, *oh what a*

> *burden was it, a heart killing thing, to take notice of her husband as one whose heart was gone from her to imbrace another; to have buried her husband would not have so Grievd her as to see him left to his hearts lusts*: To be sure such sorrow of heart as she felt did break her spirit weaken & wast her body. . . . Tis not enough y^t your wife when she was leaving the world did forgive you. what will y^t avail if god grant you not deep repentance without wch no remission[?] (AR 105–6)

No repentance could be valid before God or man unless it included repentance for contributing to Isabel's death. Miller did not want to confess to a kind of murder, but that's what he would have to do in order to truly face, acknowledge, and own the depth of his sin and crime. Only then could he know if Christ had truly forgiven him.

Clearly, this is so much more than the Hartford County court ever asked of Miller. Only by comparing the civil proceedings with the church's outreach can we fully absorb how weak, partial, and uninterested the court's rulings were. Enduring physical punishment and not reoffending was all that his sociopolitical world required of him. Justice for English colonizers in Woodland New England was transactional: commit a certain crime; pay a certain price; endure a certain punishment. Once the transaction was complete, good order was supposedly restored. Lingering resentment, guilt, and damage were ignored and even suppressed by reminders that the criminal had paid his dues and should be allowed to move forward. In contrast, the Congregational way understood that crimes were about bodies of people and the relationships that created and maintained them, not about individuals alone. Unless a crime was fully expiated in the hearts, minds, and relationships of that community, it would always be tried and retried, again and again, because the wounds would still be open. What the churches at Agawam/Rowley and Mattabeseck/Middletown were practicing was so much more time-intensive and holistic than the judicial court practice as to be incomparable, and in time this Congregational justice, already partial, would be phased out. But it was the church way, not the court's practice, that culminated in an authentic result.

The church at Agawam/Rowley concluded its letter to Miller by consenting to allow him to work with the church at Mattabeseck/Middletown. This done, they then addressed their sister church via a short letter written by Samuel Phillips in the name of the church, a missive that also included a few personal notes:

> We are glad to hear (though it be long [since]) from Tho: Miller that
> God is pleased to help him to consider of his ways in some measure....
> *I doe & the Church heer give you thanks for the love you have shoun &
> the paines you have taken to bind up & to get home that poor wandering
> Soul..... If he shall publickly & pœnitently acknowledg what has bin Evill
> yea wicked in his wayse [we] shall [take] off the censures & shall have fur-
> ther cause of thankfullness to your selves.* (AR 106)

The importance of "[gathering] home that poor wandering Soul" cannot be overstated. For more than five years, two churches had been steadfastly committed to the restoration of a single individual who had been consistently hostile and uncooperative. Their understanding of every person in terms of their relationship within the whole body was contrary to the sociopolitical settlement of not only Puritan Woodland New England but the entire European civilization from which they had come. Today it is hard to take in how strong and well defined the process was and how actively it worked in early Congregationalism.

RESTORED: THE LIVED IDEAL

It took two more years for Thomas Miller to reappear in the Agawam/Rowley church records. But when he did, on September 4, 1674, the entry celebrated what everyone had been praying for. At last he had returned to his church at Agawam/Rowley to join with the body and offer true repentance: "Septemb 4 1674 *Tho: Miller came to Rowley to seek for reconciliation wth & readmission into the Church of Christ therin*, & brought letters testimoniall from the Reverend Pastor & several brethren of the church of Middletowne wher his abode Is . . . soe now by ye manifestation of His sincere Effectuell return y^t name may be glorified, your soules refreshed, & his own indeed restored Restored & comforted" (AR 124).

While Miller's repentance was "brief," it was effective, not only because of what he said but because of where he said it. Here is how his confession was recorded:

> *By these you may be pleased to understand That Tho: Miller, who for soe many years has bin under y^t awfull sentence of excomunication out of ye church of Xst at Rowley, is now received into brotherly relation with the*

> *sayd church, their acceptance of him being manifested by a full & unanimous vote......* He has acknowledged his Evill in rending away from this church against counsell and that he went away not contented wth what accommodations he had heer to seek inlargements in worldly matters which he fears his heart was then more upon then things not seen. . . . Upon the consideration also of his carriage to his foremer wife, *he has acknowledg'd that he sined greviously filling her heart with much greif to the shortning of her life as may be justly feared; [Thus] we comitt this our restored brother wth you all & ourselves to him who is our lord & yours in whom we are Yor loving brethren in ye fayth & fellowship of the Gospell*
> Rowley 7 of Septemb: 1674 (AR 126)

The record also notes that the vote to restore Miller to full relationship with and membership in the church was "full and unanimous." In the Congregational ideal, a single body spoke with a single voice, so churches always strove to achieve unanimous votes, whether the matters were large or small. Unanimity, however, was not always possible, and many churches allowed majority votes as long as the dissenters were not discontented. In a case as contentious and important as Miller's, however, the church had to vote unanimously because its action would affect its very being.

As the record makes clear, Miller was no longer claiming to have been a good man who had made a single mistake in a single moment of weakness. Instead, he admitted that he had abruptly "rended away" from the church at Agawam/Rowley, leaving the town because he had been impatient to make money. The word *rended* is powerful, and it was deliberately chosen to demonstrate that the inauthentic departure of one member had torn away a limb from the church body, a reminder that Miller had harmed the church at Agawam/Rowley long before he had committed adultery. And now, after seven years of denial, he had also admitted that he had "*sined greviously filling her [his wife's] heart with much greif to the shortning of her life*," a conclusion that the church believed was just. Earlier he had asked for and received her pardon, but now he had asked for God's pardon—not for causing her sorrow but for contributing to her early death.

Miller's full, honest, heartfelt, and, crucially, *in-person* repentance led the church at Agawam/Rowley to vote unanimously to "receive him into memberly relation with us." The ban of excommunication was lifted. This meant that Miller, once again restored to the body of the church, could now ask the church at Agawam/Rowley to formally dismiss him to the church at

Mattabeseck/Middletown so that he could officially join the body there. This formal, orderly dismissal was the opposite of an abrupt, unfounded rending away, and the church at Agawam/Rowley was happy to "consent to grant his desire," stating that "we commit our restored brother with you all, and we commit ourselves to Him who is our Lord and yours, in whom we are your loving brethren in faith and fellowship." The ideal Congregational process of rebuke-repent-restore had been completed at last, saving not only one soul but two church bodies.

The judicial record of Thomas Miller's adultery was extremely brief, apparently objective and fair (if dated in its punishments), and ultimately effective in resolving an unfortunate incident. In reality, however, the actions of the court resolved nothing and left Miller in danger of reoffending and of becoming a social outcast in Mattabeseck/Middletown. The church record of his adultery, on the other hand, is an epic illustration of dedication to the truth, acknowledgment of guilt, and restoration of the individual to his community and to God as well as to the restoration and maintenance of the whole itself. Miller was punished by the law, but he was saved by love.

CHAPTER FIVE

Jacob Chalcom's Cases

Today, anyone who knows about Jacob Chalcom of N'ahteuk/Natick is most likely a descendant or has read his church records. While he committed a crime that was similar to Thomas Miller's, I have not found his case documented in the civil court records of the Massachusetts Bay Colony. However, his name appears in his church's records of discipline cases in 1736 and 1744, seventy-five and eighty-three years after Miller's name appeared in the Agawam/Rowley records. While the N'ahteuk/Natick records are far less complete than those, they show that the same process of rebuke-repent-restore was at work in the second century of Congregationalism in Woodland New England.

WHO WAS JACOB CHALCOM?

Fourteen individual members of the Chalcom family are mentioned in the church records, beginning with Jacob Chalcom himself, who was received to full communion on March 21, 1730 (N v56).[1] (I will discuss the phenomenon of the Halfway Covenant that made this full communion possible in chapter 8.) He married Leah Thomas, who never chose to belong to the church herself, but all of their children were baptized on their father's account: the twins Jacob and Leah on November 5, 1730; Margaret on April 7, 1734; Rachel on October 26, 1740; and a second Leah on February 3, 1745. The Chalcom parents suffered the loss of many of their children. The first Leah died at four months old, a week after her baptism. Margaret died at nine months old, seven months after her baptism. An unnamed child died in February 1742, and Rachel died at eighteen months old, sixteen months after her baptism. Young Jacob survived infancy but died at age fifteen in 1745.

Because the church records of N'ahteuk/Natick are fragmentary, I've turned to the town's vital records to fill in missing information—though, as usual, the civil records are incomplete for Indigenous and Black people. They also constantly erase Indigenous identity—for instance, neither the first infant Leah nor Margaret are identified as "Indian."[2] Such "documentary genocide" in the official record, as Jean O'Brien describes it, created and supported the myth of Indigenous disappearance even as Indigenous people continued to live on the lands to which they belonged.[3] This issue extends well beyond N'ahteuk/Natick. As Philip J. Greven Jr. writes, "the problem of the reliability of vital records, particularly in terms of the underrecording of births and deaths, is one which confronts everyone who attempts to study demographic phenomena prior to the modern period."[4] Again, this shows the vital importance of church demographic records: our historical knowledge suffers when they are not available.

Jacob Chalcom the father reappeared in the church records on January 22, 1735/36, a little less than six years after his admission into full communion, when he was accused of sexual assault against a Nipmuc woman, Hannah Ephraim, the wife of Peter Ephraim (N 9).[5] After consulting both church and civil records, I think she was Hannah Weekucks, who married Ephraim on March 7, 1734.[6] The January 1735/36 entry about Chalcom was a follow-up to what the minister and recorder Oliver Peabody referred to as a "difficult case." In it he noted that Hannah Ephraim was appearing before the church to revise her previous charge against Chalcom:

> I stay^d the Church & lay^d before them a difficult case between our brother Jacob Chalcom & Hannah, the wife of Peter Ephraim; She being present accused him of forcibly having carnal knowledge of her. She acknowledged that she had expressed it in terms too strong, ^before now as to her striving against him, upon which the Church voted the continuance of their Christian Love & Charity to her.
>
> & After this ye Church Meeting was by a vote adjourned to Fryday which will be tomorrow come three weeks, for further consideration of what relates to s^d Chalcom. (N 9)

According to Peabody, this record marked the first time he had laid this difficult case before the church, so it seems that Hannah Ephraim had made her initial accusation in private, before the minister and perhaps one or two others. Apparently Ephraim told them she had attempted to fight Chalcom off. Now, before the church, she "acknowledged" that she had not repelled him as strongly as she had claimed. Peabody's record is compressed here. Does this mean that, in the interval between private counsel and public sharing, she reevaluated the incident? Or had she not been completely truthful in making her initial accusation? We can't know because we don't have enough information in the church record and I have not found a civil record of this incident.

In this era, women appeared in church meetings to give testimony, charge people with wrongs, and respond to charges made against themselves. So if we look at the situation in isolation, we might conclude that the church had seen both parties as guilty but Ephraim as less so, given that she immediately received a vote of confidence whereas Chalcom's case needed three more years of consideration.

On February 13, 1735/36, the church met again "& further Considered ye Case of Chalcom. but Came to no votes" (N 9). Then three years later, on March 1, 1739, this entry appeared in the record book: "[A]fter many Endeavours & long waiting Jacob Chalcom Offer^d a Confession of sins Which was read before the Church; but the Churches Acceptance of it, Agreeable to his desire deferred." "Many Endeavors" likely included private meetings with committees of church members and perhaps with Peabody, and each meeting probably resulted in Chalcom's request for more time to consider his rebuke and reach real repentance. By March 1, however, he had offered a confession of sins that represented true repentance, yet he himself asked the church to postpone its vote on whether to accept it. Did Chalcom realize that his repentance was not yet complete, or did he have second thoughts about offering it? Two weeks later, on March 18, the records state, "[F]ollowing S^d Confession Read before the whole Assembly, but ye Churches Acceptance of it Still deferred" (N 9).

Again, Chalcom's confession was read to the "whole Assembly" and again a vote was deferred. Maybe this time the church felt that was something missing from the confession, that Chalcom was offering less than true repentance. Finally, on April 12, 1739, "it was put to ye Vote of the Church whether they Accepted Jacob Chalcoms Confession, & restored him to y^r Charity & passed in the Affirmatives by a great Majority of uplifted hands" (N 9). Rebuke-repent-restore had won the day, and the church body was healed. We have fewer details about the case than we had for Agawam/Rowley, but the process was the same.

Three other men had made public confessions of sins before and during the long resolution process for Jacob Chalcom: the Massachusett Joseph Ephraim Jr. confessed to drunkenness on September 8, 1734, and was restored; the

Englishman Joseph Mills confessed to forging a deed, a case that required the minister to talk "privately with him," led to "Considerable discourse & Many Questions" before the church, and meant that Mills was barred from taking communion. He confessed and was restored nine months later on February 21, 1734/35. The Massachusett Thomas Peegun, also accused of adultery, quickly confessed and was restored in February 1736/7 (N7, 8). While only Chalcom's case was apparently contested, a July 5, 1742, entry does reveal that the church wanted to ensure that no one would appeared before the body with a confession that they had not had enough time to consider: "The church being stay^d, Voted, that for the Time to Come any person that shall be so Unhappy as to fall into Scandalous Sins, & shall be brot to be willing to make a Publick Confession, & be restored to Charity, their desires should be propounded to ye Church at least one week before their Confession be read & they Restored" (N 10).

The very next entry, recorded eighteen months later on January 6, 1743/44, contains Oliver Peabody's request "to the Church to do something as to Coochuck, Nathaniel & Jacob Chalcom," noting that the church had voted to send two separate committees of three "suitable Brethren" each to each man "to discourse with them" and "make report to ye Church in due time" (N 10). The problem is not specified until four months later, on April 20, when the church met "to see what was to be done further with our Brethren":

> Coochuck was not present, but Chalcom was; Chalcom is Charged with Intemperance [and] he did not deny it nor put us to prove it; but intimated y^t he was Willing to Confess if he Could think he had truly Repented; it was mentioned to him whether he desired to have Time given him by C^{hh} to try, & ye meeting Adjourned, which he Appeared pleased with, & to which ye C^{hh} Consented.
>
> The Committee which were sent to Coochuck Reported that they had twice discoursed with him. . . . He did not discover a proper Temper, seemed to be too rough, & not inclined to give proper Satisfaction, & [it seemed] he did not much Care for ye Discipline of ye C^{hh}. What He is Charged with is Adultery.
>
> Upon y^s C^{hh} Voted to Adjourn ye Meeting till ye Second Fryday in June next, & to send to Coochuck y^t if he don't then, or before, make Satisfaction, ye C^{hh} determin to proceed According to Gospel Rule. Deacon Ephraim & Brother Jon Goodenow were desired to inform & Notify Coochuck of this. (N 10–11)

This time Jacob Chalcom seemed to be ready to work toward true repentance, while the frank description of Nathaniel Coochuck's rejection of private counsel shows that he rejected the rebuke that had prompted it and was not prepared to begin the hard work of true repentance.

The church met two months later on June 3 to consider both cases but adjourned for two weeks without result. On June 15, both men asked for more time, and the church again adjourned, this time till July 26, 1744, when, surprisingly, it was Coochuck who repented:

> Brother ^Coochuck offered a very humble Confession, of his Sin of intemperance & Adultery, after it was Read twice, the Question was put, Whether the C^{hh}. Judge this to be Gospel Satisfaction? it passed in the Affirmative. This Question was then put whether upon Condition this Confession be Read before the Congregation & acknowledged by Brother Coochuck, the Church Receive him into their Christian Charity & Communion? it passed in ye Affirmative. (N 11)

Coochuck was fully restored, after presenting a seemingly greater challenge than Chalcom. This may be a testimony to the dedication and ability of the committee of suitable brethren who had met with him so many times. Chalcom, on the other hand, "told he Church he desired to make a Confession in due Time, & after much talk he desired longer forbearances" (N 11).

The church pushed back just a little: "Being Willing to show all long suffering, a Question to this purpose was put to ye C^{hh}. Whether upon Brother Chalcoms Request of longer Time & his declareing his Resolution, to Endeavour [a] Reformation the C^{hh} would wait on him & Adjourn this meeting till our next Sacramental Lecture? it passed in ye affirmative" (N 12). The record does not state the church's reason for believing that Chalcom had already had enough time. But because he had declared that he wanted to "endeavor a reformation," the body agreed to give it to him. As we saw in Agawam/Rowley, in the context of the eternal life of the church body and the individual soul before God, a few more temporal weeks or years were nothing.

Given that time and support, Chalcom presented his confession two months later on September 7, 1744, but it was not what the church had hoped for:

> Brother Chalcom Appeared & Read a Confession of his own drawing. . . . Agreably it being put to Vote whether ye C^{hh} tho't what he had offered was sufficient to Justify us in waiting to see what might be done

by ye Spirit in him, in Order to Satisfy us in or Duty as to our further proceeding, till next Lecture, it passed in ye Affirmative & after I [had] talked seriously to him, the meeting was by Vote Adjourned. (N 12)

The church did not hear true repentance in Chalcom's confession; but rather than give up on him, they allowed him yet more time to discover it. According to Peabody, they hoped that the Holy Spirit would work within him, but clearly the committees of brethren would also have a hand in the interval, which would begin with the minister's talking "seriously" to him.

On October 18, Chalcom appeared but again failed to offer true repentance: "[A]fter some discourse with our Brother Chalcom, which did not Satisfy us, The Question was put to the Church whether, if Brother Chalcom Should not give us Some good grounds to hope that the Spirit of God had wro't a true Repentance & real Change in him the Church desired that I would prepare a proper Admonition for him" (N 12). An admonition was the precursor to excommunication, a warning that if the person did not change course, they would be excommunicated. The church voted to have Oliver Peabody prepare that admonition, which he would then "lay before the Church for their Acceptance." When December came around with no change in Chalcom, the admonition was read, "nothing was objected against it," and Peabody asked the church if he might decide when it would be made known to the congregation as well. Another confession from Chalcom was read on February 17, 1744/45, but "consideration of it" was deferred. When it was read again on February 21, the confession again fell short, leading Chalcom to ask the church to defer publicly reading the admonition against him "till we may have Opportunity to see what Evidences he shall give of Repentance & Reformation" (N 12, 13).

This rest of this page of the record book is blank, and I had to turn back to the first five pages of the book to find a transcription of the admonition, including a clear description and validation of the Congregational ideal of rebuke-repent-restore, which Peabody read aloud to Chalcom, the church, and the congregation in its entirety. Peabody took the opportunity to remind the church of what admonition and excommunication were meant to do, the loving spirit in which the church was meant to administer each, the reasons why Jacob Chalcom was receiving an admonition, and the hope for his repentance and restoration at the center of the church's work with him. It is an invaluable record of the Congregational ideal that demands and repays a close reading.

Peabody began with a statement of purpose:

> You are all sensible, I hope, that it has pleased our Lo[rd] Jesus Christ the great head of the Church [to] Ordain & Appoint a Godly discipline to be kept up in his Church to [the] End of the World. . . . Admonitions & even Excommunications then are not [for] the hurt or destruction [of] Souls, but in Order to bring such [as] have been left to fall into sin to Repentance humiliation [&] Reformation that they may Be pardoned & Saved by Jesus C[hrist.] (N 2)

Admonition and excommunication were not weapons of destruction but medicine to bring about healing. Only God could make the final judgment on a soul. Lest anyone in the church was feeling self-righteous about their own piety, the minister continued with a request that all "consider ourselves as in the flesh & lyable to temptations & While we think we Stand to take heed lest we fall. We are to have great Compassion & Lo[ving] tenderness in it, & beware of all passion or personal ill will [or] hatred or Malice, to Reprove Rebuke & Exhort with all long s[uffering;] but yet them that sin we must Rebuke before all that others [also] fear" (N 2).

Though he declared that "it is incumbent on us [to] proceed publickly & solemnly & in the Nature of our Glorious Lord, to Admonish our poor Brother Jacob Chalcom," Peabody again offered Chalcom, who was present, an alternative, saying they must admonish him only "unless by suitable tokens of his hearty Repentance he shall prevent it. Which we Should now be glad to see" (N 3). A long pause must have ensued, perhaps all eyes on Chalcom, perhaps many downcast, as the church waited to see if admonition could be avoided. He must not have spoken, for Peabody continued, now addressing him directly:

> Brother Chalcome What you stand Charged with is the Sins of Drunkenness, & sinful words & Speeches, which are sins Condemned by the Word of God; [and] now Brother you are sensible with how much Compassion tenderness and long suffering I & this C^{hh} have treated you, what means & Methods more private & more publick we have used & taken with you, in Order to your Repentance & Reformation & so in Order to your Salvation in Christ. . . . But after all, it is our great grief & Concern that we see no more evident signs & marks of true Repentance & real Change in you. . . . [W]e hope there may be mercy to ^^{be} obtained by you from God in Jesus Ch^t upon your Repentance [&] with this view &

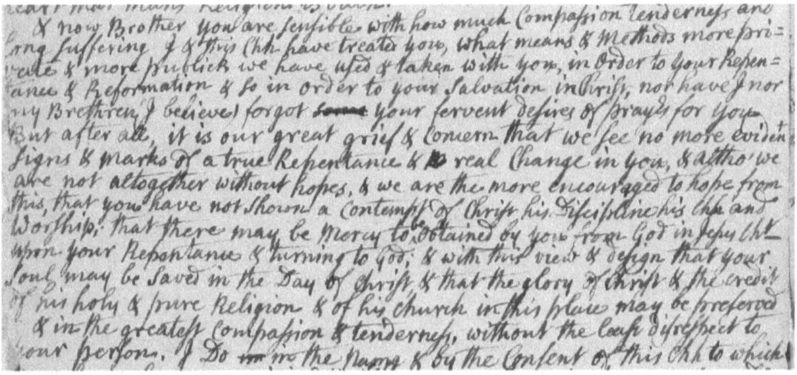

FIGURE 3. From Jacob Chalcom's admonition, undated, in "Church records, 1721–1794," in the Natick, Massachusetts, First Congregational Church records, RG 4839, Congregational Library and Archives, Boston.

> design that your Soul may be Saved in the Day of Christ & that the glory of Christ & the credit of his holy & pure Religion & of his Church in this place may be preserved & in the greatest Compassion & tenderness, without the least disrespect to your person. (N 3)

Peabody again held out hope to Chalcom that God would be merciful and lead him to true repentance and restoration. Importantly, he showed that this was crucial not just for Chalcom but for the church body, for his restoration would uphold the glory of Christ and the credit of "his Church in this place." Peabody did not mean the universal church or all Christian believers but the church body in N'ahteuk/Natick, whose limbs are gathered around their brother. If Chalcom could not find repentance and be restored, this church body would be discredited. If he could find repentance, it would be preserved, and he, as a fully restored limb, would suffer no disrespect on account of his past actions and this admonition.

Peabody then offered Chalcom yet another chance to stop the admonition from being delivered, saying he would read it "unless he [Chalcom] has Something now to Offer" (N 4). Again, Chalcom remained silent, and at last Peabody read the admonition:

> You are not thro' illwill or prejudice but very justly thot to be Chargable with [drunkenness], as well as the more secret faults, which may have provoked the Holy One to leave you to these sins. I Admonish

& beseech you in the Bowels of Christ, that you (depending on his Spirit to help you) Do go to the Blood of the Great Redeemer Christ for pardon of your past sins by true Faith, not after all despairing of Mercy thro' him & Upon your true Repentance & Faith in him who is an Almighty & Allsufficient Saviour, & that you Cry mightily to God that you may, by the powerfull working of his Holy Spirit obtain that new & soft Heart by which you may be enabled ∧not only to Confess your sins with Unfeigned sorrow; but Also to forsake them with utter & everlasting Abhorrence. (N 4)

The minister concluded by offering a final encouragement to Chalcom: "My Bowels yearn to you my Brother while I in obedience to Ch^t & in Faithfullness to your Soul thus Speak to you, [and] if you [do] indeed forsake your Sins & upon seeing good Marks of Repentance & Reformation this C^{hh} will joyfully & Cherefully Show you the marks & tokens of our Favour and Charity" (N 4). He then reiterated that if this admonition should fail to do its work, the consequences would be unthinkable:

But I must signify to you that until We see good symptoms of a penitent Heart upon you We Suspend you from our Sacred Fellowship & Comunion, & if you Continue impenitent we must proceed to such a further declaration of that Censure which will be a awfull Representation of your Eternal Banishment from the Kingdom of God, God forbid it should Come to this! & that it may not, do you do your Endeavours & we will now most humbly seek unto God for you. (N 4)

With their brother now officially under censure, the chastened church also received a final word of warning from the minister, speaking in the name of God: "Let us While we Compassionate our poor Brother & pray daily for him, Consider we are not our own keepers, [&] beware lest we fall into such sins as shall not only expose us to ye censure of the C^{hh} but to Eternal Death & Misery, & may God by his Grace & Spirit, always dwell in this church & keep us all from falling & present us faultless at last before the Throne of Glory with exceeding joy" (N 6).

Peabody left no record of the outcome of this admonition, either because his church records were incomplete or because it was recorded in another book. But Chalcom's name appears in the records of the next minister, Stephen Badger, who noted his death in 1771. As these were not civil records, Badger only recorded the deaths of church and congregation members. This

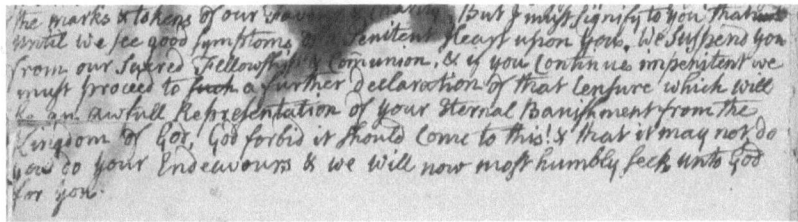

FIGURE 4. From Jacob Chalcom's admonition, undated, in "Church records, 1721–1794," records, in the Natick, Massachusetts, First Congregational church records, RG 4839, Congregational Library and Archives, Boston.

means that Chalcom was a member at the time of his death, indicating that he had found true repentance and that he and the church had been restored.

It's important to remember that this church included both English and Indigenous members and that all had been harmed by Chalcom's sin and saved by his restoration. English church limbs were dependent on the health of Indigenous church limbs and vice versa. Even without an extant record of its conclusion, the narrative of his repentance and restoration is a full and powerful manifestation of the Congregational ideal at work in N'ahteuk/Natick. Like Thomas Miller in Agawam/Rowley, Jacob Chalcom might have been punished by the law, but he was saved by the love of his church.

PART THREE

Congregational Innovation on Noepe/Martha's Vineyard and in Hassanamesit/Grafton

CHAPTER SIX

"Give him a lift toward heaven"

WAMPANOAG ASSURANCE ON NOEPE/MARTHA'S VINEYARD

In 1727, Experience Mayhew produced a report whose title conveys the scientific intent of his work: *Indian Converts, or, Some account of the lives and dying speeches of a considerable number of the Christianized Indians of Martha's Vineyard, in New-England (to which is added, some account of those English ministers who have successively presided over the Indian work in that and the adjacent islands by Mr. Prince)*. His intended audience were the men in England who funded his mission work on Noepe/Martha's Vineyard, and his purpose was to prove that the mission was successful by describing the virtuous lives of 128 Wampanoag men, women, and children. All were dead by 1727 and therefore unable to suddenly go astray after the report was shared and cast doubt on the mission.[1]

Mayhew wanted to show that these Wampanoag people were true converts—to the best of their naturally limited ability as Indigenous people with no Christian inheritance. He was careful to document their "departures" from what he would have described as orthodox Congregationalism, specifying that they gathered in "Indian churches" where certain key principles had to be modified to suit their inability to practice Congregationalism exactly as the English did. It would be easy to accept his terms and identify the Wampanoags' modifications as an attempt to resist a foreign religion and preserve Indigenous culture and identity. But that would be a mistake. *Indian Converts* actually shows that the Wampanoag faithful did exactly what the English faithful did: they evolved Congregational practice based on their lived experience and changing needs. The historian Douglas Winiarski points out that by the time Experience Mayhew was keeping his records, these Wampanoag Congregationalists "were second and even third generation Christians for whom questions of conversion had been resolved decades earlier."[2] Likewise, David Silverman writes:

> They took the lead in their own Christianization, establishing churches and courts in which the traditional elite assumed the new duty of punishing sin and spreading their people's indigenized Christianity among other Wampanoags.... By performing so many critical functions over such a long period, the Church helped communities such as Mashpee on Cape Cod and Aquinnah, Christiantown, and Chappaquiddick on Martha's Vineyard to remain Indian places long after natives were supposed to have disappeared from southeastern New England.[3]

In short, for these Wampanoags in the early 1700s, Congregationalism was no longer an outside imposition. It was intrinsic to their Indigenous identity.[4] They had made it their own.

Perhaps the most important evolution of Congregationalism that the Wampanoags led on Noepe/Martha's Vineyard was their redefinition of the concept of assurance. Rather than insist on the intensely personal, private, even secret spiritual preparation process of the English Congregationalists, a process that would ideally culminate in a moment of communication from God hidden from the rest of the world and difficult to describe to anyone else, the Wampanoags found assurance in explicit human kinship. Whereas English preparation required repeated withdrawals from family and friends in order to hear God speak, Wampanoag preparation required talking and praying together, reassuring and uplifting each other to God. English preparation was designed to lead to the discovery of individual grace, the only way to enter Heaven. Wampanoag preparation resulted in new bonds of reciprocal kinship through church belonging, kinship that mirrored the reciprocal bond between God and the faithful, which they believed God would perceive and honor by admitting the individual into Heaven after death. This allowed the Wampanoag Congregationalists to gather as church bodies without forcing their members to exhibit English assurance. Wampanoag assurance was born.[5]

Like the English, the Wampanoags ordained ministers who fulfilled the Congregational ideal, as Mayhew himself noted. Japheth Hannit, for instance, was on par with any English minister:

> He maintained a good Discipline in the Church over which the Holy Ghost had made him Overseer, knew how to *have Compassion* on those whose Case called for it, and how to save others with Fear. In difficult

Cases that occurred, he was careful to take the best Advice he could get. He was not at all inclined to *lord it over his Flock*, but willing in Meekness to instruct them. And when there was danger of Discord among his Brethren, he would not side with any Party of them, but would in such Case make most winning and obliging Speeches to them all, tending to accommodate the Matters about which they were ready to fall out; and so wonderful an Ability had he in this way, that he seldom failed of the End he aimed at.[6]

Mayhew's extended praise of Hannit covers three full pages.

Hannit and other Wampanoag ministers must have administered communion to their flocks in one of two ways: either they did not differentiate between those who had proven English-style assurance and those who had expressed Wampanoag assurance, or they differentiated between the two in a way that Mayhew did not perceive. The former seems most likely. Mayhew's accounts of Stephen Tackamasun and Joash Panu, who hesitated to join a church body out of fear of their unworthiness, may illustrate Wampanoag respect for the obligations of kinship rather than their concern over their lack of English assurance. The men wanted to be sure they could practice Wampanoag assurance, reciprocating the deep religious faith and practice of the church body, giving, receiving, and extending it through kinship, before they were joined to it as new limbs.[7]

In "A Further Account of the Progress of the Gospel," John Eliot quoted an Indigenous man named Nishouhkou, who celebrated hearts "made strong by Church-covenant, Baptism, and the Lord's Supper," without the hurdle of English assurance.[8] Wampanoag Congregationalists, too, believed that if they lived in kinship with other Christians and with God, then God would not fail to offer them reciprocal relationship in Heaven, just as he had done on Earth. A life lived in God's service would not be discounted because it lacked a human concept such as the English moment of assurance. God would not set an invisible bar and then refuse entry into his kingdom for his own kin if they failed to clear it. Rather, "those who were sorry for their sins, [would] be happy for ever in Heaven, while those who were not [would] be miserable in Hell forever."[9] Again, it's important to understand Wampanoag assurance as a practice-based evolution of Congregationalism, as the Halfway Covenant was, and not as a creolization.

Experience Mayhew's *Indian Converts* offers a number of examples of Wampanoag assurance. One involved Abigail Kesoehtaut, who said, when she still "wanted a comfortable Assurance of the Love of God to her Soul," that she was confident that "there was Mercy and Forgiveness with God through [Christ], and [she] was not excluded from the Benefits of that Redemption, which he came to work out for his People." These "considerations" gave her peace, and Mayhew posited that this allowed her to perceive assurance: "God had yet higher Degrees of Consolation in store for her, for soon after this he gave to her a firm and strong Persuasion of her own personal Interest in the everlasting Mercies of that Covenant which is well ordered in all things, and sure." Using opaque, confusing language like this to describe a crystal-clear message of salvation was business as usual for English Congregationalists. But Wampanoag Congregationalists may have noted this conundrum and questioned the validity of English assurance because of it, especially when the kinship they created as Indigenous Congregationalists was so obvious, direct, and reassuring.[10]

Mary Coshomon perceived that God had set a table for his kin so that they might "enjoy communion with him." Only a failure on her part to "draw nigh to him here, in the great Duties in which his People were bound to wait on him," would lead her to be "excluded from his Presence in the World to come, and not be admitted into the Company of such as would be then happy in the Enjoyment of him." Sarah Coomes was only six when she died, but her understanding of the true promise of Christianity was shared by the adults around her: "When she drew near her End, she desired her Grandmother not to be too much grieved for her; for, said she, I am now going to the House of God, and when you go to God's House also, we shall again see one another with Joy; and we shall there see others also, who are gone before us, [where] there is everlasting joy."[11]

Jacob Sockakonnit of Nunpaug/Edgartown was, in Mayhew's estimation, a true convert, finding joy in the practice and faith of Christianity, so much so that Mayhew was "satisfied that he was qualified for Communion with the Church of Christ, in all ordinances of the Gospel, [so] I put him on his Duty of asking an Admission to them." Sockakonnit, however, "feared that he had not yet experienced a Work of Regeneration, or saving Conversion to God, and so remained unqualified for Communion with him in his Ordinances." Mayhew, like many English ministers with their English flocks. struggled to convince Sockakonnit of his worthiness, pressing him to acknowledge evidence of English-style assurance. But when he at last seemed to have "so far overcome the Discouragements under which he thus labored," the church body Sockakonnit wanted to join was without a minister so could not admit him. Soon after, his fatal illness began, and this depressed him as a bad sign, making him "very much in the dark about the State of his Soul." When Mayhew visited him, he felt that he "did not appear to have any Assurance of the Love of God to his Soul." Sockakonnit resisted Mayhew's encouragements, and Mayhew notes, "I intended to have visited him again, but he dy'd sooner than I thought he would have done, so I missed the Opportunity."[12]

Still, other "credible Persons" did visit Jacob Sockakonnit, and they informed Mayhew that "he grew much more cheerful before he dy'd, than in the former Part of his Sickness he had been; and that he obtained a comfortable Hope of the Love of God to his Soul, insomuch as he divers times expressed his Joy . . . and lamented his having too long delayed to ask an Admission to the Communion of God's People." These "credible Persons" were probably Wampanoag Congregationalists, possibly physical as well as spiritual kin, and their visits to the dying man renewed the assurance that he had possessed before his illness. Thus, when Sockakonnit said that "he [had] obtained a comfortable Hope of the Love of God to his Soul," his hope was not a pale substitute for assurance but proof of it.[13] The English minister had tried to convince him of his individual worth, and the spiritual struggle this produced in Sockakonnit was paralleled by his illness. The Wampanoag Christians, on the other hand, demonstrated his kinship with themselves and thus with God. Where there was a Wampanoag minister, this disconnect between English and Wampanoag Congregationalism could be avoided.[14]

Eleazar Ohhumuh, just sixteen years old when he perceived his approaching death, had not experienced English assurance. So according to Mayhew, he "sent for some of the Neighbours to come and commit him to God, and as he expressed it, to give him a Lift toward Heaven, which, according to his Desire, they did. . . . Soon after this Exercise was over, the pious young Man looking up towards Heaven, and smiling as tho he had seen something that did greatly delight and comfort him, surrendred his Soul into the Hands of his Redeemer." Importantly, Mayhew followed this account with the testimony of the Wampanoag Christian kin whom Ohhumuh had called on: "Some who were with him when he died have told me, that they thought themselves as sure that he was gone into the Kingdom of God, when he left this World, as tho they had seen the Angels of God come down and convey him to that

Place of Glory." The strength of his Christian kinfolks' belief had strengthened Ohhumuh; their kinship was his assurance.[15]

Mayhew told stories of Wampanoag assurance made manifest via spectral visions delivered specifically to the kin of dying persons so that they could relay the news (another instance of an unorthodox belief in angelic visitations persistently shared by English and Indigenous Christians). When Abigail Kesoehtaut was near death, the sister tending her was frantic for confirmation that she would to go Heaven. Mayhew wrote, "She long'd for a more full Assurance of her sisters' Well-being." The unnamed sister's loving concern caused her great distress until, "about twenty four Hours before [Kesoehtaut] dy'd," the sister, who was sleeping next to her, was awakened by "a Voice in the Air over the Top of the House, saying in her own Language, *Wunnantinnea Kanaanut*, the same being diverse times repeated, [which meant], tho they are much more emphatical in *Indian*, *There is Favour now extended in Canaan*."

> [She] supposed it to be a Voice from Heaven by the Ministry of Angels, sent to give her Satisfaction in the Case that did distress her. . . . [S]he then went to her Sister and said, *Now Sister, you are going into everlasting Happiness*, to which her Sister being now speechless, could make no Answer, save that by a Sign she consented to what was said . . . and with a smiling Countenance lifted up her Eyes and Hands towards Heaven."[16]

Another case involved a dying woman named Abigail, called Ammapoo, living in Sanchecantacket in Edgartown, who was being cared for by one of her daughters. As this unnamed daughter was sitting up with her mother, trying to stay awake through the night, she "suddenly saw a Light which seemed to her brighter than that of Noon-day; when looking up, she saw two bright shining Persons, standing in white Raiment at her Mother's Bed-side, who, on her Sight of them, with the Light attending them, immediately disappeared." When she told her mother what she'd seen, Abigail/Ammapoo replied, "*[T]his is what I said to you, God taketh Care of me*." Mayhew followed this story by vouching for his long acquaintance with Abigail/Ammapoo and asserting that she was indeed "a very godly Woman." He then said that her daughter had told others about what she had seen "and still maintains the Truth of it."[17]

These examples, in which a dying person's kin received a message and relayed it to a relation, confounded the usual European experience of assurance, in which a spiritual message was delivered directly and only to the person concerned. But when Wampanoag Congregationalists expressed concern about whether or not they were qualified for communion, they sounded far more like English Congregationalists. For instance, after the mother-in-law of Hannah Sissetom of Sanchecantacket encouraged her to ask for admission to the Indian church, Sissetom, while acknowledging the assurance of kinship ("she kindly accepted of her Mother's Goodwill"), could not accept it in place of the English moment of assurance. Mayhew wrote, "[She] had not the Courage to ask an Admission to full Communion in the Church of Christ, but alleged, that she feared she was not qualified for so high a Privilege." Likewise, Martha Coomes of Nashouohkamuk/Chilmark "was under such a Sense of her sinful Unworthiness that she durst not ask an Admission to the Table of the Lord." Elizabeth Uhquat of Christian-Town was reassured by a kinswoman, "yet she was under such Discouragements a[s] never to speak with any Minister about her Case, till after she was seized with the Sickness whereof in a few Days she died." Meeksishqune/Margaret Osooit of Gayhead "was looked upon as a Person so well qualified for the Communion with the Church of Christ that many wondered that she did not ask Admission thereunto; [but] she had such Apprehensions concerning the Holiness required of those who are admitted to [communion] that she could not be persuaded that she was her self qualified for so high Privileges."[18]

Compare such statements with those made by the Englishwomen of Pequossette/Cambridge in the 1630s and 1640s, who voiced similar concerns in their conversations with the minister Thomas Shepard: they feared they were not holy enough to approach Christ.[19] Joanna Sill, for instance, "thought 'I'll go to the Lord' but could not. . . . [S]he could not believe in that blood which was shed for her." Like Elizabeth Uhquat, Jane Palfrey sought counsel for her self-doubt, and the elder she consulted encouraged her to "hope in God." Yet Palfrey "dared not lift up my eyes to the Lord. . . . I thought I should dishonor the Lord the more by going to him." Elizabeth Dunster also received encouraging counsel but "felt an inability to come [to Christ]." Like Uhquat, Alice Stedman received friendly counsel from an elder whom she had consulted during a low point in her religious seeking: "[H]e asked me what stuck upon my spirit. I said, I was afraid it was not righteousness. And he encouraged me not to give way to those fears." In other words, when the elder asked what was keeping her from believing that her preparation was sincere, Stedman replied that she was afraid she was a hypocrite. She could not accept his encouragement, and her isolated journey continued.[20]

In his account of Mary Manhut of Christian-Town, who also did not feel qualified to take communion, Mayhew commented, "Our Indians can hardly believe that they are fully in the Church, till they are admitted to full Communion in all the Ordinances there to be enjoyed: they suppose that till this be done, they are as it were but in the Porch of the House into which they would enter, in hopes of finding and enjoying God there." This seems like a strange statement for a missionary to share with his Congregational sponsors. Wasn't that what *all* Congregationalists were meant to understand and believe? Wasn't that why they went through the long, painful process of spiritual preparation? But Mayhew spoke very deliberately here, placing the Wampanoags' desire for full communion firmly in the context of their own practice of Congregationalism: "This was what this poor Woman now earnestly thirsted after, [nor] could her mind be quiet till the Church-Meeting admitted her into their Communion in the Ordinance of the Lord's-Supper." Instead of requiring Manhut to demonstrate assurance in order to join the church, the church revealed her assurance by admitting her. In the Wampanoag Congregationalist church on Noepe/Martha's Vineyard, asking for the reciprocal relationship of full Christian kinship was the requirement, not a relation of assurance,. Manhut died "comfortable" in that state.[21]

Mayhew wrote that Rachel Wompanummoo of Christian-Town, too, "durst not ask an Admission to the Table of the Lord, fearing lest she was not well qualified for it." When she was dying, she "could not be satisfied 'till she had done it"; and like Mary Manhut, she made a profession of faith and answered some questions. Mayhew was present at this moment and asked her a question that directly addressed the issue of English assurance in full communion: "I asked her, Whether the Reason why she desired to be admitted by the Church into full Communion with them was, because she thought that without being so she could not be saved?" That is, did she mistakenly believe that church membership was itself the means of salvation? "*No,* said she, *I do not think so.* Why then, said I, do you desire this, seeing probably you may not live to have any Opportunity to partake of the Lord's Supper? Unto which she answered, That [she] *thought it her Duty, to approach as Nigh to God while she lived as she could do.*" In other words, Wompanummoo understood that church kinship was as close an approximation of being in God's presence as the world afforded. While church kinship did not in itself save a soul, it brought the soul closer to God. In Wampanoag Congregationalism, church kinship paved the way for the assurance that would come *after* death, when God honored that kinship obligation and admitted his faithful people to his presence. "Which being said, the Church very gladly received her into their Communion."[22]

Some Wampanoag Congregationalists did experience conventional English assurance. Jerusha Ohquanut "asked an Admission to the Table of the Lord, [and] did it accordingly, and giving good Evidences of a Work of Grace on her Soul, was by the Church readily admitted when she was but very little above 15 Years of Age." Ohquanut gave a relation (the "good Evidences" of grace), as did Jane Pomit, who "being arrived to sixteen Years of Age [gave] so good an Account of her Knowledge of the only true God, [and] Experience of a Work of Grace on her Soul, that she was with good Satisfaction admitted to full Communion in the Church whereof Master Joash Panu was the Pastor."[23] Still, while the young woman did what her minister Panu had never done, that did not diminish his authority or their spiritual kinship.

Mayhew's accounts include other instances of Wampanoag evolutions and refinements of Congregationalism. When Wuttontaehtunnooh/Katherine of Sanchecantacket in Edgartown prayed with other Wampanoag women, "she was frequently the Person singled out among them, as their Mouth, to make known their Requests unto God." Jerusha Ompan of Takemmy/Tisbury "came to offer to pray with her Sister when her Mother was present," a "strange" occurrence that Mayhew hastened to explain: "[I]t has been a Custom amongst our Indians to teach their Children Forms of Prayers, and sometimes to call them to make use of them in their Presence, [and] I think it is better it should be so, than that for want of such Instructions they should not know so much as to how to desire a Blessing on their Food"—that is, miss a meal because they were afraid to eat without asking a proper blessing through prayer. Mayhew clearly anticipated the outrage that English Congregationalists would feel when they read that the Wampanoags were saying set prayers. Spontaneous prayer was the English Congregationalist norm, the soul's immediate response to God's stimuli, customarily taking place when the individual was alone. But for Wampanoag Congregationalists, praying together and sharing the same words to build relationship was vital.[24]

Christianity did "gradually alter" Wampanoag society by introducing new concepts into it. As Harold W. Van Lonkhuyzen writes, the disappearance argument would claim that these "pervasive new concepts . . . sucked at the very marrow of Indian identity" and led to the eventual, inevitable extinction of "true" Wampanoag culture.[25] But the real story is much different. Christianity became Congregational in Woodland New England, and English Congregationalism became Indigenous Congregationalism wherever it was practiced by Indigenous converts. This changed the converts and Congregationalism without invalidating either.

CHAPTER SEVEN

The Note Writer of Hassanamesit/Grafton

The record book for "the Church of Our Lord Jesus Christ att Hasanamisco" begins with a title page stating that the church was "Gather'd the 28th of December. Anno Dom[ini]: 1731." The large, ornate message is immediately followed by a businesslike nineteenth-century hand that intrudes on the formal white space with an urgent "Note":

> The Indian church which was gathered
> in this place was the second native ch in NE:
> it was formed either by Rev John Eliot or some one raised
> up thru his instrumentality. It is said to have been one
> of the most permanent establishments of the kind &
> yet it w[d] seem as if it continued but a short time in its
> original state. It was formed in 1671 & three years
> after contained, it is said, about 16 members living in y[e]
> [town], besides several residing in other places. But 60
> years after as appears from this book it was necessary
> to form another, & none were <u>native</u>, probably[.][1]

This brief single page is a nutshell summary of all of the erasures of Indigenous people in white histories of Congregationalism. It's also my starting point for examining Indigenous use of the Halfway Covenant in the decades after King Philip's War.

In the 1800s, someone, most likely a member of the church, held its eighteenth-century records in his hands. (Women were not officially allowed to write in church record books.) He saw two things on the title page that, to him, seemed to require clarification: the use of the name Hassanamisco (the English version of the Nipmuc place name Hassanamesit) and the date

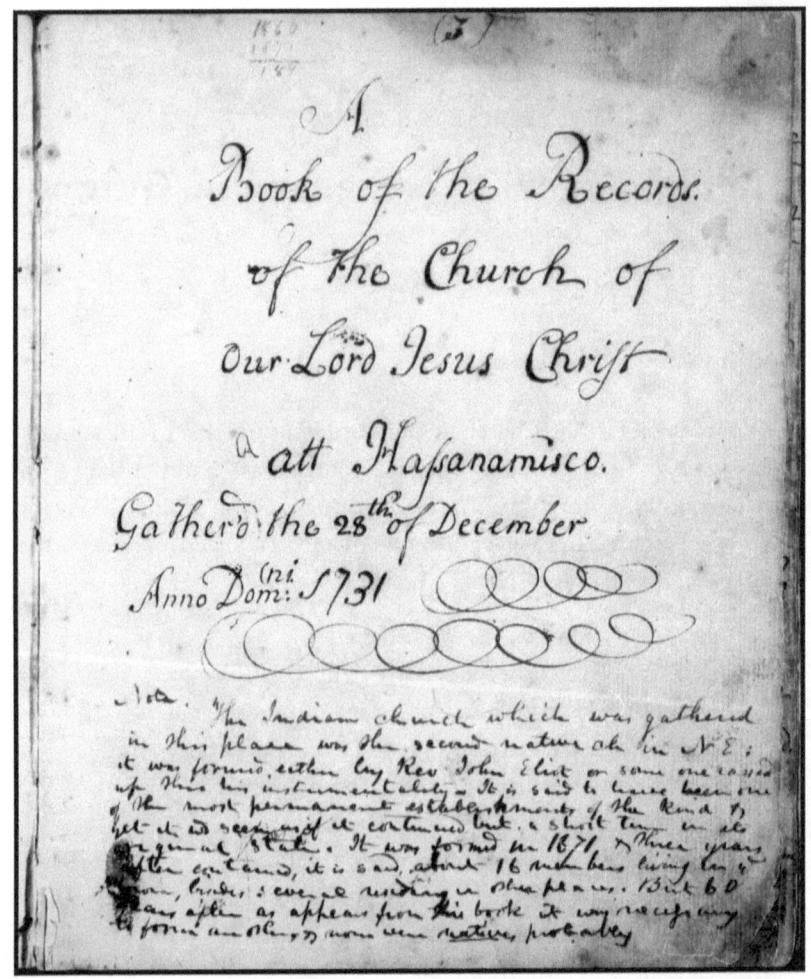

FIGURE 5. Frontispiece, "Hassanamisco church book, 1731–1774," in the Grafton, Massachusetts Evangelical Congregational Church records, RG 4921, Congregational Library and Archives, Boston.

of the church gathering. Despite the presence of the Anglicized Nipmuc name on the title page, the new church rarely used it to describe itself. In 1735, just three and a half years after the church had been gathered, the record book was referring to the place exclusively by its English town name of Grafton.[2] Why, then, was Hassanamisco on the title page? The man, whom I will call the note writer, set about to explain the situation in language that effortlessly creates a narrative, one that seems to be filled with facts and data but that is in reality a vehicle for deadly obfuscation.

Here is the note writer's narrative: There had once been an Indigenous church gathered in this place, which was notable because it had been founded either by the famous Puritan minister and missionary John Eliot or by someone who was working with him, just after Eliot had founded the first Indigenous church in nearby N'ahteuk/Natick. This Indigenous church was supposed to have been one of the most permanent ones, but it fell apart after just three years because its members had vanished. Thus, by 1731, it was necessary for the white citizens of Grafton to gather into a new church. It's hard to say for sure because Indigenous people are usually invisible in the records; but given their steady disappearance from New England and their abandonment of their own church, it's probable that none of the members of the new church were Indigenous. In contrast to this, the new church, gathered by white people, had lasted into a new century and would continue to endure for centuries to come. Thus, it was, in the note writer's view, emblematic of the natural success and steady progress of civilization and religion in New England. The Grafton church was doing what the Hassanamesit church could not, and the transition from one to the next symbolized the passing of the torch from the Indigenous residents to the New Englanders. By referring to Eliot as founder, showing knowledge of Eliot's partners in the work of founding Indian praying towns, recording solid timeframes for the Hassanamesit church's founding and foundering, and identifying the precise number of Indigenous members, the note writer displayed his authority. He knew his history—or at least he knew the most important facts about his church's origins.

Unfortunately, however, so much of this note is not only factually wrong but actively, even deliberately, harmful that I will need far more than its eleven short lines to unpack it all. The first problem is the note writer's insistence that Eliot or his colleagues "formed" the "Indian" churches. As I have already shown in this book, Congregational churches were not formed or founded by individuals and individual agency, not even by ministers. Rather, they were gathered: people left their individual identities behind and came together to be transformed by God into one living body called a church. If a church existed at Hassanamesit, it existed because Nipmuc people came together and were transformed by God into a church. The word *Hassanamesit* means "place of small stones," a fortuitous name, as in September 1673, many small stones came together at Hassanamesit to be formed into one Nipmuc church body within and before Christ. The note writer erases this Nipmuc agency, identity, and embodiment and therefore destroys the possibility of there having been a true church in Hassanamesit at all. In his telling, there was only John Eliot.

The note writer's phrase "some one raised up thru his [Eliot's] instrumentality" also erases Nipmuc lives and identity. The "some one raised up" was actually Joseph Tuckawillipin, a Nipmuc man who was the lay leader of the Christian Nipmucs at Hassanamesit. When the church was gathered, Tuckawillipin was ordained as its minister.[3] Of the course of a century in which Indigenous identities were erased from English histories, his name could easily have been lost. But the note writer's knowledge that the church's first minister was not an Englishman seems to lie behind his statement's obscure wording. It suggests that this person had been Eliot's creature, "raised up" only through Eliot's "instrumentality"; that Eliot was the channel to God who had transformed the poor clay of an Indigenous man into a potential minister.

Then comes the note writer's insidious statement that the church at Hassanamesit "is said to have been one of the most permanent establishments of the kind & yet it w^d seem as if it continued but a short time in its original state." This compact account discredits Indigenous Christianity and maturity, reducing the Nipmuc church to rumor and hearsay and implying that the Nipmuc church did not keep a record book and thus could not speak for itself. This implies that the body was not a real church but an "establishment" that was strictly for Indigenous people and therefore not part of any shared Congregational identity. Again, the note writer let rumor speak for and over the Nipmuc church by saying "yet it w^d *seem*" as if it didn't last long.

Next, the note writer represented the Nipmuc church's swift dissolution as a complete mystery: why wouldn't a strong young church have "continued"? At the same time he clearly saw no mystery at all, as he had already firmly established that Nipmucs were not real Christians and therefore had no real church. His underlying, unspoken question was "why *would* an irregular Indian establishment continue"? To bring his readers to that realization, he firmly stated that the church "was formed in 1671 & three years after contained, it is said, about 16 members living in y^e [town]." Already on its last legs, the Nipmuc establishment was destined to fail.

This claim is the very worst part of the note writer's work, because he recorded the wrong date for the Nipmuc church gathering. The church gathered in 1673, not 1671.[4] Two years is a small difference, but the note writer was surely aware that King Philip's War began in 1675 and that it devastated the Nipmucs. Thus, he must have known that the life of their church was just one more death among the thousands of Indigenous casualties.[5] The English attacked Hassanamesit during the war, burning crops and taking about two hundred prisoners, including Christians, in retaliation for their alleged treachery. Many more Nipmucs from Hassanamesit fell prey to English kidnapping and seizure and were sent into slavery or to the concentration camp on Deer Island.[6] The first Nipmuc people returned to the place in spring 1676 and did not gain in numbers until the 1680s.[7] Did the note writer deliberately choose to move the date back to 1671 so that the church's failure would fall in 1674, predating the war and therefore serving as an example of the deceit and hypocrisy of the Praying Indians? Whatever his reasoning, his refusal to state that King Philip's War had caused the collapse of the Nipmuc church and reduced the number of Nipmucs living in Hassanamesit was actually counterproductive, because its glaring absence in his statement drives readers to think specifically about it.

Finally, the note writer concluded that "60 years after as appears from this book [that is, the 1731, white, English, church record book] it was necessary to form another [church], & none [of the members] were native, probably." In other words, the newer record book stepped into the breach of hearsay and so-called Indigenous failure to affirm that a real church had replaced the suspect "Indian establishment." Its realness was affirmed by the record book itself, with its thousands of entries recorded by named, white ministers. By underlining "native" in his statement, the note taker literally underscored the division between Indigenous people and their establishments and those of white people and their Congregational churches. I can almost hear his voice saying scornfully, "Of course, an authentic church didn't have any *natives* in it, probably."

The word *probably* at the end of the note may seem small, but its damning impact is enormous. Why was it probable that no Nipmucs were part of the new Hassanamesit/Grafton church? The note writer offered many reasons in his eleven short lines: the Nipmucs had no real tradition of Christian worship; they had never been a real church, nor did they have a real minister; they had possessed only an "Indian establishment," which they abandoned suspiciously close to the start of King Philip's War, just as they abandoned Hassanamesit after the war. In short, the Nipmucs were not and never had been real Christians, and they dropped all pretense to be so—or had their pretense exposed—when real Christians arrived on the scene and composed themselves into a true church body that the Nipmucs could never join. Alongside this possibility lay the fact that all of the Nipmucs, Christian or not, may have just disappeared, as Indians were wont to do.

But it's even more harmful in that "probably" here makes it plain that accuracy was not required, that no one would fault this man's historical knowledge or call him out on his errors. Getting Nipmuc history right was not a concern. *I suppose this is true enough*, he thought, and he moved on. His note was meant only to confirm that no real church had existed in Hassanamesit/Grafton before the white church and to explain away the use of the name Hassanamisco on the title page of its records. In Marie Balsley Taylor's words, it serves as proof that "when one comes to the documents expecting that there is nothing to find, one often fails to really look."[8] Rather than raise up the Nipmucs through the instrumentality of his historical authority, the note writer named them only to erase them.

CHAPTER EIGHT

Church Belonging and the Halfway Covenant in Hassanamesit/Grafton

In 1728 English colonizers began calling Hassanamesit "Grafton," and soon afterward a new Congregational church body was gathered that they firmly defined as English. But within months of this new gathering, the church body was mixed, both Indigenous and English. Church records help retell the stories of three generations of two Nipmuc families in Hassanamesit/Grafton: the Printers and the Abrahams, as well as their friends and kin. Each entry in the records is brief, but together they add a great deal to our understanding of those families and of Indigenous Congregationalism in Woodland New England in the mid-eighteenth century. Here again, as in our understanding of events in Agawam/Rowley, the church records fill in enormous gaps that the civil records impose and normalize.

First, they reveal the extent to which the Halfway Covenant, a shared Congregational invention, shaped this church and, by extension, many others. Perhaps the most important development in Congregationalism, the Halfway Covenant originated in English lived experience. It was divisive for decades, with some Congregationalists defining it as a perverted failure and denigrating it as a half-measure (hence the name) and others welcoming it with relief and joy. Until now, scholars have studied the Halfway Covenant strictly within its English context; but as I will show, it opened a pathway to church belonging for Indigenous people who had no prior connection with a congregation, particularly after the church-destroying rupture of King Philip's War.

In 1662, a synod, or council, of Congregational ministers traveled from all over Woodland New England to meet in Pequossette/Cambridge to discuss and debate a problem. For a variety of reasons, many people who had been baptized as infants by their full-member parent or parents had never become full members themselves. Now they were adults with children of their own;

and while Congregationalists did not believe that baptism offered full or partial salvation or any protection for an individual whom God had destined for eternal damnation, baptized children were officially brought into the protection of the church, which meant they were brought up in its care and under its protective watch. Therefore, it was painful for parents to see their children go unbaptized, and they communicated their pain to their ministers, who eventually agreed to authorize a synod to meet and try to devise a solution.

The synod proposed what they described as "owning the covenant." Adults would stand before the church and testify to their belief in God and Christ, their understanding and support of the terms of the church covenant, and their willingness to uphold the core practices and responsibilities of joining the church. Once these adults owned the covenant, they would not be full church members, but they would be allowed to baptize their own children, a sacrament previously reserved only for full church members.[1] We can track how many congregations adopted the new measure and when because Congregational baptismal records almost always specify if the parents were full members, if one or both parents had owned the covenant, or if the person being baptized had owned the covenant.[2]

The Halfway Covenant was controversial, and for decades after its 1662 introduction a number of churches and congregations continued to oppose it or were seriously divided by it.[3] Two factors, however, led most to slowly but steadily adopt the measure: the growing English population and King Philip's War. As the English population expanded, churches and congregations strove to maintain ties with their burgeoning communities. Many of these people were not the children of church members. Some had never been baptized. Often they were newcomers to a town and congregation. Now the Halfway Covenant allowed such people to own the covenant and be baptized as adults.[4] By the early to mid-1700s, this natural evolution of purpose of the Halfway Covenant—to include strangers—was an element of all of the churches that had voted to accept the measure. The hope was that it would bring people into a deeper connection with their new sisters and brothers, putting them on a path of spiritual seeking that would one day result in their discovering assurance/salvation and joining the church body. But even if that hope were never realized, the Halfway Covenant kept congregations and churches from dwindling away simply because fewer and fewer people had blood ancestors who had been full church members.[5]

The role of King Philip's War in the adoption of the Halfway Covenant acts like an invisible hand throughout standard histories of the intervention—unmentioned but at work between every line. The scholar Robert Pope is an outlier in this regard. He describes how the shock of the war led English Congregationalists to recognize that they needed to renew and replenish their covenant with God. Ten of their towns had been abandoned during the war, and many more had been attacked. Their losses included not only houses, livestock, and human casualties but also church bodies. Rebuilding towns and regathering churches was the work of the postwar decade. The carnage also led the English government in London to reconsider the Massachusetts Bay Colony's ability to govern itself and to revoke the colony's charter in 1684. Thus, the war attacked and destabilized every part of colonizing society, and English people responded by restoring and rededicating their churches. As Pope says, "the broad implementation of the half-way covenant that occurred between 1676 and 1692 can only be understood in the context of crisis."[6] Regathering church bodies that had suffered human losses meant two things: people who had been baptized as children but had never become full church members needed to be brought into church covenant along with their own unbaptized children; and people who had no connection to a congregation, often new colonizers who were resettling towns shaken by the war, had to be brought into the work of reestablishing or restoring congregations. "After 1690 the clergy increasingly courted inhabitants of [a] town who had no church connection and invited them to share in the renewals."[7]

But the fast-rising number of baptisms that took place in the postwar decade—most of them making use of the Halfway Covenant—were not restricted to English members. Indigenous believers were actively reclaiming their own Congregationalism. After King Philip's War, Indigenous Congregationalists whose churches had been destroyed were usually unable to regather in purely Indigenous bodies, as even the old praying towns such as Hassanamesit had been taken over by the English. So those who wanted to reclaim their church belonging had to join the new English congregations, and they could do so only through the Halfway Covenant.

Before the digitization of thousands of pages of church records, historians had to rely on available data from a limited number of communities, most of them in or near Boston. But now we can begin to document when and where churches in Woodland New England admitted Indigenous members via the Halfway Covenant, from the decade after King Philip's War through the First Great Awakening. This leads to an interesting question: how might the number of Indigenous baptisms have influenced the number of English baptisms? It is tantalizing to speculate that watching Indigenous people—the recent enemy—own the covenant and join English congregations or even church bodies may have spurred English people who had been wary of the intervention to take advantage of the Halfway Covenant themselves. If, as the historian James Cooper says, "the laity would determine the outcome of this explosive controversy" over the validity of the Halfway Covenant, then the English laity had to decide whether to allow Indigenous people to join them by owning the covenant, and their own commitment to the intervention in response. Church records tell us that they did both, and this act of the laity had "lasting repercussions upon the development of Congregationalism."[8] Laypeople worked together to shape their faith and practice, and that laity was, very soon after King Philip's War, once again mixed, both Indigenous and English.

Boles notes that "the impressive extent of black and Indian participation in northern Protestant churches . . . was varied and not inherently connected to the Great Awakening."[9] It's possible to detach Indigenous participation from the perceived loosening of Congregational standards in the 1730s and 1740s by studying how many Indigenous people joined churches and congregations via the Halfway Covenant long before the First Great Awakening began. According to Cooper, "by 1690, three-quarters of the churches in Massachusetts Bay practiced the innovation, and [a] majority of the laity may have supported the change all along."[10] This timing points to Indigenous involvement, for in the 1680s those who had not been enslaved or killed after the war often returned to the places to which they belonged. There, many reclaimed their Congregational heritage via the Halfway Covenant, which then provoked or inspired English Congregationalists who had passively supported the intervention to actively use it to reclaim their own church identity and belonging. Recall the reciprocal nature of church membership, in which admitting new full members validated both the individual member and the church body. Admitting Indigenous people through the Halfway Covenant validated both them and the intervention itself, making it even more acceptable for English people to use.

The records of dozens of churches, stretching back over two centuries, support this hypothesis. They list Halfway Covenant members—Indigenous, Black, and English—without documenting any pushback or rejection from orthodox English church or congregation members. English, Indigenous, and Black people frequently owned the covenant on the same day and were joined in the same record. This contrasts with the historian Richard A. Bailey's repeated assertions that Indigenous and Black people had to use force to join the churches: "Native Americans and Africans seized the opportunity to enter the doors and pulpits of the northern colonists' churches, forcing puritans to make a place for them within their communities of faith.... Those awakened spiritually and socially by the [revivals] forced New England puritanism to open ever wider to include them within its boundaries."[11] But if English people had protested against Indigenous halfway membership, they would have been casting doubt on the concept itself and thus implicating their own English halfway members. Therefore, Indigenous use of the Halfway Covenant may well have helped to seal its place in Congregational practice and so to change Congregationalism itself. This was not simply an example of, in Bailey's words, "a focus on white members inadvertently [creating] opportunities for non-white membership."[12] Through this successful evolution, a still unknown number of Indigenous Congregationalists were restored to kinship within congregation and church and kept their religious practice alive for future generations. As the scholar Gregory Michna writes:

> Issues of ecclesiology and conversion within these English and Indian communities intersected for a period as ministers simultaneously navigated the boundaries of membership for all potential members, culminating in the Halfway Covenant of 1662.... While ministers fail to cite Indian progress as the deciding factor informing their support for the [Halfway] covenant, it is hardly coincidental that they supported both widening the communal boundaries of the church to allow Indians to enter as fellow members along with efforts to include third-generation "children of the church."[13]

FIRST FRUITS OF THE HALFWAY COVENANT IN HASSANAMESIT/GRAFTON

The Printers were a Nipmuc family rooted in Hassanamesit. Naoas, a prominent man, had converted to Christianity and had sent his son Wawaus (1640–1709) to live in an English household, where he was called James. James attended the Indian Charity School at Harvard College and became an apprentice to the printer Samuel Green, where he became known as James the Printer or James Printer. With John Eliot he translated the Bible into the Massachusett language and set the type for an "Indian Bible," the first Bible published in the Western Hemisphere. James Printer's return to Hassanamesit during King Philip's War, his determination to serve and protect his Nipmuc kin, his remarkable survivance during and after the war, and his role as a teacher and leader in Hassanamesit have been well documented, particularly in Lisa Brooks's *Our Beloved Kin*.[14]

The English record is not explicit, but it seems that James Printer had no children. Moses Printer (1665?–1729) and Ami Printer (died 1741) may have been his nephews, cousins, or other near relatives who took his name in his honor.[15] Moses and his wife Mary Pogenit Printer had a daughter Sarah (born circa 1715–20). Ami and his wife Sarah Printer had two daughters, Sarah Jr. (born circa 1717) and Abigail (born circa 1718). Each couple had other children, but these daughters are the Printers on whom I will focus.[16] In 1731, when the records of the second church at Hassanamesit/Grafton begin, the sisters Sarah Jr. and Abigail Printer were living with their parents while their cousin Sarah Printer, the orphan of Moses and Mary, was apparently apprenticed to an English household in Hassanamesit/Grafton.[17] All three girls were about fourteen years old. The Hassanamesit/Grafton second church records have no information on any of them to this point, which seems to show that neither Printer family had any connection with the new church body.

The first Indigenous name appears in the church record book just four months after the church was gathered, on April 30, 1732: "Andrew Abraham Indian Ju^r. Owned ye Covenant And was Baptized" by the minister Solomon Prentice (HG 13).[18] This brief record reveals two pieces of linked information about Andrew Abraham Jr.: he had no current tie to the congregation, yet he became part of it. Perhaps his ancestors had belonged to the first church body in Hassanamesit/Grafton. Nonetheless, in 1732, his decision to join the second incarnation, which included none of his neighbors or kin, may have been a difficult one. It's possible, however, that he had crucial support: the church record book tells us that on February 4, 1733/34, ten months after her son had owned the covenant and was baptized, his mother, Deborah Abraham, followed suit:

> Deborah Abraham the Wife of
> Andrew Abraham ^Indian own^d. the Covenant

Church Belonging and the Halfway Covenant in Hassanamesit/Grafton   111

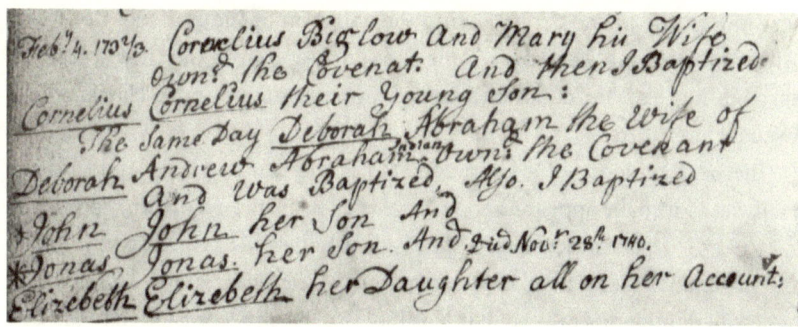

FIGURE 6. Record of the Abraham family's Halfway Covenant, February 4, 1733/34, in "Hassanamisco church book, 1731–1774," in the Grafton, Massachusetts, Evangelical Congregational Church records, RG 4921, Congregational Library and Archives, Boston.

> And was Baptized Also. I Baptized
> *John her Son And
> *Jonas her Son. And (Died Nov$_r$: 28th. 1740.)
> Elizabeth her Daughter *all on her [Deborah's] Account*: (HG 16)

This single baptism record miraculously restores one vital component of the identities of five Nipmuc people—Andrew Sr., Deborah, John, Jonas, and Elizabeth Abraham—by restoring their relationship to and decisions about Congregational Christianity.

Andrew Abraham Sr. was of some importance in the town; yet unlike his wife and children, he did not become a member, either halfway or full, of the second church. In Woodland New England it was common for Congregational congregations and churches, whether English or Indigenous, to have more female members than male. Scholars have floated many reasons for this imbalance, which grew even more pronounced after the Revolutionary War.[19] For now, I simply note that it was not an Indigenous anomaly for Deborah Abraham to own the covenant without her husband's participation and to have her three remaining children baptized. Most Congregational children who were baptized by a single covenant-owning parent were baptized "on their mother's account," as the records phrased it.[20] It was also common for a person who owned the covenant to have their children baptized on the same day, as Deborah Abraham did, or very soon afterward. Parents wanted their children to be formally under the protection and watch of the church; this was indeed the prime driver behind the adoption of the Halfway Covenant. Although Deborah Abraham's name does not reappear in the church records, through her and her children, Nipmuc Congregationalism at Hassanamesit lived on after 1676.

The next evidence of a Nipmuc person's baptism and admission via the Halfway Covenant appeared about a year later, in the record for January 5, 1735/36: "George Muc'kamuck <u>Alias</u> Read an Indian Man Aged 20 yrs Owned the Covenant here and was Baptized per me S. Prentice. After he had made an acknowledgment for ye Sin of lying" (HG 21). Church records often noted that someone had acknowledged a sin at the same time they had owned the covenant, for a frank admission of spiritual struggle was part of putting oneself under the watch and support of the congregation. Here was another young Nipmuc man following Andrew Abraham Jr.'s example. On his own initiative, he had taken advantage of the Halfway Covenant to put himself under church discipline and gain the support and care of the church and congregation; no parent had presented him for baptism. This tells us that neither his mother, the powerful matriarch Sarah Robins Muckamaug, nor his father, Peter Muckamaug, were members of the second church, either full or halfway.[21] These two cases may begin a generational pattern in which children born in the first two decades of the eighteenth century committed to the second church at Hassanamesit/Grafton of their own accord, perhaps reclaiming a spiritual identity that their grandparents had established and from which their parents had been forcibly separated by war. As Linford Fisher notes, participation via the Halfway Covenant "was a continuation of, not a break with, prior [Indigenous] religious engagement.... This point is worth lingering over because the trope of the sudden conversion obscures the far more interesting ongoing process of religious engagement and cultural change."[22] In this way, the Halfway Covenant was functioning precisely as it was meant to: reclaiming the grandchildren of church members after a generational failure or gap. Sarah Robins Muckamaug never chose to belong to the church. Her son George did, but her daughter Sarah did not. Ami Printer chose not to belong, but his daughter Sarah did. Father and daughter Moses and Abigail Printer chose not to belong, but Abigail connected herself through marriage to the Abrahams, all of whom belonged, except for Andrew Sr. And all but one of Abigail's own children would be baptized in the church she never chose to join.

Despite a possible lack of parental encouragement or connection, we know that George Muckamaug was serious about his spiritual seeking, for on June

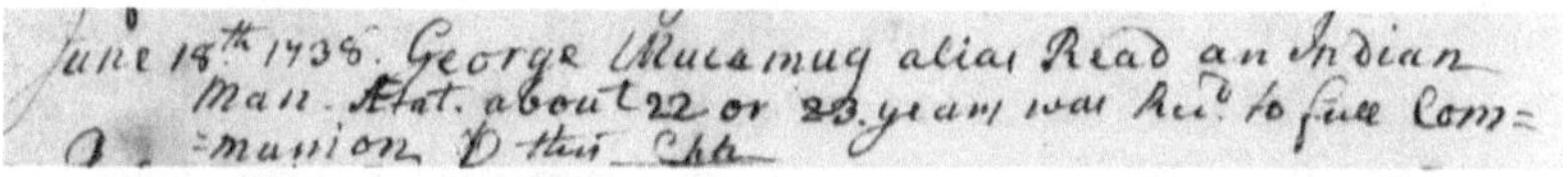

Church Belonging and the Halfway Covenant in Hassanamesit/Grafton 113

[handwritten record] June 19th 1738. George Mucamug alias Read an Indian Man Ætat. about 22 or 23. years was Rec.d to full Com=munion ℗ this Chh

FIGURE 7. Full communion record of George Muckamaug, January 5, 1735/36, in "Hassanamisco church book, 1731–1774," in the Grafton, Massachusetts, Evangelical Congregational Church records, Congregational Library and Archives, Boston.

18, 1738, "George Mucamug alias Read an Indian Man Ætat. About 22 or 23. years was Rec^d. to full Communion per this C^{hh}" (HG 34). Muckamaug was the first Nipmuc person to become a full member of the second church body in Hassanamesit/Grafton. This meant that he was a pillar of the second church and an exemplar to everyone in the congregation and the town. He was equal in spiritual status to any Englishwoman or man who had experienced the same discovery of election. Unlike the English town and its government, the Congregational church had offered him full inclusion and the reciprocal relation of mutual care and responsibility. This new and important state of being makes it likely that George Muckamaug served as counsel to the next young Nipmuc person who had no parental involvement in her decision to belong to the congregation: Sarah Printer, who "owned the Covenant, & was baptized" just six months later on December 31, 1738 (H/G 26). I feel confident that this was orphan Sarah Printer, the daughter of Moses and the cousin of Abigail, not Abigail's mother, Sarah Printer Sr., because the record does not list a husband or children. Moreover, because neither Abigail nor Sarah Sr. ever chose to belong to the church, the record probably does not refer to Abigail's sister, Sarah Jr. Like Andrew Abraham Jr. and George Muckamaug, this Sarah Printer was the first member of her family to join the second church body. Her parents, Moses and Mary Printer, may have belonged to the first Nipmuc Congregational church body in the town. However, like her cousins, Sarah Printer was born in the gap between the demise of the first church and the gathering of the second, so there are no baptism records for her. Her decision to join the second church body may represent a continuation of her own family belonging or her creation of a new web of relation with that body, one made easier by the presence of her kin, Andrew Abraham Jr. and George Muckamaug.

Unfortunately, George Muckamaug did not have much time to serve as an example or a help to any other Nipmucs in their spiritual seeking. After writing out the list of people admitted to the church, the minister Solomon Prentice inserted a small note next to Muckamaug's name: "Died at Cape Bretton." This indicates that he died between six and nine years after his admission to full membership, during the siege of Cape Breton Island in Canada, presumably as a soldier in King George's War (1744–48). Muckamaug's death is a reminder of the minister Stephen Badger's assertion that one factor driving the decline in the local Indigenous population was the men's participation in the many "military expeditions set on foot."[23]

On February 29, 1740, two years after George Muckamaug and Sarah Printer joined Andrew Abraham Jr. in the church body, Abigail Printer's name appeared in the church record book when she married Abraham: "Andrew Abraham ^Jur. (Indian) ^(both of this Town) To Abigail Printer Indian" (HG 63).[24] They must have known each other all their lives; and despite her own unchanging decision not to belong to the church, she was apparently comfortable with his devout Christianity and Congregational belonging. Almost the entire Abraham family, as we've seen, were active in the church and congregation, so she would have been familiar with this aspect of his life.[25] Her decision not to seek church belonging was not a dealbreaker for Andrew Jr. As Neal Salisbury explains, Indigenous people who chose Congregationalism, "while identifying themselves as distinct from the non-Christian segments of their communities, [nevertheless] maintained contact with people in these segments, many of whom were kin and longtime neighbors."[26] Six months later, on July 13, 1740, Abigail Printer Abraham's sister-in-law Elizabeth also appeared in the record: "Elizabeth Abram Daughter of Andrew Abram Indian was Rec^d. into full Communion w this C^{hh}" (HG 35).

On December 27, 1741, Samuel John "An Indian Own^d ye Cov^t and was Baptized," continuing the flow of Nipmucs into covenant belonging through the Halfway Covenant (HG 76). Almost two years later, on May 17, 1742, Andrew Abraham Jr. and Abigail Printer Abraham baptized their first child: "Jonas Son of Andrew & Abigail Abram Ju^r. Indian on his Account" (HG 36). This record shows that Abigail still had not owned the covenant as Jonas was baptized on his father's account.

On April 8, 1743, the couple baptized their second child: "David Abram (Indian) Son of Andrew & Abigail Abram. Indian (nee Abigail Printer)" (HG 79). There is no baptism record for the Abrahams' third son, John, although the vital records for Grafton list his date of birth as June 10, 1747.[27] That year must be an error, as in his will, written a year earlier on August 1, 1746, Andrew

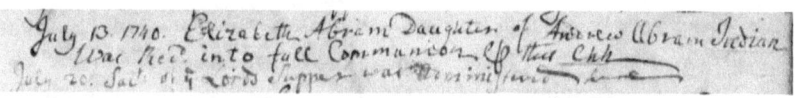

FIGURE 8. Full communion record of Elizabeth Abraham, July 13, 1740, in the "Hassanamisco church book, 1731–1774," in the Grafton, Massachusetts, Evangelical Congregational Church records, RG 4921, Congregational Library and Archives, Boston.

Abraham Jr. listed "my children Jonas David and John Abraham." Why was John Abraham the only son whose baptism was not recorded in the church records? It's possible that the minister, Solomon Prentice, made an error. But it's also possible that Andrew Abraham Jr. was not in Hassanamesit when John was born. It was against Congregational practice to baptize infants if the parent or guardian on whose account they were being baptized was not physically present. Abigail was not a member, either halfway or full, and so could not present John to the church for baptism. While this baby was welcomed into his Nipmuc family in other ways, he could not be baptized in his father's church without his father present.

The wording of the will itself suggests that Andrew Abraham Jr. was not present for his son's birth but had followed George Muckamaug and so many other Indigenous men into English military service during King George's War: "I Andrew Abraham Junr . . . a soldier Considering the shortness and uncertainty of life do make my Last will and Testament."[28] Perhaps the financial demands of his growing family had made it necessary for him to enlist; it may have seemed preferable to hiring himself out to English employers or selling land. The official document noting his death describes him as a "planter," meaning that he had adopted English farming, so selling his land would have also stripped him of his livelihood. Both indenture and enlistment would have taken him away from his family for months or years at a time, but at least military service was less likely to have led to permanent servitude.

Whatever his reasons, Andrew Abraham Jr. knew that his choice to enlist was dangerous, so he left a will and, like other Christian men of his time, made his first bequeathment to God: "Imprimis Recommending my Precious Soul into ye hands of Jesus Christ and my Body to ye Dust In hopes of a Resurrection to a glorious Immortality, I do will and dispose of my worldly Estate which god hath mercifully gave me in ye manner following." He went on to leave his "beloved wife Abigail . . . 20 pounds old tenor that is in Col^o Brattles hand and all my Wages that is or shall be due to me by going into ye Kings Serve (If any there Be) Likewise ye Benefits of that Tract of land of mine... so long as she remaineth my widow and no Longer." To his sons he left "that lot of land of mine at Natick to be equally divided amongst them and also that tract of land that I give... unto my wife... they to come into possession of it at ye time of her marriage or in case she never marries at her decease." Abigail was the sole executrix of this will, which her husband signed.[29]

Andrew Abraham Jr. was prescient in making a will because he was reported dead almost exactly a year after filing it. The next document in his file in the Worcester probate records is a short statement by Aaron Wilder: "I certify that James Printer and Andrew Abraham Two Indian soldiers who went to Port Royal under Capt. [Innis] are both dead & [I] saw them buried. Worcester August 31: 1747." This testimony was witnessed by the trustee John Chandler.[30] Abraham's estate was inventoried and the records were filed a year later, on August 30, 1748. His twenty-three acres of land were valued at £280, and Abigail Abraham witnessed this inventory as the sole executrix.[31] Her grief must have been compounded by concern for her widowed mother, Sarah Printer Sr., who was suffering from a long-term disabling condition in one of her legs. Her husband Ami Printer Sr. had died in 1741, so she may have been living with her daughter Abigail.

Her husband's death meant that Abigail Abraham's most immediate tie to the church at Hassanamesit/Grafton was broken. Her three sons were young—ages five, four, and one. Would she honor her husband's desire that his sons be raised in the church that she had chosen not to belong to? Or would she break the connection he had claimed or reclaimed through the Halfway Covenant? The church records contain no entries for any of her sons after the first two baptisms, and the Grafton vital records are similarly barren: there are no marriage or death records for Jonas, David, or John. This suggests two possibilities: they left the church while continuing to live in the town but were erased from the civil record, or they left the church and the town.

I'll come back to this question of Abigail's sons and the durability of Halfway Covenant membership. For now, my focus is on the struggles she faced as a landowning Indigenous widow outside of church belonging. Her husband had left her with a fairly comfortable estate, which he may have hoped would protect her from the insistent land grabbing that was building the town of Grafton on the lands of Hassanamesit. But with her sons too young to work, she struggled to maintain the English-style farm her husband had founded.

Church kinship, as we've seen, was rarely if ever powerful enough to override economic competition, even among full members who were English. An Indigenous woman standing outside the church would be treated no differently from any other Indigenous woman who stood between colonizers and a land purchase.

In October 1748, increasing financial difficulties likely led Abigail Abraham and her mother Sarah Printer Sr. to petition the General Court to be "empowered" to sell some of the land they belonged to by birth and owned by colonization.[32] They were not the only Nipmuc women who were being driven to sell parts of their land: Abigail's sister-in-law Elizabeth Abraham and their kin Sarah Muckamaug Burnee also appear in the civil records. Only Elizabeth was a church member at the time she sold her land, but this counted for little or nothing in terms of being forced to the extremity of making a sale.

Abigail Abraham and Sarah Printer Sr. had to petition the General Court for permission to sell their own land because Governor William Shirley had signed an act on March 2, 1746/47, stating that, to prevent sales from being "imposed on" Indigenous people by "evil minded men[,] ... for the future no Petitions for selling Indians land be received, unless such Petitions be recommended by the respective Guardians of the said Indians." The two women, identifying themselves as "widows & Indians of Grafton, together with a minor child named Martha Printer," petitioned for empowerment to sell two thirty-acre lots out of their "valuable estate of land," which the court judged to be worth £150 old tenor.[33] The plan was that "if said two lots were sold & the money arising from the sale was faithfully laid out under the imposition of some prudent English person, it might without all doubt turn to the great comfort of your petitioners—and as your petitioners have nothing else in view—they humbly pray an order may pass [to] enable them to make sale of said two lots."[34] The petition was granted a month later, on November 19, 1748.

The statement that the women "had nothing else in view" is telling. It reveals how bleak their outlook was and how few options the English would give them. Abigail Abraham had to provide for a sick and aging mother, a lame younger sister, and three little boys. She couldn't hire herself out to work for someone else without abandoning her own farm and household. She didn't have the money to hire men to help her plant and harvest. Her mother's and sister's medical bills were adding up every month. Crucially, she was allowed to remain in this untenable position for as long as it took to ensure that she would have to sell part of her land to make ends meet. If Abigail had "nothing else in view" but a sale, that was because her prudent English neighbors had made sure of this. As I will show, they would be the ones to buy her land and to make their own fortunes by establishing their families on it. They benefited from Andrew Abraham Jr's labor to make their way, reducing his sons' chances of doing the same.

In 1749, Sarah Muckamaug Burnee was also caring for her ailing mother Sarah Sr. (Sarah Robins Muckamaug English), who died sometime that year. Sarah Sr. left her daughter their land, the Robins parcel, and her descendants were able to keep their Nipmuc culture alive on their land, where it lives on today.[35] A petition from the daughter ("Sarah Burnee an Indian of Grafton Als Hassanamisco") appears in the records of the General Court dated March 22, 1749/50.[36] Sarah Jr. had married Fortune Burnee at some point between her return to Hassanamesit/Grafton from Providence in 1741 and the birth of her daughter Sarah Muckamaug Burnee (Sarah III) on November 27, 1744.[37] Both Sarah Jr. and Fortune Burnee remained outside of the church at Hassanamesit and do not appear in its records. This is unfortunate as it forces me to rely on the Grafton town records, which are almost always less detailed and careful, as I showed in the case of John Abraham's erroneous town birth record. Sarah III's birth record reads "Burnee _____, d. Forten (negro) and Sarah (Indian), Nov. 27, 1744." Sarah III's name reappeared in the Grafton town records when she married, but neither her Indigenous and Black identity nor her husband Boston Philips's Black identity were recorded: "Burnee, Sarah and Boston Philips, July 9, 1786."[38]

Sarah Jr.'s petition was successful: the English recognized her as her mother's heir, so she was "empowered" to sell a portion of the land she had inherited in order to build a house and buy cattle. The two lots were sold a week later, on April 2, 1750: Hezekiah Ward bought the forty-six-acre lot, and Abraham Temple bought the thirty-acre lot, each "being the highest bidder." This last phrase served as a kind of boilerplate in the English records; I have to take their word for it, as other bids were not recorded.[39]

Just as the Hassanamesit/Grafton church records reveal a fuller understanding of these Nipmuc women as complete human beings rather than simply the subjects or objects of legal transactions, they also reveal more about the four Englishmen who bought the women's land—Hezekiah Ward, Abraham Temple, Ephraim Sherman, and his brother Nathaniel Sherman—and fill in the gaps of the civil records. Hezekiah Ward was born in Whipsuppenicke/Marlborough in 1703, the son of William Ward, a powerful magistrate and landowner and one of the men who had petitioned to create the town of Southborough at Ockoogangansett.[40] Hezekiah Ward would have arrived in Hassanamesit/Grafton with money, standing (he was listed as a selectman in 1749), and a plan to rapidly amass land. On August 5, 1750, four months after his purchase of Sarah Jr.'s land, the church records show that "Hezekiah Ward & Sarah his wife were recieved into full Com^n. with this C^{hh}. being dismissed from the C^{hh} in Southb.gh" (HG 39). On January 27, 1750/51, his adult son Hezekiah Ward Jr. and his son's wife Hannah owned the church covenant and presented their adult daughter Abigail Ward for baptism. She would become a full member of the church two months later, on March 3, 1750/51 (HG 85, 39). Hezekiah Ward Jr., baptized on his parents' full-member account but never a full member himself, took advantage of the Halfway Covenant to put himself and his family under church watch and protection. Then, like Elizabeth Abraham, Abigail Ward moved from being baptized on her parents' account to becoming a full member of the church in her own right.[41]

The English buyer Abraham Temple first appeared in the church records on February 3, 1733/34, when he and his wife Elizabeth Temple owned the covenant and baptized their son Joseph Temple (born in 1732). The Temples then reappeared in the church records repeatedly as seven more children were born. According to an entry dated May 3, 1752, their infant son Silas Temple was baptized in an emergency situation on his mother's account: "Silas Son of Abraham Temple & Elizabeth his wife at Her Desire & on her Right, he also desiring it on her Acct at his House by a vote of ye C^{hh} ye Sabbath before she engaging before a number of Brethren for the child; it being imperfect & much indisposed. Baptized May 18. 1752" (HG 86).

Because baptism was a sacrament, it was supposed to take place in the meetinghouse, the only building likely to be large enough to allow all of the church body to be present as witnesses. Thus, many churches went through an agonizing decision when parents requested the home-based baptism of an infant who was clearly too sick to live until the next Sabbath day or too sick to be moved from a house.[42] This particular record is confusing, however, given that both parents had owned the covenant in Hassanamesit/Grafton. Why, then, was Silas baptized at his mother's "Desire & on her Right," with his father also "desiring it on her Acct"? The previous entry for the Temples was for an infant baptism in 1749. Could it be that, at some time over the course of those three years, Abraham Temple had left the church body? In the 1730s and 1740s, the Great Awakening was sweeping through Woodland New England,

and he might have joined the separatists who had left their Congregational church bodies to worship in one of the movement's new and exciting forms while his wife remained firm in her commitment to the established Congregational way. Or the Temples may have experienced a different religious rift, which could also explain the three-year gap between the births of their sons Timothy and Silas. Silas was baptized at home and died two months later, on July 30. Abraham Temple's next child, Persis, was baptized slightly more than a year later, on October 2, 1753, again on her mother's account. Abraham Temple made no further appearance in the Hassanamesit/Grafton church records (HG 90).

On January 9, 1750/51, less than a year after Sarah Muckamaug Burnee's March 1749/50 petition, Elizabeth Abraham and Abigail Printer Abraham each petitioned the court separately to be recognized as a female heir and to be empowered to sell part of the land they were to inherit. Elizabeth Abraham's petition was entered into the record first and was granted the next day.[43] She was empowered to sell her "aged mother" Deborah Abraham's land whenever she chose, provided that "the house on the premises be reserved for the mother during life."[44] This happened quickly: on March 11, 1750/51, fifty acres of "Elizabeth Abrahams Land An Indian of Grafton" were sold to Ephraim Sherman, "the highest bidder," for £81.

He and his wife Thankfull Sherman had owned the covenant and had their son Ephraim Sherman Jr. baptized on June 30, 1734, just four months after Deborah Abraham had owned the covenant and had her three children baptized (HG 20). Thankfull Sherman would go on to become a full member decades later, on June 7, 1763, though her husband would need more time: "Thankful wife of Ephraim Sherman was received into full Com^n with y^s C^{hh}. at the Same time ye C^{hh} voted to [postpone] their Receiving Ephraim Sherman into the full com^n. for the present. The Pastor after proposed the next Lecture for his offering himself again" (HG 43). Three months later, on September 1, he "was received into full Com^n. with this C^{hh}" (HG 43) and would go on to serve as a deacon of the church until his death on July 9, 1775, at age sixty-six.[45]

On May 30, 1750, Sarah Printer Sr. and Abigail Printer Abraham sold the two lots composing about 122 acres that they had been empowered to sell back in 1748 to Ephraim Sherman's brother Nathaniel Sherman, "freeholder, he being the highest bidder for the sum of £163 via "old Tenor bills of Credit."[46] His son Nathaniel Sherman Jr. had been baptized just four days after Andrew Abraham Jr. had owned the covenant and was baptized (HG 13). Like his brother, Nathaniel Sr. was a constant church committee member and town officer. They bought land from Indigenous women at the same time, perhaps pooling their connections to secure the sales, and Nathaniel Sherman was open about his resistance to supporting Indigenous people in Hassanamesit/Grafton. In January 1738 he was one of seven signatories to a petition demanding that the proprietors, or first founders, of the town be relieved of their obligation to "support and maintain Preaching and schooling, and all without charge to the Indians of s^d Grafton"—a commitment included in the terms of purchase of the land to create the town. Representatives of the town filed a counter-petition claiming that these men did not act in their name and clearly stating that they understood that this subset of proprietors was proposing a harmful abandonment: "[A]s soon as [we] heard what the committee had done, [we] called a meeting and dismissed said committee, [and] voted that the petition should be withdrawn [and] by which [we] do not by any means propose to hurt the Indians or original proprietors, but are sincerely desirous that both may be served, and that all the good ends and purposes designed by the General Court, relating to the Indians, might be fully answered."[47] They may have protested too much as the issue was not formally resolved until 1773, an "unaccountable and inexcusable neglect" that allowed the commitment to Indigenous religious inclusion and education to languish in limbo, contributing to Indigenous civil and religious marginalization in the town.[48]

Hezekiah Ward, Abraham Temple, Ephraim Sherman, and Nathaniel Sherman were all full church members. Ideally, this should have meant that they would not lowball the Printer, Burnee, and Abraham women but pay true value for their land. All of these families, both Indigenous and English, were limbs of the same church body. But the parallel universe that existed for English people in Woodland New England meant that a religious relationship did not override their fear of scarcity or their competition for resources. The Shermans, Temples, and Wards had a spiritual connection with the Printers and Abrahams in the church body, but that did not stop them from buying the women's land rather than helping them in some other way—for instance, by negotiating with creditors or lending their labor on the farm. The men could have stepped in immediately after their brother Andrew Abraham Jr.'s death. They could have helped to care for the women he had left without then demanding that this debt be repaid with the women's only asset—land.[49] It would have been relatively easy for large, well-established English families such as the Shermans, Temples, and Wards to overcome economic difficulty and forestall land sales for their sisters in Christ. But they chose not to help in any of these ways, thus contributing to the circumstances that led to the women's land sales. This makes the fact that they allegedly paid a fair price for the land even less impressive.

I return now to the question of what might have happened to Jonas, David, and John Abraham. None of their names appear in church or civil records after their birth entries. That absence is part of a larger pattern in which Indigenous people disappeared from both sets of records in Hassanamesit/Grafton after the 1760s. In the 1770s, the church and the town underwent turnover and conflict linked to the contentious dismissal of the minister Aaron Hutchinson in 1771, the belated arrival of his successor David Grosvenor in 1785, the advent of a Baptist congregation in town, and the Revolutionary War. While a full study of the situation is outside of my scope, I can conjecture that dissension in the church, the introduction of a Baptist option, and the repair of the meetinghouse in 1779—a costly undertaking to which few Indigenous people would have been able to contribute—may have led to their marginalization in the church.

Service in the Continental Army could have been another factor explaining the absence of Indigenous men who might have continued their church membership. The widow Abigail Printer Abraham married William Anthony (who did not belong to the church), and her son from that second marriage, Joseph Anthony, died during his military service in 1778. He left land in Hassanamesit/Grafton, which he had inherited from his mother, to his half-brother David Abraham. In December 1778, David, also serving in the Continental Army, made his will using the same deeply Christian language that his father had used before serving in an earlier English war. According to this will, David Abraham was living in Alstead, New Hampshire; he is traceable in searches for the Abraham brothers of Hassanamesit/Grafton only because he gave Joseph's land there to Joseph Prentice, an English resident of the town.[50] David Abraham's stepfather Fortune Burnee, the widower of Sarah Muckamaug Jr., whom Abigail Printer Abraham Anthony had married in 1757, contested this bequest, claiming that he himself should have the land. (His petition was denied.)[51] Perhaps the animosity between Burnee and his stepsons kept David, Jonas, and John Abraham away from Hassanamesit/Grafton. David lived until 1784, and his Christian faith seems evident. Jonas and John may also have remained strong in their Congregationalism, offering proof of the durability of Halfway Covenant membership.

Abigail Printer Abraham Anthony Burnee died in December 1776, a year after she was forced to petition the General Court for delayed interest payments that were due to her from the Indian trustees.[52] Her death was not recorded in the official vital records of Grafton, an absence that seems deliberate. The determined expansion of Grafton's English town government was built in part on its deliberate marginalization of the Indigenous residents. But in the John Milton Earle Papers, an archive linked to Hassanamesit/Grafton, there is an anonymous, undated note: "The wife of Fortunatus Burnee, known by the name of Nab Fortune, having become intoxicated, was frozen near the brook that runs into Dorothy Pond. An Indian Jury brought in a verdict that she came to her death by reason of the water in the rum freezing in her."[53] It's tragic that this is the only English epitaph we have for a strong and important woman who engaged deeply with so many of the key events and movements of the period. But what made this Nipmuc woman notable to the anonymous writer? Like the note writer I discussed in chapter 7, I think he was using the note to prove a point. He continued by saying that each May, when the Indigenous people were supposed to receive their interest payments from the trustees, "the Indians always had a drunken frolic, a dance &c." Abigail Burnee died in December, but this note writer seems to link her death to habitual Indigenous drunkenness. More importantly, the note ends with the detail that, when the payments were made, the Indigenous people "received not only money, but a blanket, a psalter or a psalm book according to the age of the individual." [54] The note thus reveals ongoing Congregational identity amongst the Nipmucs of Hassanamesit/Grafton in the latter half of the eighteenth century, even as multiple forces were working to remove them from the church and the town.

TWO WOMEN, TWO CHOICES

In June 1753, a surprising entry appeared in the Grafton town records: "Tommack, Andrew (alias Andrew Abraham), s. Sampson and Elisabeth Abraham, March 6, 1754."[55] Elizabeth Abraham, who had turned twenty-two in February, had given birth to a child by a man she was not married to and had named him after his uncle Andrew. She did marry Samson Tommack a year later, on May 30, 1756, when she was five months pregnant with their daughter Deborah Tommack, a marriage that is recorded in the town records only. She made no further appearance in the records of her church body, although she and Samson continued to live in the place and they had another child, a son named Silvanus Tommack, born on March 3, 1762.[56]

If Elizabeth Abraham Tommack had stopped attending services and had refused to take communion, thus withdrawing from the church, a committee should have been sent to visit her, and this would have been recorded in the church record book. But there are no records of such outreach. Did she separate from the church body before the pregnancy, responding to the call of the Great Awakening? Did she come to agree with her sister-in-law Abigail's firm stance against belonging to the second church in town? Or did her husband lead her away from her family tradition?

The church records offer no answers. After 1747 and the great crisis that tore apart the second church at Hassanamesit/Grafton apart (see chapter 9), entries for Indigenous people drop almost to zero. There are twenty-four entries for Nipmuc people between Andrew Abraham Jr.'s owning of the covenant in 1732 and the final entry for Ezekiel Cole in 1747 (also discussed in chapter 9). After that, only one Nipmuc person, Esther Lawrence, appears in the church records, between 1755 and 1763. Although Esther was the daughter of Abigail Printer's cousin Sarah Printer and Sarah's husband Peter Lawrence, there is no record of a baptism, which is unusual, given that her mother belonged to the church. However, as she was married in 1763, I estimate that she was born in the early 1740s because most women in the records were married in their early twenties. Sarah Printer Lawrence must have raised Esther within the church because she followed in her mother's footsteps and even surpassed her owning of the covenant: on July 27, 1755, "Esther Lawrance Ind^a. was recieved into full Comm^n. with y^s C^{hh} & baptized after her Confession of faith & Relation rece^{d}" (HG 41). Esther Lawrence, like her cousin Elizabeth Abraham before her, became a full member of the church body, joining just four months after Elizabeth bore her son out of wedlock.

The next entry for Esther Lawrence invites even closer comparison with her cousin: on January 11, 1762, she "made a publick confession for the sin of Fornication and was restored" (HG 42). Although fornication in Puritan Woodland New England is often conflated with the heavy sin of adultery, it was very different. The church records of all towns abound with regular entries for couples of every race who had confessed their sins of fornication and were instantly forgiven by their churches and immediately "restored." In almost all of these cases, couples who committed fornication had either had sex before marriage, as evidenced by the birth of a child less than eight months after marriage, or on a fast day. Fornication confessions were so routine that some ministers grouped them like baptisms or marriages; they didn't stand apart as transgressions that had to be addressed in church meetings. In the second Hassanamesit/Grafton church record book (1774–1828), the minister Daniel Grosvenor grouped fornication along with other "Confessions etc." on page 45. Even couples who had sex before marriage were usually restored immediately. Only rarely was fornication more complicated, necessitating fuller explanations in the church record book.⁵⁷

So what was the case when Esther Lawrence made a confession of fornication and was instantly restored? The answer lies in a record just two weeks later: "Lawrence, Peter, s. Esther, bap. Jan 25, 1761" (HG 97). Like her cousin Elizabeth Abraham, Esther Lawrence had given birth to a child out of wedlock. Both women were full members of their church, and both had transgressed the terms of belonging with their pregnancies. But while Elizabeth seems to have chosen not to belong to the church body by the time her child was born, Esther chose to stay. She stood before other members of that body and confessed her sin—obvious to all by that time—and was immediately restored to them. We can only conjecture about why the women made different choices, but it is possible to discount the idea that racism had driven the church body to cast out Elizabeth Abraham. Esther Lawrence was a Nipmuc woman, but she was not cast out for her transgression. Her son Peter Lawrence was baptized in the meetinghouse on her account; and when she married Sharp Freeborn, the father of her child, more than a year later on July 6, 1763, the minister Aaron Hutchinson performed the ceremony: "July 6 1763 Sharp Foreborn ^a Negro man of Licester and Esther Lawrence of Grafton an Indian woman were married together [in] Grafton pʳ Aaron Hutchinson pastor." Hutchinson sent this record "to [the town] clerk Febʸ 28 1766" (HG, no page number).

This small record reveals the ever-dual workings of church kinship in Woodland New England. Issues that remained entirely within the church body, such as unwed pregnancy, were subject to the ultimately rehabilitative and loving process of rebuke-repent-restore, while issues that crossed over into the economic combat zone of land grabbing were not. Church sisters who came to the attention of their sisters and brothers for a personal reason experienced church kinship. Those who were forced into appearing in the civil, economic realm did not. Perhaps Elizabeth Abraham Tommack's experience with the self-interested church brethren who bought her land so "fairly" in 1751 led to her eventual disappearance from the church records by 1755.

Church records can never tell the whole story of the Printer, Abraham, Lawrence, and Muckamaug family members who belonged to Hassanamesit/Grafton in the early to mid-1700s and the decisions they made about love, marriage, and living as Nipmuc people. But their histories have an enormous impact on our understanding of how the Halfway Covenant was used by Indigenous people to reclaim their Congregational heritage and identity after King Philip's War—and how and why this mattered to their English counterparts. By the turn of the eighteenth century, each relied on the other for validation of their congregation or church status attained through use of the Halfway Covenant. This halfway membership seems to have been durable across generations, and further research will produce valuable insights into Indigenous Congregationalism in the eighteenth century and beyond.

PART FOUR

Mixed Church Bodies Sabotaged in Hassanamesit/Grafton and N'ahteuk/Natick

CHAPTER NINE

Finding Ezekiel Cole

If you are familiar at all with Ezekiel Cole, a Nipmuc man who belonged to Hassanamesit/Grafton, you most likely know him as a minor footnote in the story of the English minister Solomon Prentice. I will tell both men's narratives in this chapter, bringing Cole out of that footnote, where he has long served as shorthand for radical, unaccountable, outsider forces that challenged Congregationalism during the Great Awakening. For Ezekiel Cole was no outsider to Congregationalism; he was not a random "Indian" whose identity adds to the perceived chaos of the Great Awakening in Woodland New England. As with Thomas Miller, the English civil records that concern him pale in comparison with the church records that tell us so much more of his story. Those records, written by Prentice, also give us much more information about the minister than was previously available.

Historians without access to the full Hassanamesit/Grafton church records have already told a version of Solomon Prentice's story.[1] They have presented him as an originally orthodox Congregational minister who eventually became a New Light—someone who abandoned Congregationalism for the experiential religion of the Great Awakening—though the split he knew this would cause in the church body grieved him and made him hesitate to fully break away. But the story I tell here is completely different. It comes directly from the church records that Prentice wrote, which differ from his letters, sermons, and public writings as well as from third-party reports. That's because he understood the church records to be communications he was making before God, where telling the truth was a matter of life and death.

The accuracy of Ezekiel Cole's story also relies on church records. Without access to the full Hassanamesit/Grafton church records, historians over the centuries confused him with another Ezekiel Cole, a contemporaneous English separatist minister living in nearby Manchauge/Sutton. In the nineteenth century, historians apparently saw (or cherrypicked) a few entries in the Hassanamesit/Grafton church records out of context, which led them to mix up data about the English Cole with those about the Nipmuc Cole. The two men's identities have been merged and confused ever since, even though a quick check of the Worcester County probate files reveals that Reverend Ezekiel Cole of Manchauge/Sutton died in 1799 and in his will left $1,000 each to five of his children, also dividing a farm between two of them. His estate totaled nearly $14,000, a fortune that his children fought over for decades.[2] No Indigenous separatist preacher would have been given the title *reverend* or been able to amass such an estate. Moreover, the invaluable Worthley inventory for the church at "Sutton, Separate" says that the minister of the New Lights church gathered there was Ezekiel Cole (ordained in 1751, died in 1799). If this Ezekiel had been a Nipmuc, that information would have been noted in the inventory.[3]

A few historians, among them Isaac Backus in his 1871 history, were able to keep the two men separate, but others who had read only snippets from the Hassanamesit/Grafton church records generated more confusion, proof of the importance of access to those records in their entirety.[4] Though it's not clear how the historian Frederick Clifton Pierce was able to consult these partial entries, his 728-page history of the town of Grafton (published in 1879) includes an impressively apocryphal anecdote about Solomon Prentice shooting a bear on his way to the meetinghouse, "where he undoubtedly led the devotions of the assembly with more concentration and fervor of mind than he could have commanded, if he had suffered the wild beast to roam through the neighborhood in freedom." The footnote to this passage addresses the question of whether a minister would have fired a gun on the Sabbath, which Congregationalism prohibited. According to Pierce, however, Prentice's "apprehension [for] the safety of children . . . would justify it" to even the most exacting conscience. The historian then contrasted the minister's heroic action with another, clearly criminal one: "It seems to us more in keeping with the spirit of the age, that 'Brother Ezekiel Cole' should have 'come before the church,' as the records say he did, on the 13th of February, 1743, 'and acknowledged his fault for going a gunning on the public thanksgiving day appointed for the King's deliverance in the late battle on the river Mayne in Germany.'"[5]

I have confirmed this reference on page 111 of the Hassanamesit/Grafton church record book:

> 1. Bro^r Ezekil Cole Came before the C^{hh} & acknowledg^d
> he had been rash & unchristian, in charging y^e Pastor
> with Preaching Damnable Doctrine and Said he was
> Sorry there fore, and ask^d forgiveness of Pastor & C^{hh}
> who accordingly manifested their <u>forgiveness</u>
> 2. Bro^r Ezekil Cole also acknowledged his fault for
> going a Guning on the Publick Thanksgiving Day ap=
> =pointed for the Kings Deliverance in the late Battle
> On the River Mayne in Germany[.] (HG 111)[6]

The full entry makes it clear that Pierce saw only a snippet from the record—entry 2. If he had seen the whole, he would likely have shared the much more remarkable entry 1, in which Cole charged the minister with "preaching damnable doctrine." (I will return to this record later in the chapter.)

Two pages later, Pierce's history refers to Ezekiel Cole in the context of the Great Awakening that tore apart the Hassanamesit/Grafton church and congregation: "Ezekiel Coal (or Cole), a member of this church, and an Indian, Solomon Paine, Elihu Marsh, and others, who had been ordained as lay preachers or exhorters, also came among the people at this period and preached."[7] The church records do include the names of Deacon Marsh and Solomon Paine as "lay Exhorters" whom Solomon Prentice had "countenanced" in an entry for March 25, 1746 (HG 139), and I will discuss the Nipmuc Cole's role as a lay exhorter. For the moment, though, I want to focus on the fact that Pierce did not refer to Cole as "an Indian" in his first reference but did in his second. This may be evidence that he knew or suspected that there were two Ezekiel Coles.

Later scholars have identified the Nipmuc Cole with anarchy and separatism. For instance, Ross Beales Jr. describes "the appearance of an Indian, Ezekiel Cole, in the Grafton pulpit" as one of the alarming events that led to dissension in the church; and Douglas Winiarski confuses the two Coles, stating that "the Sutton dissenters were led by Ezekiel Cole, a zealous Native American revival convert from the neighboring town of Grafton who claimed to be the typological descendant of the 'Captain of the Lords hosts' described in Joshua 5:14. Soon, rumors were circulating that the 'separating Brethren' had rejected their infant baptisms and embraced 'familistical' errors, including the controversial practice of spiritual wifery."[8]

In this chapter, I focus on the Nipmuc Ezekiel Cole, using the church records to help answer some of the questions that the scholars Stephen Mrozowski and Heather Law Pezzarossi have also asked about him: "Did Cole reflect an enthusiasm that he shared with his Hassanamisco community members? Did this movement empower the Native community, young or old, or both? We do not know how the Native community reacted to this event, but it seems that the acceptance of 'uneducated exhorters and itinerants into his pulpit' [soon] became a source of much contention among the settlers."[9] Paradoxically, I begin this history of Ezekiel Cole and Solomon Prentice in Hassanamesit/Grafton with a record from the diary of the Whipsuppenicke/ Westborough minister Ebenezer Parkman, who mentioned Cole in passing on November 28, 1742:

> Was pritty Comfortable in the Day But was feverish at Eve. N.B. a remarkable meeting at Mr. Harwoods (upon the Borders) last night. Great awakenings there and several Children of Mr. William Nurse and one of Mr. James Fay much wrought on. N.B. An Indian Youth one [ ] Cole, greatly carry'd out at those Meetings. Some of Westborough people that were present greatly question'd their regularity and Soundness, particularly Mr. Eliezer Rice. May the Spirit of Truth lead us and guide us into all Truth for his Name's Sake! Grant us by all Means the Blessing and preserve us from the Evil! Old Mr. Mainard settling his Estate. At Eve Mr. Edward Goddard here. Thomas Winchester thrashing Rye.[10]

Why begin with yet another record in which Ezekiel Cole was hardly more than footnote? Because Parkman's mention was far more balanced than those that appeared in later histories. As he recorded New Light activity in his area with worry and skepticism, he named three Englishmen and some of their children as well as another young person, one of them Indigenous, who were all swept up in the fervor of revival, whether "much wrought on" or "greatly carry'd out" by it. Parkman prayed that this revivalism would be abandoned, then moved on to other local news.

Parkman's diary entry dates from November 1742, and the minister Solomon Prentice may have been preaching to Cole at about the same time. In his self-serving 1744 narrative of the Great Awakening, Prentice recorded that he was preaching by request in many neighboring towns during the winter of 1742–43. In January 1742/43, "I Preached the Sab. Evening [at] one of our Indian Famalys: where the Lords was pleased to meet with us again, and Manifested Himselfe in the Extraordinary Convictions sundry Persons were under."[11] Prentice recorded the spiritual frenzy characteristic of the Great Awakening, and his language was transparently unorthodox. He was clearly preaching revivalism to these "Indian Famalys," perhaps with the hope or assumption that his change to a New Light could be kept secret if he were to reveal it only to a fringe population. If so, he was wrong; the change became obvious to his congregation within the year, despite his protestations that he had had nothing to do with the new unorthodoxy. His influence would have been complex for a young person such as Ezekiel Cole. The Congregational minister was preaching unorthodoxy in Nipmuc households while publicly denying that he was doing so. He was also continuing to perform his duties as minister, including his baptism of Cole on February 17, 1742/43:

> Ezekil Cole an Indian about 21 or 22 years old was
> Baptiz^d & Rec^d to full Communion, as also Hannah Willard, Silence Holbrook, and Eunice Foster, were Rec^d per this C^{hh} on Lect. Day[.]
> (HG 37)

Ezekiel, along with three Englishwomen, became a full member of the church body. Very unusually, this entry doesn't describe whether they owned the covenant or were received on a parent's account. However, a later entry in the church record book makes it explicit for one of them: "Ezekil Cole. Ezekil Cole an Indian Youth. Ow^d. y^e. Cov^t. was Baptizd.^{d} & Rec^d. to full Comunion Feb. 20" (HG 78).

Ezekiel owned the covenant five years after George Muckamaug and Sarah Printer (Abigail Printer's cousin) became full members and fewer than three years after Elizabeth Abraham did. Like them, he had no living tie to the church body. Two months after Ezekiel joined, Andrew Abraham Jr. and Abigail Printer Abraham baptized their third son, David. For some of the younger generation of Nipmucs in Hassanamesit/Grafton, this was clearly a moment of growing engagement with the church. George Muckamaug was still alive, Andrew Abraham Jr. was regularly bringing his sons into relationship with the congregation and the church, and his mother Deborah Abraham and two of his brothers were Halfway Covenant members. Perhaps this was the influence that led Ezekiel away from revivalism, despite the minister's preaching.

For guidance, he might have looked more to these Nipmuc neighbors and kin than to English revivalists.

The church records show that Ezekiel Cole and Hannah Willard were admitted to full communion together. Cole had a difficult history with the Willard family. The single English civil court record I have found for him is dated a year later, on May 8, 1744, and is equal parts alarming and baffling:

> Ezekiel Cole a negro or mulatto living in Grafton a freedman & laborer came into court and Confessed that in the latter end of January last past on the Sabbath day he greatly abused ye body of a young infant about ten months old son of Benjamin Willard of said Grafton there appearing no prosecutor the Court order that for his offence he pay a fine to our Lord the king of twenty shillings that he pay cost & fees & send surety for his peaceable & good behavior till the next court and stand committed till sentence be performed, which he did.[12]

A few months later, on August 20, 1744, a short note in the civil records reports, "Ezekiell Cole recog discharged": he was released from jail on his own recognizance. That is the end of the civil record regarding this incident. But what does " greatly abused ye body" of a ten-month-old tell us? Colonial records in Woodland New England did not shy away from clearly identifying crimes of child abuse.[13] These crimes were thoroughly investigated and publicized, and ministers referred to them in sermons. The case of an Indigenous man who had assaulted an English baby would have been a recurring topic in English personal letters and diaries. It would not have been limited to a single eight-line entry in the Worcester court records, which did not mention any witness testimony and specifically noted that no prosecutor had been present in the court. Like Thomas Miller before him, Ezekiel Cole was fined, jailed, and then released on promises of good behavior going forward. That was that. The only commentary I can find on the case is from Ebenezer Parkman, who noted the day after Ezekiel appeared in court that he had "heard that Ezekiel Cole's Case was try'd yesterday at our County Court in Worcester, and that he was fined, etc."[14] Parkman went on to comment on another court case involving a woman charged with defamation of a minister. No note of horror accompanies his short note.

In the civil record, Ezekiel Cole was described as "a freedman and laborer." Was he employed by Benjamin Willard? Perhaps he had been indentured to the Willard family in his youth and had grown up with the Willard children.

English families were supposed to offer Christian instruction to children, servants, and the enslaved; so in such circumstances Cole, too, would have been instructed. It's possible that he and Hannah Willard joined the church at the same time because they had received instruction together. We know that Cole was not enslaved by the Willards when he joined the church; if he had been, the church record would have stated that he had been "presented" by Benjamin Willard, and he would have been described as "belonging to" Willard. At some point, then, Cole became a freedman and began to do paid labor for the family. Here I enter the realm of informed speculation. What if Cole was working at the Willard household in January 1743/44 and in some way injured ten-month-old Benjamin Jr. in the course of his work? He may have been recklessly working near the baby, which would explain the charge of abuse. The actual physical injury must have been relatively minor. But the actual physical injury may not have been what alarmed the Willards. It might have been their perception of Ezekiel Cole's state of mind, for the next church record after the incident with Benjamin Jr. appeared two weeks later, on February 13, 1743/44, and featured Cole asking the church's pardon for two "rash" acts that we've seen before:

1. Bro^r Ezekil Cole Came before the C^{hh} & acknowledgd he had been rash & unchristian, in charging ye Pastor with Preaching Damnable Doctrine and Said he was
Sorry therefore, and ask^d forgiveness of Pastor & C^{hh} who accordingly manifested their forgiveness
2. Bro^r Ezekil Cole also acknowledged his fault for going a Guning on the Publick Thanksgiving Day appointed for the Kings Deliverance in the late Battle On the River Mayne in Germany
Asked forgiveness of God and ye C^{hh} ye C^{hh} Satisfyed[.] (HG 111)

Reading this full record in the context of previous entries gives us so much more than a snippet could tell earlier historians. Cole seems to have committed a trio of provocative acts in the year after he became a full church member: endangering the Willard baby, accusing the minister of fraud, and violating a religious day of thanksgiving. The short entry on his challenge to Solomon Prentice is revelatory when read against Cole's earlier exposure to the minister's revivalist preaching. As an orthodox church member, he was condemning that preaching as "damnable doctrine," but he then acknowledged that he had been wrong to attack Prentice in public. This must have confirmed some other members' suspicions about their minister. The fact that the church forgave Cole immediately seems to cement this reading. That he was still their brother in good standing is made evident by their willingness to also forgive his violation of the day of thanksgiving.

According to the next entry in the church records that mentions Ezekiel Cole, he was back to working for the Willards, less than two months after the incident with Benjamin Jr. Once again he had done harm to a Willard child. This time, however, there is no civil record, only the church record from March 8, 1743/44:

> Ezekil Coal! Acknowledgment.
> I Ezekil Coal do Acknowledge that I was wholly out of the way of my Duty & Over born
> by Temptation, w^n. I thought it my Duty to Whipp Benj^a: Willards Child, So as I did. But
> I hope the Lord has bro't me to See the Evil of itt; & Now I would Earnestly ask
> forgiveness of God & this C^{hh} & Congregation beging that ye would forgive me, & Pray
> that ye Lord God would forgive me; And lift up ye Light of his Countenance upon Me
> And Lead me in ye way to Evlasting Life.
> Voted by the C^{hh} here to Accept the above Acknowledgm^t. And Reicve S^d. Ezek. into full
> Charity again[.] (HG 50)

Again we are left to wonder what had happened between Cole and a Willard child and pressed to extrapolate meaning from a short record. Cole described himself as being "Over born by Temptation" when he "thought it my Duty" to whip the child. Most likely, the problem for the Willards, the church, and the town was not that he had whipped a child but that he had whipped someone else's child. What temptation he had experienced we can't know. What we do know is that, again, the Willards did not take him to court, and Cole seems to have voluntarily confessed the whipping as a sin before the church body, which included Captain Benjamin Willard, the grandfather of both of the injured children. Captain Willard was one of the original members of both the second church body and of the third gathering in 1750. He joined with the rest of the church body in receiving Cole into "full Charity again."

What the church records tell us, then, is that Ezekiel Cole was an orthodox Congregationalist who was an early opponent of Solomon Prentice. In the battle for the Hassanamesit/Grafton church body that began in 1743, his name would reappear many times, not as an innocuous footnote to Prentice's story but as a powerful internal counterweight.

THE CHURCH BODY BROKEN: AGGRIEVED BRETHREN

On January 9, 1743/44, almost a year after Ezekiel Cole had joined the church, its record book records the first entry about the conflict brewing in the church at Hassanamesit/Grafton: "An account of the C^{hh}. meetings, and thier proceedings about the Seven breth^n: that absented from Comunion at the Lords table &c" (HG 110). These men were "aggrieved" enough to withdraw from communion with the rest of the body, and their concerns would dominate the church records for the next four years. According to this entry, members who were present at a church meeting voted to question each of the men privately about his reasons for withdrawing. In response, all seven stated that they had already "lodged the reasons of their conduct with the pastor, but had not desired him to lay them before the Church" (HG 110).

This short statement reveals an enormous problem. The men had already approached Prentice, asking for a private conversation in order to resolve a still-unstated issue, and they had specifically asked him not to bring that issue into the more public forum of a church meeting. But for some reason, the minister chose to move immediately to a public church meeting rather than meet with them. Therefore, the men asked for more time to prepare more public statements suitable for the church to hear. Prentice's refusal to follow the Congregational way of private conversation first, public conversation second, is inexplicable at this point in the record.

A month later, on February 13, 1743/44, the seven "aggrieved" brethren decided to make their case against Solomon Prentice public. They "read their Articles of Complaint against me their Pastor, containing their reasons for withdrawing from the Sacrament as they have done. Read also my answers to them ... and [they] desired a weeks time farther to Consider my Answers" (HG 111). Notably, this is the same church record in which Ezekiel Cole had sought pardon for charging the minister with teaching "damnable doctrine." In fact, Cole's apology had begun the meeting. He was not one of the seven brethren, but he was clearly aligned with them and was willing to begin the process of challenging the minister. Did he feel he had to act alone because the others would not include him, presumably because he wasn't English? Or did he choose to remain independent? We don't know for certain, but it's clear from the record that Ezekiel Cole, far from being a threatening, chaotic force of revival, helped to initiate the fight to save Congregationalism in Hassanamesit/Grafton.

From February 1743/44 on, divisions in the church body worsened as the brethren—the Old Lights—who were opposing the minister's New Light preaching drew some but not all members to their side of the issue. The Old Lights gave Solomon Prentice a list of their complaints against him, which he answered; but on February 20, in another church meeting, they declared themselves to be dissatisfied with many of those answers. The church voted on whether to move forward with the Old Lights' complaints, given that they had violated Congregational kinship by withdrawing from communion. The body decided to continue, and a committee was formed to hear both sides. But over the course of the long meeting, this vote was questioned and then overturned. Then, after a brief recess, the members present at the meeting began the arduous process of going over each of the Old Lights' twenty-three complaints and each of Prentice's twenty-three responses. Like some other ministers, he did not describe the content of each complaint in the record, only noting that each "article" was put to the vote: was the complaint serious enough to justify withdrawing from communion? All twenty-three were voted down; the members saw "[no] sufficient reason for these brethren to withdraw from Communion with us as they have done." Prentice described these votes as "mostly unanimous." Faced with this setback, the determined Old Lights asked for an ecclesiastical council to be called "to hear and consider of their affairs," which the church voted to do—as long as the Old Lights fully bore the "Cost and Charge" of the council's travel expenses (HG 111–13).

What Is an Ecclesiastical Council?

Councils were a Congregational invention that allowed each church to operate independently while remaining in relationship with other churches. If a church body experienced long-term difficulties that it could not resolve using the Congregational way (that is, private counsel, rounds of mediation, and rebuke-repent-restore), it could call for a council. Members of the body sent letters to churches with which they felt a special connection, asking them to send delegates (usually the minister and one or two others). The number of churches involved could vary, and agreeing on which churches to invite could be difficult when the parties were very divided. (This was the case in Hassanamesit/Grafton, where it turned out to be almost impossible to decide on a roster.) Once a quorum of churches agreed to send delegates, a date could be quickly set. Then the delegates would travel to the suffering church to hear the argument from all sides, often a time-consuming task.

The minister Ebenezer Parkman was not prone to revealing large emotions in his diaries, but his descriptions of serving on ecclesiastical councils overflow with feeling. These entries offers priceless insights into the councils' disagreements and their strenuous efforts to come to agreement. On July 15, 1736, for instance, he described being part of a council in Naquag/Rutland. He grieved over the state of the church and the weakness of its minister Thomas Frink:

> The Council in great Perplexity and Distress [at] the Prospect of the Desperate State of this Flock. . . . When the Brethren came to us [they] were exceedingly [impatient] with Mr. F[rink] [for] it became evident that Mr. F. made a most lame, trifling Defence. . . . Divers of the Church resolved not to hear Mr. F. again. Matters at a Dreadful Extremity. The Brethren would by no means hear of our Dissolving. . . . [A]djourned the Council (in great Distress of Heart) to tomorrow Morning Six o'Clock.[15]

In October 1758, Parkman was part of a council in Manchauge/Sutton, where division was deep until the group experienced a sudden miraculous breakthrough:

> 1758 October 4 (Wednesday). Matters are very difficult—a.m. labouring with the contending Partys. . . . All is dark and Sad.

> 1758 October 5 (Thursday). Nothing can be darker and more sad—the Partys extremely stiff and resolute against one another. Mr. Welman and his Brethren urging that we do what we came for, and give them a Result. . . . When we [were trying] to Support our Spirits [by] observing that it was darkest just before morning—Ensign Goddard and Mr. Daniel Greenwood came with new Proposals and Offers. . . . We ripen this Scheme, and it proves Successful thus far.[16]

In other words, restoration was on the horizon.

Councils were meant to act efficiently because they were called in as a last resort and time was of the essence in helping a church get back on the right path. But council members were not judges. A council would offer its "Result" at the end of its deliberations, and the church that had called the council was under no obligation whatsoever to take that advice. Indeed, if a church found a council's result deeply unacceptable, it could simply call another council with representatives from different churches. Or, in keeping with Congregational practice, a council might advise a church to resolve its differences itself, not out of perversity of spirit but with an abundance of caution: the Congregationalists did not want a presbyterian hierarchy or governing body to develop out of the practice of calling for a council.

In short, the council did not dictate what the church should do but gave loving advice meant to rebuild and strengthen personal relationships within the church to make it stronger—and to strengthen ties between churches by validating the sense of kinship that had led the troubled church to call on its sister churches for help. By giving good advice and then dissolving, the council provided help for healing while honoring the autonomy of its sister church.

Deepening Division

Trying hard to avoid a complete rift with the Old Lights, the church at Hassanamesit/Grafton voted to reverse itself at the next meeting on March 1 and not require them to pay the council expenses. That meeting was devoted to trying to agree on which churches should be asked to form the council, but "this Church could not choose," and the meeting adjourned (HG 114). Another meeting was called for March 8, 1744—the sixth church meeting in three weeks, an eloquent expression of the seriousness of the problem. Church meetings were usually scheduled for regular monthly or quarterly intervals or called once to handle a short-term problem. They did not happen twice a week for three weeks. The wear and tear of so many long, contentious, existential meetings became evident in later church records: Prentice recorded that people were begging to go home as arguments lasted well into the night.

Yet another church meeting was scheduled for March 20, and this time the body sent messengers to several ministers who happened to be in Hassanamesit/Grafton on other business, including "the Rev. Mr Parkman," asking them to come to the meetinghouse to "give us their advice." Unfortunately, that informal council offered only the usual measured Congregational response: "[They] advised us if we Could to Accommodate matters among our Selves."

But the situation was out of hand. "It appeared no ways probable to accommodate matters among ourselves," so members at the church meeting resumed their tortuous attempts to agree on which churches to call for a council. Every choice the Old Lights suggested was "negatived," and eventually "all the aggrieved brethren present declar^d they would not nominate another." At an impasse, a committee was chosen to meet privately with the Old Lights to try to find acceptable choices, and the meeting adjourned (HG 115).

The respite was brief. The next meeting was held six days later, and the committee reported success in finding candidates that they felt that the church could approve. But without missing a beat, their opponents voted down every single choice. This was an abuse of the Congregational way, one that made a mockery of the committee and the very premise of talking privately in order to come to a public agreement. Like the previous meetings, this one failed.

Meanwhile, the moderator of all of these meetings, Solomon Prentice, remained maddeningly passive throughout, doing nothing to intervene in the growing dissension. He should have stepped up to ensure that the Congregational process—private meetings before public hearings, respectful engagement—was in use and being honored. He should have stopped the increasingly disdainful disregard for kinship that was beginning to run rampant in the church. His apparent lack of investment in or care for the health of the church body became even clearer as time went on. In his narrative, written in 1744 in the midst of this turmoil and intended for possible circulation or publication, Prentice made a shocking comment about the church: "Im verily perswaded [that] three years ago, there was but a very Small Number in the Town, that knew anything really and Savingly of Js. Ct. Its awfull to think of; but I have been so Free with my People of Late that I dare not think otherwise.... Its true, Im blamed by many for being so Stingy in my Charity towards my People; and have been highly censured by Some therefor." He also claimed, against all evidence in the church record book that he himself kept, that he had exhausted every effort to call a council but had been rebuffed by haughty and uncaring fellow ministers: "Neighbouring Ministers [I] have Intreated Collectively and Seperatly in the Bowles and Compassion of the Dear Redeemer to Come and See us and Examine, and if possible Detect our Errors and Delusions, (if there by any among us): but as yet can perswade None to come: but the Language of their Practice is, You'r deluded, and So you may [continue].'"[17]

Exhausted by these contentious and too-frequent meetings and stymied by the deadlock that their minister was refusing to manage, the church met several times during the summer to try to find seven neighboring churches they could call on for a council. Finally, on October 11, they came to an agreement. Solomon Prentice did not record the result of the council or its advice and opinion on the troubles, but he did record his response to it, which reveals that the result did not go his way:

> My Decleration to ye C^{hh} upon ye result.
> Brethren, I can't but declare I find & feel my Selfe very much hurt & press^d in & with the
> Result of the Venerable Council . . . Which I humbly hope and believe, have actd uprightly,
> [I] do therefore with Meekness & Patience, . . . Submitt there unto, so far as I can & not
> Infringe upon my Conscience. . . . Octobr 11. 1744 S. Prentice (HG 132)

After casting subtle doubt on the good faith of the council, Prentice agreed to submit to its recommendation—apparently, that he should renounce his unorthodox teaching and preaching and work with the church in true partnership—but only "so far as I can & not infringe upon my Conscience." He had created a critical loophole for himself. With amazing boldness, Prentice then "proposed it to the aggrieved brethren, whether they accepted of the result of the venerable council, which they signified they did, as their pastor had done." In other words, the pastor accepted the result only so far as it would serve him and rejected its main recommendation. The "aggrieved brethren," on the other hand, made a good-faith agreement to work with him, relieved to see an end to their troubles, and "the church meetings which had been long subsisting were dismissed for a season" (HG 133).

The Hassanamesit/Grafton church records do not mention the conflict within the church for almost two years. Nor does Ezekiel Cole's name appear in the records during this time, which might suggest that he was quietly staying out of the differences within the church. However, the resumption of the church records makes it clear that he did no such thing. By March 1746, the unresolved conflict was boiling over again, and the name "Brother Coal" appears repeatedly as one of two main reasons for the uproar. Between October 1744 and March 1746, he had begun to go beyond lay exhortation to actual preaching around the town, and Solomon was not only making no effort to stop him but tolerated and even promoted it.

What led Ezekiel Cole to do this? One guess is that somehow, over the course of two years, he had been won over by the New Lights in the church and was preaching separatism. But the church record refutes that idea. The March 19, 1746, entry notes that, once again, a number of church members had withdrawn from communion. Just five days later, those men stated that they had done so because they believed that Solomon Prentice was "denying the result of the late council in 1744 in word and practice and countenancing lay exhorters" (HG 139). The word *exhorter* did not necessarily imply New Light; orthodox Congregationalists who were not ministers but preached informally were common and respected. John Winthrop, for instance, was one of the first lay exhorters in the Massachusetts Bay Colony. The problem in this case was that Ezekiel Cole was not seen as qualified to be a lay exhorter because he wasn't an elder. Thus, Prentice's "countenancing" of an unqualified layman was problematic. Allowing such a person to preach in his stead was seen as an open strategy to degrade preaching in the town and allow the minister to disengage from his most important duty.

On March 28, the church voted on the question of "whether it appear to the church the Rev Mr Prentice our Pastor Came in with the Judgment and advise of the Venerable Council [in] every particular." The result was a resoundingly unanimous *no*. This particular vote would become a sticking point, as Prentice would repeatedly state that he had honored the result and was doing his utmost to carry out its recommendations. Coldly, he described this long, damaging meeting in the church records: "[B]y this time ye C^{hh} was tyrd and many of y^m beged they might go home, [and] others drew off with out Leave" (HG 139). The futility of the situation must have weighed heavily on the church by this point.

Members would have been astounded if they had known what Prentice had written in a postscript to that record: "NB. I here, take this Oppertunity to Reccord, that it may be transmitt^d to posterity, that it Never was in My heart to comply with the judgment of Said Council ^$^{\text{in Every Particular}}$ because I should in So doing go directly against the Light of Conscience, because in Sundry places the Question is beg^d so y^e Conclusion is false. S. Prentice" (HG 139). He couldn't have been plainer. He had lied to the council, and he had lied to the church. If orthodox Congregationalism were really against his conscience, he should have stepped down from his ministry. Instead, he had continued his attempt to break the church down through a passive-aggressive war of

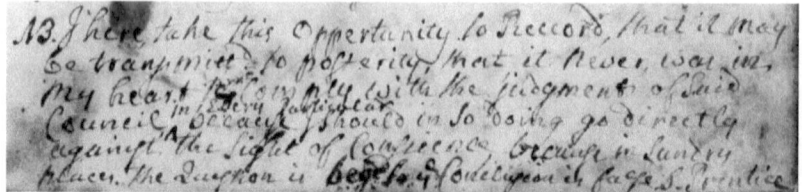

FIGURE 9. Solomon Prentice, note, March 28, 1746, in "Hassanamisco church book, 1731–1774," in the Grafton, Massachusetts, Evangelical Congregational records, RG 4921, Congregational Library and Archives, Boston.

attrition, letting the body tear itself apart so that he could pick up whatever pieces were left and begin anew as he chose.

One of Prentice's chief strategies in this offensive was to continue to allow lay exhorters, including Deacon Marsh and Solomon Paine, along with Ezekiel Cole (whose name appears as "Coal" in the church record from this point onward), to take his place. On April 23, 1746, the church met again, unaware of their minister's explicitly toxic intentions, to hear a group of members give their reasons for withdrawing from communion. Four men by name and an unknown number of others specifically identified Cole's preaching—sometimes in tandem with a complaint against Prentice's denial of the council result, sometimes on its own—as their main complaint: "Under the Complaint against Bro^r Coal for publickly preaching & teaching. . . . Complaints against Bro^r Ezekeil Coal for taking upon Publickly to teach & preach. . . . [T]he Case of Coal." After all of the men had made their public statements, Prentice noted that it was "Propos^d (after much discourse upon itt) Whither bro^r Coal. did not appear to ye C^{hh} [with] only with his pressent Qualifications to be Justifiable in publickly preaching and teaching. . . . [P]ass^d Negative." That is, the church did not consider Cole to be qualified to preach and teach. However, the vote was not unanimous and was cast only after lengthy discussion.

Now that Cole had been voted as unqualified to serve as a lay exhorter, some of the membership asked "whither the C^{hh} wont look upon Such of their brethren Offenders who for the future Shall Invite Ezekeil Coal, publickly to teach & preach in their houses, or Else where or Countenance him ther in." In other words, should anyone who invited him to preach be considered an offender against the church and possibly barred from communion? This vote also passed, again not unanimously. Finally, the church voted to forgive and restore "our Brethren who have Invited Said Coal [as they] did not mean to do itt as a publick preacher, and upon their refraining inviting Or Countenancing of him (in this way) for the time to Come." A committee of three men was created "to discourse with Said Coal, and about his preaching & to Endeavour to know [what] his aim & Desighn is in preaching as he dos, & whither he be determind So to proceed . . . & in Case ye Comt^{ee} can't have an oppertunity to discourse with him, he be desired to refrain Coming to ye Next [sacrament] with us" (HG 144–45).

None of these entries accuse Ezekiel Cole of preaching unorthodoxy, and he was still attending Congregational church services and taking communion as a member of the church. Only if he were to refuse to talk with the committee would he be barred from the sacrament. In the church records, Prentice noted that Cole did in fact meet with the committee and provided a written response to the church about what his "aim and design in preaching" had been, whether he was "determined so to proceed," and what "qualifications" he might prove to have that members would be unaware of. Unfortunately, Prentice also wrote that Cole's "Answer in Writing [was] . . . lodged with ye Councils" rather than recorded in the church book—a dereliction of duty on the minister's part—so we cannot know what it said.

On October 29, 1746, Solomon Prentice continued to sit back as the church debated "the affair [of] Coal" (HG 147). On November 3, the church voted:

> [P]rovided our bro^r Coal should reassume his Late practice of publickly preaching & Exhorting which he (as we think) unwarrantably and Unscripturably Sett up to the Dissatisfaction of many of the C^{hh}, the C^{hh} may call him to account therfor In Order to deale with him as an Offender
>
> But in Case he ye S^d Coal desist and practice So No More to the offence of his Brethren; then the C^{hh}, do Overlook, and pass by what he has done therin, (hoping he is Come to a Better Mind) and Accordingly we do Receive him to our Charity; Solemnly warning & Cautioning our [said] bro.^{r} Coal, against Such practice for the time to Come Seing ye ill & hurtfull tendancy [thereof] in time pass^d. (HG 148)

The first line is important: after meeting with the church committee, Ezekiel stopped preaching. This vote, then, was about what the church would do if he were to "reassume his Late practice of publickly preaching." The threat of being barred from communion was meaningful to Cole, as was the Congregational way of offering even an erring brother continued communion so long as he continued to "desist and practice So No More." While his preaching was considered to be "Unscripturably Sett up," this again did not necessarily indicate unorthodox content. The wording could refer to Cole's lack of education or to the problem of having a minister who was allowing—or using—a lay exhorter to preach in his stead.

Needless to say, the vote was not unanimous. "The vote regarding our brother Coal" would be mentioned in many subsequent meetings as a point of contention among those who believed that the now-lost written record of his response to the committee showed no sign of true repentance and remorse or proof that he had really stopped preaching. Without his written response, I can't judge their claim. However, Ebenezer Parkman did mention Ezekiel Cole in his diary, in an entry written two weeks later:

> 1746 November 14 (Friday). At Eve Mr. Noah Brooks of Grafton here—being in much perplexity and Difficulty not knowing what was his Duty respecting their approaching Sacrament. Since he and others had complain'd of Ezekiel Cole for his preaching and the Church had condemm'd him as disorderly, yet had lately voted him forgiveness if he would reform, notwithstanding they have had no Signs of his Repentence—nay have reason to fear he has had not Conviction of his offence.[18]

Noah Brooks was Benjamin Willard's brother-in-law, married to Sarah Willard. He likely knew Ezekiel Cole as well as any of the Willards did. It seems that Brooks had voted to restore Cole yet doubted his sincerity. As an orthodox Congregationalist, Brooks was afraid that if he were to take the sacrament with a person with whom he had an unresolved disagreement or whom he believed to be violating the sacrament through hypocrisy, he himself would be committing a terrible sin. In this situation, he felt bound to withdraw from the sacrament himself. Ever low key, Parkman did not record what advice he gave to Brooks.

Church meetings on December 30, 1746, and January 19 and 26, 1746/47, revolved around continuing complaints against Solomon Prentice and Ezekiel Cole. "The vote about Coal and the doctrine I deliver" became Prentice's shorthand for these complaints. The fatigue of the church was clear in the December 30 entry: after seven brethren had made their complaints, the eighth, Edward Cobb, said "Nothing but [his] wife was not well & it was Exceeding Rainy" (HG 148–49). It's unclear if this was Cobb's bitter sarcasm about the by-now empty ritual of restating complaints that would never be resolved or a plain record of the personal struggle required to spend night after freezing night in church meetings rather than attend to business at home. What is clear is that Prentice seems to have thrived on these meetings and the frustration they produced. The meeting on January 19 almost didn't take place because it lacked a quorum of attendees. But when Prentice was told that "I Should take the Liberty to go about my other business," he perversely sat for two more hours in the meetinghouse, waiting for the rest of the brethren to appear (HG 150). They reluctantly did, and at that meeting the church voted unanimously not to reconsider their March 28, 1746, vote declaring that Solomon had denied the council result.

On January 26, dissatisfaction with the previous March's vote to restore Ezekiel Cole emerged yet again, and finally the church agreed to "reconsider the [Vote] about Coal ... with which So many had manifstd y^m Selves Uneasy: which perhaps Answer^d No other End, than to make as Many Uneasy as were before[,] for upon this Ebenezer Wadsworth Neh: Bachellor & Jacob Whipple Ask^d a Dismission from this C^{hh}" (HG 151–25). That is, three members of the church body who had not previously appeared as aggrieved brethren were now asking to be dismissed so they could join another, functioning body. This new crisis spurred the church to vote to call another council; and this time, without delay, they rapidly decided on five sister churches to invite. The church met ten more times between February 5 and July 5, 1747, to thrash through its issues before and during the council. On July 8, 1747, the council finally agreed that there was no way to heal the breach in Hassanamesit/Grafton and recommended "dissolving the Pastoral Relation of the Revd Mr Solomon Prentice [with] this C^{hh} of Christ in Grafton." So the church, at long last, "voted that [it] conceives that there is no possible Method to continue the Pastoral Relation but do Desire the dissolution therof" (HG 87). Solomon Prentice at last left the church body he had done so much to injure. The church eventually called a new minister, Aaron Hutchinson, on June 6, 1750.

Ezekiel Cole's name appears nowhere in the council result or the church records. In fact, after the January 26, 1747, record, it is absent for decades. This absence is mostly a mystery, one that historians used to resolve by turning to records of the Englishman Ezekiel Cole's actions in Manchauge/Sutton and extrapolating that they referred to the Nipmuc Cole. We do know that the Nipmuc Cole may have spent some amount of time in Manchauge/Sutton but only from a single, brief, slighting mention in the diary of the minister David Hall. The church body at Manchauge/Sutton had been torn apart by the same separatist strife that befell the body in Hassanamesit/Grafton, and Hall's diary includes many long passionate entries about the wrongdoing and "wildness" he perceived. On October 7, 1748, he wrote of visiting a group of "Seperating Brethren," whom he described as "wild boars," when an interesting event occurred: "[O]ne asked if I could pray for them in faith as men wandring from God. I told y^m I could and did often [yea] Daily[.] after ys a Molatto fellow fell to Exhorting I strove to check him but could not stay him speaking with a haughty [Air] as I thought." This "Molatto fellow" may have been the Nipmuc Ezekiel Cole.

It's not clear from Hall's entry if the man was one of the separatists. According to the minister, the separatists challenged him, and he replied; then a man began exhorting, and Hall tried to stop him. Was Cole stepping over Hall to exhort the separatists to return to orthodoxy? Did he size up Hall, as he'd sized up Solomon Prentice, as a man who was unable or unwilling to turn the separatists so decide to do it himself? Hall's entry suggests that he was refusing partnership with a "Molatto" lay exhorter rather than rejecting a separatist.

In an entry made five years later, on October 22, 1752, David Hall did mention an Ezekiel Cole, but he was almost certainly referring to the Englishman: "Last Sabath Cole ye Separate Exhorter made a Long Confession among us and again to day attended worship."[19] Why do I assume this? Because Hall did not mention the man's race, as he had in the 1748 entry. Also, this Cole was returning to communion with the church body in Manchauge/Sutton, while the Nipmuc Cole had never left the body in Hassanamesit/Grafton. The English Cole's journey back to orthodoxy is confirmed by a final entry in Ebenezer Parkman's diary:

> 1756 December 17 (Friday). Cold Snow Storm. Mr. Hall of Sutton on his Journey home, turns in and tarrys with us. He purposes to me this Question, Whether a Child baptized by Ezekiel Cole, shall be baptized again? ... [T]he Father of the Child desires it might be baptized notwithstanding all that was done by Cole; yet it is allowed that Coles Ordination was as good as Wadsworth's and the rest of the Separate Teachers, who have baptized many.... I told him I believ'd that if the Case was mine I Should baptize the Child, at least under those Circumstances.[20]

It seems clear that that the ministers were referring to the English Cole. There is no record of a non-white man being ordained or baptizing children in

Manchauge/Sutton, and this entry is about ironing out the final wrinkles of the Englishman's bout with separatism.

Almost everything we think we might know about the Nipmuc Ezekiel Cole after the Hassanamesit/Grafton January 26, 1747, church record depends on a single entry in David Hall's diary that doesn't even use his name. Thankfully, however, volume 2 of the Hassanamesit/Grafton church records rescues Cole from complete oblivion. On October 19, 1774, the minister Daniel Grosvenor wrote "A list of the C^{hh} of Christ in Grafton." The last name in the list of males is "Ezekiel Cole, Indian Man" (HG 2:v7).[21] His full belonging is confirmed in two more short entries. On September 7, 1775, Grosvenor wrote that it was "Voted, y^t a letter be wrote to Ezekiel Cole, Reminding him of his neglect of Ordinances w^h us & to Desire his attendance at our next C^{hh} meeting, y^t the C^{hh} may discourse w^h him[.] Voted that Deacon Stow, Deacon Meriam, & B^r. Noah Brooks be a Committee to assist the Pastor in sending the above letter to Ezekiel Cole" (H/G 2:v95). Nearly thirty years later, Noah Brooks, the man who had consulted Ebenezer Parkman in November 1746 about whether he could take communion alongside brethren who had voted to restore Cole, was now part of a committee to reach out to his brother to find out why he was not attending communion. This means, of course, that Ezekiel *had* been in communion, and therefore in good standing as a part of the church body, for some time.

The final entry for Cole, on April 2, 1778, leaves the answer hanging: "Since no Return had been made the C^{hh} from B^r Ezekiel Cole, upon a Letter wrote him by the Pastor in the name of the C^{hh} requesting his attendance at a meeting of the C^{hh}, voted, that the Pastor again write him, Requesting in the name of the C^{hh} his reasons for non-attendance to Special Ordinances with us" (HG 2:v95) Two and a half years after he had stopped taking communion, he was approached once again by his church to ask why, again by letter. The church was not giving up on him, but it was also not taking the extra step of sending a committee to him wherever he was living at the time—at least not yet. The fact that this is the final entry for Ezekiel Cole only raises more questions. There's no record of his death in the church records or in the town's vital records, so he may have died in another place. But that should not have stopped Daniel Grosvenor from recording his death in the church record book. Perhaps news or reliable confirmation of Cole's death never reached the minister.

Ezekiel Cole's relationship with and role within his church body were in many ways deeply representative of the lifelong, complex, living, reciprocal relationship that was true Congregationalism. His story is not a footnote to a more important story about a more famous Englishman. In Cole's story we learn what Congregational Christianity meant to one intelligent, passionate, dedicated Nipmuc man and how he negotiated his relationship to it and his relationships within it, without ever breaking faith.

CHAPTER TEN

The Note Writer of N'ahteuk/Natick

On the last ten pages left blank by the eighteenth-century ministers who wrote in the church record book for N'ahteuk/Natick, two notes appear in a nineteenth-century hand. The first, titled "The Peabody Church Records," recounts the 1885 efforts of a church librarian named Daniel Wight to recover the lost church records (identified with the minister Oliver Peabody) that I mentioned in the introduction. The second, "The Origins of the Cong! Church in Natick" (dated 1890), is my focus here.

By the late nineteenth century, Congregationalism no longer practiced rebuke-repent-restore, the buildings in which congregations met were called churches, and there was no separate church body. It was simply a denomination of Protestantism with a long history that some of its current practitioners were curious about, mostly because their towns' Congregational churches had existential connections with the colonizing town founders. Gargantuan town histories were the bread and butter of nineteenth-century gentlemen, and some gentlewomen, and they dedicated large portions of those histories to church history.

Reverend Daniel Wight was one of those history writers, as well as being the librarian of the Congregational church in N'ahteuk/Natick. He was the author of a short volume titled *First Congregational Church, Natick, Mass.: The Confession of Faith, Covenant, Forms of Admission, Ecclesiastical Principles and Rules, with an Historical Sketch, and List of Members, 1877*, which in 1890 qualified him in the eyes of the town to offer expert advice on how to commemorate the church's history. So in a trembling, elderly hand, Wight wrote a two-page note on the last pages of the church record book. "The Origins of the Cong! Church in Natick" is full of citations from his own book (which he referred to as the *Historical Sketch)*, and both are remarkable in their full acknowledgment of the first Indigenous Congregational church, including its minister Daniel Takawombpait, who was "associated with [John] Eliot till his death in May 1690, after which, D. T. became the sole pastor of the church & continued as such probably till his death, Sept 17, 1716" (N 74).[1]

Then Wight diverged from history to invent an Indigenous church death, just as the Hassanamesit/Grafton note writer did. He noted that, after Daniel Takawombpait, two Indigenous men served the church "for a brief time" until 1721, when "Oliver Peabody entered on his labors as a missionary Aug 6 of that year.... A new church was gather[ed] Dec. 3 1729 & prospered under Mr Peabody's labors till his death Feb 2 1752" (N v74–75). Here again, a new church seems to have gathered as if the old one had completely, willfully disbanded, and Wight transmitted the strong impression that this church, ministered to by an Englishman, was all-English. A reader might well conclude that the Indigenous Congregationalists of N'ahteuk/Natick had disappeared.

In reality, when Oliver Peabody began to preach in the town in 1725 (he was formally ordained in 1729), the congregation was almost entirely Indigenous, made up of Nipmuc and Massachusett people, and only gradually became mixed. The original group of men who gathered into the second church body with Peabody on December 3, 1729, were John Brooks, Joseph Ephraim Sr., Joseph Ephraim Jr., Ebenezer Felch, James Beal, Samuel Ames, and Thomas Dunton. John Brooks and the Ephraims were Indigenous, and Peabody wrote that he had begun working with them some weeks before his ordination, taking "much pains with them" so that they could be propounded to "full communion in the Intended Church" on November 13, 1729 (N 5). Peabody was ordained on December 17, and on January 16, 1730, Joseph Ephraim was "chosen Deacon by a fair Majority of written votes & he accepted N.B. He being an Indian I think every English man in the Church voted for him & ye Indians voted for English men not unanimously" (N 3). Many Indigenous people chose church membership in the second church, In 1726 twenty-seven people were baptized, although, because the church was not yet gathered and had no minister, these baptisms were performed by ministers visiting from Tiot/Needham and Quinnebeggin/Medway. In 1729 five were baptized and in 1730 thirteen. They included members of the Abraham, Ephraim, Thomas, Coochuck, Peetimee, Peegun, Comacho, Womsquon, George, Waban, Weekucks, Lawrence, and Chalcom families.

Of course, this positive mixing existed in parallel to the negative issues linked to ramped-up English colonizing after King Philip's War. As the scholar

Harold Worthley notes, the second church was gathered "with an eye to accommodating the English now living in Natick."² The Harvard Corporation, which paid the salaries of ministers who served in Indigenous Congregational churches, sent a committee to N'ahteuk/Natick in February 1728/29 before the church was gathered and Oliver Peabody ordained "to Inquire into ye State of Religion there." The committee reported back on October 28, 1729, that because "the Indians" there were generally so "negligent," it would be beneficial to ordain Peabody so he could help them. But even that negative report is alive with evidence of a strong Indigenous Congregational inheritance and practice as well as a shared, mixed congregation and church that were alive and well in N'ahteuk/Natick:

> [T]he English & Indians agree well together in their attendance on publick Worship and the Indians are willing the English should attend with them.—The Indians and English also (of whom there are 8 Familys in Natick & about 13 Familys in other towns who attend there) were askt if they desired a Church might be gathered in Natick and Mr. Peabody ordained a Pastor there—and they particularly & expressly manifested their desire that it might be so and that the Church might at first consist of Indians and English of the town of Natick If suitable persons could be found for that End and afterwards those of Neighbouring Towns that desired admission & were qualified might be admitted into the Church of Natick[.] Upon the whole we with the Neighbouring Ministers who were there and heard the Examination in the meeting House rejoicing in their unamity were of opinion That it might be proper to answer the desire of the English and Indians to have a Church gathered & Mr. Peabody ordained their Pastor.³

Eventually, this ideal situation would be erased. The first Congregational church gathered in N'ahteuk/Natick would be retroactively redefined as an "Indian church" that was not quite authentic, and the second church gathered there in 1729 would be referred to as the first church.

Today first-church status is still important in Woodland New England, a label that's considered prestigious in a region in which connecting with the earliest colonizing period remains so important for non-Indigenous residents. Congregations proudly identify themselves as "First Church" on signs and sometimes vie with other congregations in town for the title.⁴ Scholars and town historians alike generally supported this pride in being first. But by assuming that the maelstrom of King Philip's War marked the end of real and effective Indigenous participation in Congregationalism in N'ahteuk/ Natick, even sympathetic scholars have contributed to the erasure or reduction of the Indigenous church body. Julius H. Rubin, for instance, wrote, "The Natick 'tribe' of praying Indians did not survive this dark age. . . . Those who resettled in Natick after the war [did] not successfully reinvent themselves as a traditional enclave. [They] suffered 'dispossession by degrees' and progressive psychological and physical abandonment of what was becoming an English village."[5] While it's true that N'ahteuk/Natick was no longer a "traditional enclave" with a majority Indigenous population and town government when it was resettled after the war, Indigenous people remained strong within the congregation and church throughout the eighteenth century. The church records include entries for multiple generations of forty-one Indigenous families and sixteen individuals without family name—nearly six hundred Indigenous people over the seventy-three years between 1721 and 1794. This is a testimony to Indigenous survivance after the war and through the decades of intensifying colonization, testimony also to the staying power of Indigenous Congregational faith and participation.

Daniel Wight, the inheritor of a false history of Indigenous church disappearance, concluded his 1890 historical account with a profoundly inaccurate summary:

> March 27 1753, Rev Stephen Badger was ordained a missionary over this Church & a third M H was commenced 1754 but not completed till 1767. (Id. 50) Mr Badger continued his services till July 1799 (Id. p. 657) He died Aug 1803. In 1797 four families signed off to Dover, 12 to Sherborn & 17 to Needham, 33 families in all(.) The third M H was falling out of repair & a new M H was erected at the center in 1799, & a new Church organized Feb 1802, consisting of 23 members [at] least six of whom were received by letter from Mr. Badger's Church which then became extinct. The organization of 1802 continues till the present, with a good prospect for the future. (N v75)

This eight-line summary tells a story of natural English outmigration from the town of N'ahteuk/Natick, leaving a much smaller congregation and church that struggled to keep the meetinghouse in repair. Fortunately, they were able to build a new one, proudly located in the center of town, in 1799. There the minister Stephen Badger gracefully dismissed the remaining members of the old church to the new one, which in Wight's telling was still going strong nearly a hundred years later.

The real story is very different. In it, English families who had been allowed to settle in N'ahteuk/Natick by Indigenous invitation in the 1720s began to agitate in the 1740s for a separate, all-white, all-English meetinghouse, congregation, and church body in the town. English members of the church and congregation wrenched themselves away from their Indigenous sisters, brothers, and neighbors, both physically and spiritually, starting a horrible battle with Badger and their Indigenous sisters and brothers to move the new meetinghouse away from its historical location in South Natick to Natick Center, the new, segregated English part of town. They eventually succeeded, and a new meetinghouse was built in the center of town in 1767. For decades, two congregations, both calling themselves "First Church," met separately until Badger was dismissed for refusing to preach in the new, English-only meetinghouse in 1798. As a statement, "Mr. Badger's Church became extinct" was meant to continue the erasure of modern Indigenous Congregationalism in N'ahteuk/Natick. In fact, however, Indigenous members carried on after Badger's death in 1803, eventually reorganizing in 1828 and building a new meetinghouse in South N'ahteuk/Natick. It became Unitarian in 1870 and continues to thrive today.[6]

How could Daniel Wight be so forthright about the Indigenous origin and heritage of the Congregational church in N'ahteuk/Natick and then whitewash the violent erasure of both by white racism? In his last lines, he revealed his purpose in writing this nutshell history—to influence the wording of a historical marker—and made an enigmatic statement:

> In view of this broken history, I would suggest the following for the Tablet
>
> The Congregational Church.
> 1660,–1729,–1802.

He saw the church history as "broken" because three church bodies had been gathered over the centuries. His dating was symbolic: a seventeenth-century date for the Indigenous body, an eighteenth-century date for an English body that broke up naturally, and a nineteenth-century date for the new English body that formed afterward. Wight was born six years after the third body was gathered, and he had grown up within it. It must have seemed natural to describe a progression from non-white to white over the modern century. His note brims with facts while creating myth in the service of Indigenous disappearance.

In this way, his note is on par with the one written on the first page of the Hassanamesit/Grafton church record book: not a real addition to the record but a subtraction that removed Indigenous people and churches to create a blank slate for new English-majority churches. White residents had to step into the breach created by disappearing Indians. The causes of this so-called disappearance were left unspoken; indeed, no cause really seemed to be needed. The Indians disappeared because that's what they did, whether through God's will, English superiority, or mysterious reasons of their own. But erasing Indigenous history in this way also erased white history. All of the violence that English people used to remove Indigenous people from Woodland New England was transformed into a voluntary Indigenous disappearance. As Stephen A. Mrozowski and Rae Gould write, while the production of this kind of "local [history] predicated on the assumed extinction of the Indigenous peoples of New England" is an "active step taken to end the history of a group," in reality, it erases the histories of both groups.[7]

CHAPTER ELEVEN

Death of a Church Body

OLIVER PEABODY IN N'AHTEUK/NATICK

The voluminous church records of Agawam/Rowley are exceptional, a result of and tribute to the commitment of the ministers serving between 1651 and 1839 who contributed to the single record book that documented the years 1664 to 1835.[1] Samuel Phillips, as I've shown, was particularly dedicated to noting every part of church life and business. Most ministers, even devoted ones, did not leave such detailed records. But with a few glaring exceptions that I've noted, even malevolent ones like Solomon Prentice kept fairly complete records. Therefore, when encountering a church body such as N'ahteuk/Natick's, whose life spanned centuries but has only one record book, I have to ask myself why.

Perhaps there were multiple books that have since been lost. Many churches in the eighteenth century had a book for financial records; one for births, marriages, and deaths; one for church meetings; and one for correspondence. Every church body made its own decision about whether and how to keep these books. So if a church chose to store records in more than one place, they may easily have gotten lost over time. Any small and seemingly incomplete church record book is a warning sign that we've been left with only part of the story. That may be the case with the N'ahteuk/Natick records.

Currently there is just one slim volume of records for the church, seventy-five manuscript pages in total. The first thirty-two pages comprise Oliver Peabody's records, and the rest belong to his successor, Stephen Badger. On the first page, Peabody noted that that the forthcoming records would be "faithfully made by me, Oliver Peabody, Pastor of the Church of Natick." In detailing the dismemberment of the church body at N'ahteuk/Natick in the mid-1700s, even this slim volume is a useful reference for understanding the calamity that befell the church.

Among other things, the records reveal elements of Peabody's role in that calamity, for the division and death of the church body began during his ministry. Was he to blame? Daniel Mandell, who has studied the event, quotes a seemingly damning note that the minister wrote in 1726, bemoaning his cultural isolation: "[It is] very lonesome, uncomfortable and disadvantageous to be at such a distance from Neighbours as I am from any English [and] if I might have two or three English [families] near me, it would (I believe) render my Life much more pleasant & Easy." Mandell reads this as evidence of "a cultural gap" between the minister and the congregation and suggests that Peabody "may not have been happy with his new assembly of uneducated natives; in turn, his listeners may have been more bewildered than enlightened by his sermons."[2] The historian Richard Boles shares this negative assessment: "Peabody had a condescending attitude toward the Natick Indians."[3]

In fact, however, the note from which Mandell quotes was appended to a 1726 petition by the Nipmuc Samuel Abram, who was asking to sell land to an Englishman named Samuel Ames. (Ames would eventually be one of the seven Indigenous men and Englishmen who first gathered into the church body in 1729.) Abram wrote that he was "pretty well landed and Very well Respecting the Revd Mr Peabody Our Minist^r & Desireous that he Should have an English Neighbour Settle Near him."[4] This thoughtfulness is touching; Abram seems to have taken no offense over Peabody's desire for an English neighbor.

There is no evidence that Peabody held himself apart from his Indigenous congregation or that its members did not fully embrace or benefit from him. After interviewing him for the position of minister, the Indigenous Congregationalists in N'ahteuk/Natick accepted him warmly. In their May 29, 1722, report to John Leverett, the president of Harvard College, they agreed to give Peabody the land "intended then for ye ministry" or any other good parcels of land "Equal to that in quantity & quality (which of them he shall see cause to chuse.) in order to Encourage him to settle among us in ye Gospel ministry in our said town of Natick." The report was signed by Massachusett representatives Thomas Waban, Solomon Thomas, and Benjamin Tray.[5] This cordiality seems to have lasted. Fourteen years after Samuel Abram's request, Tray petitioned to sell land directly to Peabody "as a token of his Respect & Gratitude" for the minister.[6]

Why, then, did the process of dismembering the church body in N'ahteuk/Natick begin during Peabody's ministry? I believe his case illustrates how English civil society destroyed the Congregational ideal via the powerful economic weapon of impoverishing ministers. He may have been less a villain than a pawn in a larger racist game played by two related groups: the men of the Harvard Corporation and the new English inhabitants of the town. Both were driven by colonizing greed, and both contributed to Peabody's struggle to carry out his sincere ministry to the Massachusett and Nipmuc people of his congregation and church.

As I've noted, the terms for paying ministers' salaries were convoluted and confusing, and those payments were often years in arrears. The civil records are replete with cases brought by ministers against their town governments after years of failed attempts to get their pay, and those cases could be drawn out for months or years. In my search for Indigenous church members from N'ahteuk/Natick in the Middlesex Court records, I scrolled past many examples—among them the long sad case of Reverend John Fox of Naumkeag/Woburn, who was trying to get many years of back pay. The case began in August 1732, was then deferred, reappeared two years later, and was deferred again. In March 1736 the case was still continuing, and two months later Fox stated that he had not been paid anything at all since September 1734. The congregation sent a lawyer to ask for a jury trial, but this was refused, and the members were ordered to pay Fox what he was owed by December—a staggering £140. The court also sent a tax assessor to the town to levy the money. This case was now apparently closed. However, when a minister won his case, his town representatives—including members of the congregation or even the church—almost always immediately appealed the ruling and often won a reversal. That seems to have happened here, for in April 1737 Fox's original petition appeared again, and he clearly was not paid by December 1736. Finally, in August 1737 a single line reveals that he gave up: "The Revd Mr John Fox, upon his Motion, as on file is allowed to withdraw his Petition." Fox was not alone in his long five-year struggle. At the same time a "Mr Swift" was going through an identical war of attrition in Washakamaug/Framingham.[7]

Even if a minister gave up, his widow or adult children often fought for years after his deaths to get the money that he had been owed and that they needed. But the civil records show that the men who were supposed to pay him and support his family routinely had no compassion for his plight or any interest in meeting their obligations to care for him financially. Their unapologetic indifference was rooted in the contradiction that lay at the heart of their colonizing society, a world in which a minister was at once the most and least valuable person. He represented a church before God. That was vitally important. But the church made no profit; and in the secular world of colonization, a man who relied on someone else for his entire financial support was bound to be disdained as childlike, at least to some extent. Ministers were meant to wield no secular power, and they were completely dependent on men who did.

Ministers who were trying to recover their back pay wrote pleading letters to the powerful men in their town, to the Harvard Corporation, to the courts, and even to the governor, yet these attempts to document their mistreatment seemed to work against them. By recounting the meager sums they had been promised as well as their town and congregation's easy readiness to cheat them, the ministers made themselves look ridiculous rather than sympathetic. Towns focused on growth were loath to spend even a penny more on their minister than they had originally contracted. They expected men who went into the ministry to understand that they had willingly taken on a life of relative poverty in the service of God. Towns passed the buck to the congregations, demanding that they fulfill their obligations to their minister, and the congregations passed the buck back to the towns, demanding that they raise funds for his salary through general taxation.

Many ministers were forced to participate in the marketplace to survive, often working small farms on the less-than-profitable homesteads that were usually allotted to town ministers. This took away from the time they could spend ministering to members of their congregation and preparing sermons. A vicious circle developed: any minister engaged in private commerce to supplement or fill in for his salary was seen as not really needing a salary anymore, given that he was doing less for the congregation while also making money on his own. Towns seem to have deliberately driven ministers into private commerce in order to justify not paying them. Ministers who held out, as Oliver Peabody did for many years, often emphasized that they did not want to divert from their role as minister by taking on other jobs. But this stance did not help them either. Instead, they were criticized for being helpless and for relying on others to pay their salary.

ECONOMIC HARDBALL IN AGAWAM/ROWLEY

Edward Payson, who worked as a teacher alongside the minister Samuel Philips at Agawam/Rowley (1682–96) and then taught on his own after

Philips's death (until 1732), wrote a long entry in the church record book about this very situation. The minister in Agawam/Rowley was paid out of a bequest that an individual had included in his will. This was a good arrangement for the town because it didn't have to levy a tax to fund the ministry. Philips was paid out of this bequest. The teacher, however, was paid through taxation, though his position was also considered a church office. After Payson was made teacher, Philips became "uneasie about his Sallary, and told me y^t y^s Town was not able to keep two Ministers." That is, the town would be unwilling to tax its inhabitants to do so, whether or not it could actually afford it. Payson wrote, "I found my own Salary very scanty while we were two together, [£53] in grain was my whole allowance (wth my Wood) by ye year; five of wch was yearly taken off for Parsonage Lands y^t I improved" (AR 249).[8] In other words, because he was so underpaid by the town, Payson had to start farming on his allotted parsonage lands, and his small income from this work led the town to cut his salary.

When Philips died in 1696, Agawam/Rowley was left without a minister. In 1699, town officials, anticipating that a new minister would be called, recognized that the incoming man's salary negotiations might prompt Payson to attempt to renegotiate his own meager pay. They asked "what Sallery I would be willing to take up with, both while alone, & also in case another Minister should be called." He offered several options, but "nothing was acted upon them, & so ye matter lay silent" (AR 247). Meanwhile, officials came up with a fiendish plan. For as long as the church had no minister, they would refuse to renegotiate with Payson, using the excuse that they couldn't decide on a salary for one man when there would soon be two and that second man's demands were as yet unknown. Churches often took years to choose a new minister, so the town could feel secure about this stalling tactic. "The Generality of ye Town appear^d very dull ab^t acting any thing on my Proposition," Payson noted (AR 248). Still, some church members persisted in asking the town to settle a higher salary on him, and the town retorted with a vengeance:

> On or ab^t ye twenty third day of Feb^{ry} at this [town] meeting my aboves^d propositions were brought afoot & many appeared as willing to comply with ye first, ^while I was alone, but as to ye latter y^t referred to ^calling another Minister, y^y most were dull & would not stirr to decide a vote.—I had told some of the chief of ye Town before this meeting, y^t seeing they had not taken up with my propositions, it was now their turn to make proposalls to me; accordingly ye Deacon on ^The Towns behalf abated five

pounds from my 2ᵈ proposition referring to calling another Minister which took off 30 pounds from my Salary. . . . I was Informed [that] it was said amongst Some, yᵗ I must take what the Town would give me. (AR 248, 249)

According to Payson, several town selectmen visited him at home to say that certain men were calling for a town meeting on his behalf. They asked if he wanted this, and he replied, "I did not desire yᵗ yᵉ Town should be convened meerly on yᵗ account; But if they had anything further to transact in reference to calling another Minister, [I] would hindʳ nothing of that, they night warn a meeting as soon as they pleased." This selfless answer seems to have confirmed the selectmen's contempt for a man who wouldn't put his own self-interest first: "The Selectmen seemed satisfied, and not Inclinable to warn any meeting on that accᵗ" (AR 248).

PEABODY'S ODYSSEY IN N'AHTEUK/NATICK

In N'ahteuk/Natick, ministerial poverty was used as a tool to manipulate Oliver Peabody and as a weapon to destroy the mixed church body. The records of the Harvard Corporation at Harvard College fully document of the origin of his lifelong financial struggles and the corporation's role in fomenting them. The tortuous financial finagling began on November 16, 1719, at a meeting "in the Library" of the president and fellows of Harvard College. There they voted that £45 from a private donation should be given "for One Year (beginning from the Commencement last past) [to] Peabody to encourage him to Qualify himself for preaching the Gospel among the Indians, and to Devote himself to that Service; Provided That he continuing his Inclination so to do." This statement is important in two ways. First, it reveals that Peabody had enrolled at Harvard College with the specific "Inclination" of ministering to Indigenous people. The position was not forced on him, nor was he reluctant to take it. He had known from the start that the ministry might well involve living in isolation from English society; the prospect wasn't a dealbreaker. Second, the statement shows that his £45 scholarship became a curse: Peabody would spend years trying to get the money he was owed from this subsidy, and confusion about his initial grant would be used against him in all future salary negotiations.

The confusion spans many entries in the Harvard College records. For instance, Peabody was required to "give proper Security to refund s^d Money [in] case he sh^d afterward divert from the Indian Service."[9] A year later, on May 4, 1720, he gave that security, signing a contract stating that he was "firmly bound, & obliged unto Mr John White of Boston Treasurer of Harvard College [for] the full, & compleat sum of two hundred pounds." Why £200 was required to secure £45 is unclear. A year later, in an April 4, 1721, meeting, the college recorded that it had given £45 to Peabody to "*further* to encourage him to Qualify himself for Preaching the Gospel among the Indians and to devote himself to that Service, he continuing his Intentions so to do, and having given Security to refund what he has or shall receive, if he diverts from it."[10] At this point, he was about to graduate, and ministering to the Nipmuc and Massachusett Congregationalists at N'ahteuk/Natick was no longer speculative. Peabody had met with them well before his commencement that spring. As I have already noted, in May 1722 they had written to the president of Harvard College to formally accept his settlement "in ye Gospel ministry" with them.

On October 3, 1722, the corporation voted that Peabody "be allow'd for preaching to the Indians at Natick one Moiety [of] £45 [for] the year now running."[11] A stipulation that he be paid quarterly was removed. In February 1722/23 the corporation presented its proposal "for the Allowing Mr Oliver Peabody £40 p Annum for his Constant Labours in Gospelizing the Aborigines at Natick, and £50 towards his [Settlement] there; . . . agreeing to pay also towards [his] Support the Sum of £40 p Annum, and fifty pounds towards his Settlm^t. . . . Agreed and Voted, that the sum of forty pounds p Annum towards [his] Support, and fifty pounds towards his Settlm^t be paid [by] the College Treasurer."[12] In other words, Peabody was being set up with an initial £50 settlement followed by yearly payments of £40 from the corporation.

In August 1724, however, "[t]he Corporation have Looked over the several Votes relating to Mr Peabody & Mr Treasurer having laid before the Corporation the several payments made to him We Judg that Mr Peabody has received all the Moneys that the Corporation have Voted or meant to vote him from time to time."[13] Those "several Votes" are not documented, so we can't know what happened. By October, Peabody was pleading for a reversal:

> [H]aving received of the Treasurer as much money as we apprehend was Voted for him[,] yet not having allowed him more Support for his

freshmanship than for one half of that year & No Support for one other year of his being Undergraduate and he having pleaded his present Necessity of further help to forwd his Settlement at Natick[,] Wherefore now Voted That the Treasurer Pay to the said Mr Peabody fifty pounds and that no more shal be paid to him with reference to any Services or Charges that are past.[14]

The note about his tuition remission suggests that he had received only a small part of the money he had been promised to defray his college expenses, but we never learn why. Presented with their breach of contract—a contract in which Peabody and his father had taken on an outsized financial penalty and the corporation had taken on none—the corporation now curtly agreed to give him a one-time payment of £50. Clearly it was impatient to be rid of him.

Because Peabody was ministering to Indigenous people, the Harvard Corporation rather than the congregation was responsible for his salary. His petitions for more money appeared before the corporation in June 1726, November 1727, April 1732, April 1733, April 1736, and September 1741.[15] Again and again he "pray[ed] for some Addition to his Salary," pleas that emphasize his shoestring earnings. After 1741, he began taking on duties at Harvard College to earn money. In 1744 he became "Scholar of the House," in 1746 he became "Butler," and in 1748 and 1749 he became "Library-Keeper."[16] In 1749, in the saddest entry, the aging and chronically unwell minister received fifteen shillings for "taking Care of the Chambers in the College, Cellars &c in the last Vacation."[17] In May 1750, the corporation heard his final petition, in which he requested more than £22, which he was owed but had never received due to "a Failure in the Remittance of that Stock, wch he was to be paid from." In this petition, Peabody said that "He hath been paid his Salary yearly, yet not at such Advance as he suppos'd He had a Right to." The corporation voted to pay him "such Addition [as] may answer him to the proper Advance," but only when "the Treasurer shall receive the full Remittances that have been wanting."[18]

Those stocks never did turn around. Three months after Peabody's death in February 1752, his son, Oliver Peabody Jr., wrote a furious letter to the corporation, lacerating them for the financial hardship his father had suffered during his long tenure in N'ahteuk/Natick:

[M]y Father was sent to Natick [with] what (he judged) an Assurance from the Gentlemen then in Office, (especially of the Corporation) of a decent Maintenance proportionate to ye Difficulty & Importance of the Service. . . . he had repeated Invitations to Settle in the Ministry elsewhere with a prospect of considerable private Advantage; and from Time to Time was at no small Expense in relieving many of his Indian Parishioners, in their Poverty & Distresses [yet maintained] his Steady Adherence to the Interest of Religion among the Indians [yet] for ye Space of Near Twenty Years past, he had not [a] salary equal to ye Necessary Expenses of his Family; nay at a Moderate Computation Scarcely enough to support it with comfortable Food & Drink, exclusive of any Cloathing, as I believe cannot but appear, from what has been Annually voted him as a Salary.[19]

Peabody Jr. may have been biased, and certainly he was trying to portray his father in the best possible light, but his angry letter doesn't come across as misrepresentation. The details he provided about his father's ministry are important. He noted that his father could have left N'ahteuk/Natick and earned far more money as a minister in another town, but he chose not to. Like a good sachem and an ideal Congregational minister, he had given his own resources to his church, even when he didn't have enough to provide for his own family.

If Oliver Peabody had indeed been so committed to his Indigenous ministry, then why did he write the note saying that he wished English families would settle in N'ahteuk/Natick? The answer may lie in the next part of his son's letter:

[H]is Annual Support has been so slender, that Notwithstanding his Industry & Fatigues in ye Management of his Farm; and all that he has receiv'd from his English Parishioners, & the Generosity of his private Friends; He was Obliged not only to Sell a Considerable part of ye Lands given him as a Settlement by ye Indians; but also to involve his Estate in a Debt of Five or Six Hundred Pounds. . . . my Fathers Farm has been of late Years somewhat profitable to him, & [he] could not have Subsisted his Family upon his Salary without it; Nevertheless the Net Profits of that was but small by Reason of ye price of Labour. . . . but supposing his Profits therefrom ever so great, yet I must beg Leave to say, I cannot see why that should be a Reason for his not having a Support adequate to his Services.[20]

The letter shows that Peabody supplemented his official salary by growing food for the local market, by selling land, and, crucially, by receiving money from "his English Parishioners." This casts light on what eventually happened in the town, congregation, and church. The English people who came into N'ahteuk/Natick knew that Peabody was not paid by his Indigenous parishioners. They also learned that the corporation was not paying him in full, and they knew that the town government would not vote to pay a minister if it could have his services for free. So these Englishmen stepped in, giving Peabody gifts of money and goods and creating a divide: on the one side, Indigenous people took wealth from the minister; on the other, English people shared it with him. They even helped by buying Peabody's land when he needed money, something the impoverished Indigenous people were unable to do. Benjamin Tray's 1741 petition to give Oliver six acres of land freely, out of respect and love, was the exception that proved the rule: real support came only from the English.

The bitter irony is that these Englishmen could have voted in town meeting to raise money for the minister whom they claimed to love, or they could have moved to raise a special collection in the church and congregation from time to time. Instead, they refused to use their power to increase his salary in these formal ways.[21] In fact, we see that by buying his land, they acted the same part Englishmen had played with the Abraham and Muckamaug women in Hassanamesit/Grafton. They stood by, watching the situation and allowing the minister to fall into ever more helpless poverty. Then they swooped in to "aid" him by buying his land. This guaranteed that the seller's poverty would increase over time, permanently cementing the unequal power relationship. By the late 1740s, when Oliver Peabody, in the final decade of his life, was working as a janitor at Harvard to earn extra money, these apparent allies were agitating for an all-English, all-white congregation and meetinghouse, and they must have believed they had the minister in their power, both emotionally and financially. As Richard Boles writes, the "white Christians" of N'ahteuk/Natick, who had originally "seemed to acknowledge the primacy of the Indian identity of this church and accepted some Indian leadership therein," were no longer willing to do so.[22] If Peabody would not support their move to break the church body in half, they could call in his debts, stop buying his land, and stop the flow of their self-interested "Generosity."

This supposition is validated by another astonishing statement in Peabody Jr.'s letter: "And further, The Charges of his Funeral have Necessarily added considerably to ye beforementioned Debts, which Charges his English Parishioners will not defray (as is Customary in most Other Parishes in the like Case) inasmuch as they esteemed my father to be an Indian Missionary." This was frank hypocrisy. When Peabody might help them gain something, he was an English minister. When he might cost them something, he was "an Indian Missionary." Other churches detailed the funerals they paid for when their ministers died. In Agawam/Wenham in January 1720, "a vast multitude of Peop[le]" attended the funeral of Reverend Joseph Gerrish, "being present to do him honour at his burial."[23] In Massebequash/Marblehead in October 1800, the church met to "[take] into serious Consideration the afflicting Dispensation of Gods Providence in the removal by Death of our Pastor the Rev[d] Ebenezer Hubbard [and] what is necessary to be done to pay our last Tribute of respect to the Dec[d]—Voted that this Church be at the expence of the Interment of our Dec'd Pastor. . . . Voted that the Treasurer do give to the widow Hubbard the Sum of Twenty Dollars out of this Churchs Stock."[24] Peabody's treatment after death was shocking.

The English parishioners won the battle to cut the church body in half and move the meetinghouse from Indigenous South N'ahteuk/Natick to all-English Natick Center. Currently, there are no available personal records belonging to Oliver Peabody to show if he fought against those Englishmen and their families and, if so, how hard. But in a long and angry 1799 letter describing the break, including the deliberate denigration of and attacks on the Nipmuc and Massachusett people of N'ahteuk/Natick, his successor, Stephen Badger, made no mention of Peabody's support of the English malevolence. If Peabody had, Badger's exposé would surely have mentioned it. Moreover, his deepening poverty and the English parishioners' refusal to honor him in death with a funeral suggest that he did not give in to that pressure. They would have rewarded Peabody if he had.

Evidence in the extant church record book from N'ahteuk/Natick indicates that Oliver Peabody was a good minister to everyone in his mixed church and congregation. It shows that he worked within a mixed church government and that he recorded all baptisms, both Indigenous and English, in dedicated detail. In 1743, He wrote a letter to a convention of ministers in which he said, "Among my people [there] have been very apparent strivings and operations of the Holy Ghost among English and Indians, young and old, male and female."[25] His choice to call both Indigenous and English "my people" suggests that he didn't support the English coup, as does his claim that the Holy Ghost was at work equally in both populations. Perhaps Peabody didn't see them as two separate populations but as one congregation and, crucially, as one church body.

CONCLUSION

Haunted Houses

In her book *The Name of War*, the historian Jill Lepore describes the extent to which English colonizers conflated "the burning of houses" with "the spilling of blood" during King Philip's War.[1] As she notes, "English accountings of the war's casualties . . . tallied houses first, then people." Towns were collections of houses, and houses were "the bosom of the town."[2] For the English, the ruins of burned houses that dotted the landscape during the war were like unburied dead bodies. More had been lost, in their owners' reckoning, than four walls and some possessions.

In Lepore's view, this was because houses expressed and shored up English identity. Life in a permanently situated house was what separated the colonizers from the Indigenous people. She states that "property became the defining character of social relations" in Old England over the course of the seventeenth century and posits that, in Woodland New England, this character was not purely economic but cultural: "In the decades of settlement leading up to King Philip's War, the idea of property as identity had much more to do with distinguishing an Indian from an Englishman than a merchant from a servant." Thus, she argues, "for most colonists, the loss of habitations became the central crisis of the war."[3]

However, the primary sources don't seem to support this argument of identity insecurity. Indeed, they seem to prove the opposite: that the English colonizers were fatally incapable of questioning their identity; that they barreled through the Eastern Woodlands secure in their English parallel universe. The end result was new houses, cleared land, and dead Indians.

In Woodland New England, the English house was a sign of one's claim to colonizing wealth and station. To have that house burnt was, then, a complete catastrophe for the colonizer, erasing his struggle, his effort, and, crucially, his success in changing his station by becoming wealthy and powerful. Men who lost their houses were back at the starting line, faced with an expanse of empty, unimproved land. It was a disaster, but not, as Lepore claims, because "the houses they lived in and the things they owned were a good part of what differentiated the English from the Indians."[4] Their Englishness was never at stake in this way. It was their *New* Englishness that was in peril—the difference between the independent New England proprietor and the subservient Old England tenant. That is why men whose houses had been burnt during King Philip's War felt as if they had been "stripped naked." They had lost all of the wealth that their house had both literally held and metaphorically represented. To be houseless was not to be "Indian." It was to be *poor*: thrown out of the wealth of Woodland New England and forcibly returned to the poverty of Old England. This may explain why some Englishmen died in their houses trying to stave off Indigenous attacks during the war. Without the house, what life was left?

Perhaps that's why there are so many historic houses in Woodland New England today. The people who inherited them, directly as descendants with ownership or indirectly as townspeople, felt the pressure of everything that those houses represented. Historic houses are almost always named for a family: the Russell House, the Royall House, the Edmund Fowle House, the Cooper-Frost-Austin House, the Sanderson House, the Willard House, the Platts-Bradstreet House. The list is long. Visitors who read those names begin thinking of these unknown people from the moment they step onto the property. If the houses are open for tours, the guides talk about the men who built them, later generations of men, eventually some women, and perhaps some enslaved men and women associated with the place. The intent of such talks is to cement the connection between a house and the people to whom it belonged—and to whom it still belongs. Sometimes mannequins or cutouts of the inhabitants sit in chairs or stand beside the eternally cold fireplace, encouraging visitors to pretend that they are actually spending time with these people in their house. But given the smallness of the rooms, there's not room for everyone, and you are the one who will eventually leave. As you walk away, you may turn back to glimpse those figures through the windows.

These houses are haunted by their former inhabitants, who left so much of themselves within them. All of their things are there—generations of spinning wheels, chairs, tankards, cupboards, blankets, andirons, pots, cradles, saltcellars, chests, clocks, pewter, tables, and beds. The one thing missing is the full story of how the people came to live in the houses. Did they build them, or did they scoop them up at bargain prices from Indigenous women in distress such as Abigail Printer Abraham and Sarah Muckamaug Burnee? Is the oldest part of the house actually the original English-style structure proudly built by an Indigenous man such as Andrew Abraham Jr., a way to lay claim to full membership in English society? It's a rare for a historic house tour to end without the tale of a ghostly presence in one of the rooms. Whose ghost might it be?

"We are greatly confounded because our dwelling places have cast us out," wrote Increase Mather during King Philip's War.[5] Yet the family houses that survived that conflict have not quite cast out their original dwellers, either Indigenous or English. To our great confounding, the houses still wait for them, and we are the ones who are cast out.

The meetinghouses, though, did indeed cast out their original dwellers. As their congregations dwindled to nothing or moved on to bigger and better buildings, structures they eventually referred to as *churches,* the Congregational ideal of the church body within a congregation died. Its spirit cannot haunt the buildings that once fleetingly incorporated that ideal, for the Congregational ideal was not about identifying people with property. Old meetinghouses are not filled with relics of past worshippers. There are no tales of haunted meetinghouses in Woodland New England.

There are, however, some meetinghouses that have been preserved as historic landmarks, although they receive fewer visitors than historic houses do. These buildings are almost exclusively the preserve of their small descendant congregations, whose members bear most of the burden of raising money for preservation and upkeep, even as they worship exclusively in modest modern buildings. The congregations may hold special events in the "old meetinghouse," but they are more likely to host concerts or other events on the lawn, keeping the careless public out of their increasingly fragile buildings. As a public historian, I have given talks for town historical societies in Woodland New England in the faceless cinderblock annexes attached to and standing in for the old meetinghouses. I was deeply touched by the loving tours I was taken on before or after my talk, led by elderly members of the church body who had lain awake for decades worrying about the present safety and future existence of their old buildings. A steel fire-door in a linoleum-lined annex would open onto a musty staircase or passageway, which in turn would open into the wooden meetinghouse. The place would be enveloped in silence—shadowed, airless, heavy with centuries of past use and present cocooning, tense with fragility and risk. The limits of the walkable floor would be marked with ropes and stanchions or by masking tape so that no one could fall through and cause unrepairable damage. A few quiet words might be spoken, and then we would withdraw, back into our own time and space, where we could do no damage.

Of course, this reverence is itself a contradiction of the Congregational ideal, something that would have shocked and grieved true Congregationalists in Noepe/Martha's Vineyard, Agawam/Rowley, Hassanamesit/Grafton, N'ahteuk/Natick, and elsewhere in Woodland New England. When it was not filled by the church body and the congregation, the meetinghouse was an empty husk without meaning; it was not meant to inspire reverence or nostalgia. As a meetinghouse began to age, the town was eager to replace it as soon as finances would allow. By the late 1700s, large, established, prosperous towns considered the old graceless meetinghouses sitting squarely in the midst of their thriving modern trade center to be embarrassing eyesores. But a meetinghouse couldn't be replaced as quickly as an English house could: it was a large building, and the expense of materials and labor required town funding. As the eighteenth century drew to a close and the nineteenth began, Congregationalism had lost its status as the only authorized denomination in town. Arguments over who should pay to update or rebuild a meetinghouse were opportunities for ministers and churches to try to reestablish their importance and for non-Congregationalists, including town officials, to try to shake off the financial claims of the old religion once and for all. By the mid-1800s, the transition from meetinghouse to church building was in full swing.

Those meetinghouses that do remain standing are, to me, even more haunted than the family houses. They are testaments to their own disappearance, their former selves, their ghosts of gathered bodies past. Humans often identify death as the spirit leaving the body. The spirit of the gathered body has left the wooden shell of the old meetinghouse, leaving it far emptier than the family house. The meetinghouse has no abundance of furniture or personal items to summon back former owners. It has no fanciful stories of battles fought within its walls, spies passing messages in its halls, or romances blooming in the parlor. It is truly empty. Its only furnishings are an empty pulpit, benches, or pews. The people who are missing are deeply felt through their absence. When I look up at the second story, if there is one, or into the gallery in the back of the meetinghouse, where the Indigenous Congregationalists were once segregated, the absence is even more profound, for they are usually invisible even through memory among the elderly caretakers of the twenty-first century. Old meetinghouses are sad monuments to lost opportunity, markers of an original connection between English colonizers and Indigenous people in the Eastern Woodlands. Their decay and their rarity reiterate the message that the Congregational ideal, which offered a way of living completely opposed to secular English politics and society, was overpowered and overthrown by that secular civil world. The scope of the loss is breathtaking. We're living with its consequences to this day.

I've stood in those old meetinghouses, down by the pulpit and up in the gallery where the Indigenous faithful worshiped, and felt the complex emptiness of spaces that seem to be waiting for the church body to return and restore them. Their current physical fragility seems to prove that, without an eternal body to gather within them, the buildings are dead. But there is one manifestation of eternity that lives on with undimmed vitality: the church records. As we work to preserve historic meetinghouses, we can also focus on preserving the invaluable records that the churches kept to document what took place in those buildings, records that add so much to our understanding of the first three centuries of colonization in Woodland New England. They tell of the Indigenous people who rose to the challenge of overcoming annihilation, of the English people who brought their psychic distress and fear of scarcity to this place, and of the idealistic religion that members of both groups helped to create—a tenuous, bounded, but very real middle ground made possible by the ideal of the Congregational church body. The people who wrote in the church records believed that those books existed on both a physical plane and a spiritual one; that the physical bound book would be visible to God as well as to successive generations of church members, that its pages would be translated beyond this Earth to live forever in heaven as a testament to the people whom God had gathered into churches. The messages they contain—about human struggles to perceive and honor God's will, to work through internal divisions to true healing, and to engage in mutual care—still speak to us today. As more church records become available, they will continue to serve as the closest thing humans have to immortality—the chance to be known and valued long after they were first created.

I began this book by expressing my hope that it will contribute to new scholarship in the fields of Puritan, early American, colonizing, Indigenous, and religious studies, and I end in the same way. There are staggering numbers of church records waiting to be explored, engaged with, placed in relation with known primary sources, and applied to existing hypotheses. Each step taken in that direction is a step toward better understanding the histories of the countless thousands of people whose houses we visit and whose decisions we inherit, for better or for worse. It's crucial for public historians to share that new understanding with a wide audience. Perhaps four hundred years after those first record books were begun, on the brink of planetary collapse and civil war, more Americans are ready now to sit down together on those parcels of land where meetinghouses once stood and gather as one living body, undifferentiated by race, sex, or anything else, bound together by mutual care.

Notes

A NOTE ON NAMING

1. *Records of the governor and company of the Massachusetts bay in New England* (Boston: White, 1853), 271.
2. I'm grateful to my colleague and friend Lance Young for this name and its differentiation from the Dawnland, a translation of the name for the lands that now make up northern New England, as I learned from Lisa Brooks's magnificent *Our Beloved Kin: A New History of King Philip's War* (New Haven, CT: Yale University Press, 2018).
3. For instance, in *Our Beloved Kin*, Lisa Brooks uses the term *protectors* to describe Nipmuc men who took up arms during King Philip's War, but they are usually labeled as *warriors* in our histories.
4. Jean O'Brien, *Firsting and Lasting: Writing Indians Out of Existence in New England* (Minneapolis: University of Minnesota Press, 2010), 57.

INTRODUCTION

1. Epigraph cites Francis J. Bremer, "Women and Sermons in the Early Modern Anglo-Atlantic World," recorded presentation (2023), Congregational Library and Archives, Boston (hereafter CLA), https://www.youtube.com/watch?v=qQMOauI1c3U&t=5s.
2. "Church Records, 1728–1798, First Congregational Church in Stoneham, Mass.," viewer 213, New England's Hidden Histories, Congregational Library and Archives, Boston (hereafter NEHH, CLA).
3. "Granville, Collection History," 160, NEHH, CLA.
4. The extant records for the church at Mattabeseck/Middleborough, for example, run from 1707 to 1865. Naumkeag/Danvers's book covers 1689 to 1845.
5. "Account book, 1672–1735, First Church of Danvers, Mass.," viewer 337, NEHH, CLA.
6. "Church records, 1704–1802, First Congregational Church in Marlborough, Mass.," viewer 128, NEHH, CLA.

7. "Natick, Massachusetts. First Congregational Church Records, 1721–1862," viewer 65, NEHH, CLA.
8. "The extent of interracial religious activity during the eighteenth and early nineteenth centuries in northern churches has been obscured because historians have not fully utilized the church records where congregants of color are documented and because American Christians themselves have forgotten or glossed over this history" (Richard J. Boles, *Dividing the Faith: The Rise of Segregated Churches in the Early American North* [New York: New York University Press, 2020], 2, 3).
9. Richard J. Boles, "Enslaved Christians: Black Church Members in an Era of Cotton Mather," recorded presentation, November 30, 2023, Partnership of Historic Bostons.
10. Margaret Ellen Newell, *Brethren by Nature: New England Indians, Colonists, and the Origins of American Slavery* (Ithaca, NY: Cornell University Press, 2015), 86.
11. Linford D. Fisher, "Native Americans, Conversion, and Christian Practice in Colonial New England, 1640–1730," *Harvard Theological Review* 102, no. 1 (2009): 103, 107.
12. Marie Balsley Taylor, *Indigenous Kinship, Colonial Texts, and the Contested Space of Early New England* (Amherst: University of Massachusetts Press, 2023), 10–11.
13. Marie Balsley Taylor, "Recovering Indigenous Kinship: Community, Conversion, and the Digital Turn," in *The Afterlives of Indigenous Archives*, ed. Gordon Henry Jr. and Ivy Schweitzer (Lebanon, NH: University Press of New England, 2019), 17.

CHAPTER ONE

1. Epigraph cites George E. Ellis, "Introduction," in Arthur B. Ellis, *History of the First Church in Boston* (Boston: Wilson and Son, 1881), 30.
2. Francis J. Bremer, *Puritanism: A Very Short Introduction* (New York: Oxford University Press, 2009), 39, 40.
3. "Nathaniel Sparrowhawk experienced assurance after physical fasting made his spiritual hunger more painfully apparent to him than ever before. [Assurance] overwhelm[ed] the starving soul with nourishment and provoke[d] an ecstatic response that [wa]s emotional ('rejoicing') and physical ('weeping' and being unable to 'refrain from speaking to others')" (Lori Rogers-Stokes, "Making Sense of the Shepard Conversion Narratives," *New England Quarterly* 89, no. 1 [2016]: 135–36). For a quick outline of preparation and the "single ineffable moment" of assurance, see Charles L. Cohen, "The Post-Puritan Paradigm of Early American Religious History," *William and Mary Quarterly* 54, no. 4 (1997): 703.
4. For a concise description of this requirement, which was unique to New England, see David D. Hall, ed., *The Antinomian Controversy, 1636–1638: A Documentary History* (Durham, NC: Duke University Press, 1990), 12–14. The first anecdotal evidence of New England Puritans giving relations of faith in the course of, or as a requirement for, church membership comes from Roger Clap of Dorchester, who described "many in their Relations [speaking] of their great Terrors and deep Sense of their lost Condition" (*Memoirs of Roger Clap 1630* [Boston: David Clapp, 1844], 24).

5. Ralph Partridge, "Modell of Church Discipline," c. 1648, viewer 2, NEHH, CLA.
6. James F. Cooper, *Tenacious of their Liberties: The Congregationalists in Colonial Massachusetts* (Oxford: Oxford University Press, 1999), 101.
7. James Savage, Richard Dunn, and Laetitia Yandle, eds., *The Journal of John Winthrop, 1630–1649* (Cambridge, MA: Harvard University Press, 1996), 168–69.
8. Adam McKeown's fascinating study of civil dissent and reconciliation during the first two decades of the Massachusetts Bay Colony and the crucial role of John Winthrop in documenting reconciliation efforts and results (and in carefully shaping that documentation) adds to this distinction between civil reconciliation and church restoration. Crucially, McKeown's work shows that civil reconciliation did not have full restoration of the divided parties as its goal. Doing the painstaking and long-term work of fully resolving all parties' complaints (as churches strove to do, to bring about authentic, intrinsic restoration) was not part of the civil approach, which settled for quieting complaints and burying them in the past as quickly as possible to preserve extrinsic peace ("Reconciliation in John Winthrop's *History of New England*," *Early American Literature* 59, no. 2 [2024]: 267–92).
9. David D. Hall, "New England Background," in *The Cambridge Companion to Jonathan Edwards*, ed. Stephen J. Stein (New York: Cambridge University Press, 2007), 74.
10. Cooper, *Tenacious of their Liberties*, 198.
11. Marie Balsley Taylor, *Indigenous Kinship, Colonial Texts, and the Contested Space of Early New England* (Amherst: University of Massachusetts Press, 2023), 11.
12. Lisa Brooks, *Our Beloved Kin: A New History of King Philip's War* (New Haven, CT: Yale University Press, 2018), 4.
13. Daniel R. Mandell, *Behind the Frontier: Indians in Eighteenth-Century Eastern Massachusetts* (Lincoln: University of Nebraska Press, 1996), 5.
14. Brooks, *Our Beloved Kin*, 19, 20.
15. "'Foreigners and Strangers' [were] persons resident in a town who had not yet been officially admitted as town inhabitants—a legal status which usually bestowed rights to use common land and to benefit from land distributions" (Scott McDermott, "'Wandering Jacobites': The Ideology of Puritan Mobility to, from, and within New England in the Seventeenth Century," https://www.academia.edu. These individuals had to be explicitly granted rights by the 1641 Massachusetts Bay Colony Body of Liberties because traditionally they possessed none.
16. Brooks, *Our Beloved Kin*, 19.
17. Brooks, *Our Beloved Kin*, 29.
18. Linford Fisher, "Native Americans, Conversion, and Christian Practice in Colonial New England, 1640–1730," *Harvard Theological Review* 102, no. 1 (2009): 108.
19. "The Indians query Eliot as early as 1646, but not until the tracts of 1649 and 1651 do their questions appear exclusively in lists. Formally, too, Jack Goody writes, 'lists differ from the products of oral communication' and 'stand opposed to the continuity, the flux, the connectedness of . . . conversation, oratory, etc.' The remainder of the Massachuset questions appears in a very different format that, antedating the lists, represents the 'connectedness' of the Indians' rhetorical

strategies" (Craig White, "The Praying Indians' Speeches as Texts of Massachusett Oral Culture," *Early American Literature* 38, no. 3 [2003]: 441, 444).
20. White, "The Praying Indians' Speeches," 441, 449. White also observes, "Recorded performances of [the conversion] genre indicate that the Puritan and Indian peoples, rather than representing antipodal mentalities of orality and literacy, inhabited distinct positions on a continuum of speech and writing" (448).
21. Balsley Taylor, *Indigenous Kinship*, 135, 136.
22. Brooks, *Our Beloved Kin*, 17, 19.
23. David J. Silverman, "Indians, Missionaries, and Religious Translation: Creating Wampanoag Christianity in Seventeenth-Century Martha's Vineyard," *William and Mary Quarterly*, 3rd ser., 62, no. 2 (2005): 167.
24. Cooper, *Tenacious of their Liberties*, 123.
25. "Church Records, 1820–1848, Old First Congregational Church of Bennington, Vt.," viewer 137, NEHH, CLA.
26. "Church Records, 1798–1840, First Congregational Church in Stoneham, Mass.," viewer 195, NEHH, CLA.
27. All citations of church records are from "The Phillips Diary (church records), 1664–1784, First Congregational Church in Rowley, Mass.," NEHH, CLA. For simplicity's sake, I've included shortened references in the text. The page numbers refer to the number the minister wrote on the page of the actual record book (e.g., AR 249). Edward Payson was minister at Agawam/Rowley from 1682 to 1732.
28. "The economics of being a minister, though favorable in some respects, were deteriorating; the downward pressure on ministerial salaries during the troubled 1680s and early 1690s, when war-related expenses forced Massachusetts to issue paper currency that rapidly became worthless, was manifested in the shortfalls that accumulated in many towns. Well before this moment, every installation of a new minister was already requiring extensive negotiations about the level of salary, modes of payment, and access to land and housing. When inflation struck in the 1720s, salaries fixed in calmer times depreciated in value to the point where some ministers fell into financial difficulty" (Hall, "The New England Background," 62).
29. David Hall, diaries, 1704–89, church records of Wenham, Massachusetts, 110, P-363, reel 5.1–2, Massachusetts Historical Society, Boston (hereafter MHS).
30. Brooks, *Our Beloved Kin*, 30, 34.
31. For descriptions of sachems and sons of sachems who became ministers on Noepe/Martha's Vineyard, see James Ronda, "Generations of Faith: The Christian Indians of Martha's Vineyard," *William and Mary Quarterly* 38, no. 3 (1981): 372–73, 374, 381. Ronda's article offers more illustrations of the overlap of those roles.
32. Jason Eden notes that many ministers turned to mission work simply for economic reasons: "Such missionaries probably had a variety of motives for preaching to Indians, but it seems clear that earning money was one of the most important. These individuals were often ministers in small communities where English congregations could offer only meager salaries. [As] such, these men frequently complained about their lack of income and readily pursued missionary work and the supplemental funds provided by the English missionary societies"

("'Therefore ye Are no More Strangers and Foreigners'": Indians, Christianity, and Political Engagement in Colonial Plimouth and on Martha's Vineyard," *American Indian Quarterly* 38, no. 1 [2014]: 39).

CHAPTER TWO

1. Jeremy Dupertuis Bangs, *Indian Deeds: Land Transactions in Plymouth Colony, 1620–1691* (Boston: New England Historical and Genealogical Society, 2002), 54.
2. Scott McDermott, *The Puritan Ideology of Mobility: Corporatism, the Politics of Place, and the Founding of New England Towns before 1650* (London: Anthem, 2022). Chapter 1, "Puritans and Society in the Stour Valley," is an excellent description of real and perceived scarcity, with a focus on enclosure and resulting vagrancy.
3. John Lauritz Larson, *Laid Waste! The Culture of Exploitation in Early America* (Philadelphia: University of Pennsylvania Press, 2020), 14.
4. In her article on eighteenth-century narratives involving Indigenous people convicted of crimes, Katherine Grandjean writes that "the . . . century was a crystallizing moment in the intellectual history of race, a time 'when the myriad of human physical differences collapsed into simple types privileging skin-color differences.' They also help to pinpoint the latter part of the century, more specifically, as an age in which inflexible notions of racial difference took hold, and with a much firmer grip" ("'Our Fellow-Creatures & our Fellow-Christians': Race and Religion in Eighteenth Century Narratives of Indian Crime," *American Quarterly* 62, no. 4 [2010]: 926). See also James Warren Springer, "American Indians and the Law of Real Property in New England," *American Journal of Legal History* 30, no. 1 (1986): 27: "While the English regarded themselves as religiously and culturally superior, they did not regard themselves as racially superior." Of course, this was the situation only in the early years of colonization.
5. Larson, *Laid Waste*, 16–17.
6. Larson, *Laid Waste*, 13.
7. Larson, *Laid Waste*, 14.
8. Neal Salisbury, *Manitou and Providence: Indians, Europeans, and the Making of New England, 1500–1643* (Oxford, UK: Oxford University Press, 1984), 166–67. Salisbury notes that this trend was particularly pronounced in the southeastern counties of England, from where most of those who made up the Great Migration to Woodland New England emigrated. See his chapter 6, which focuses at length on the deep psychic distress that this upheaval created.
9. Thomas Shepard, *The Parable of the Ten Virgins opened & applied . . . (London: J. H. for John Rothwell, 1660)*, 54.
10. Salisbury, *Manitou and Providence*, 167.
11. "[The] process we call modernization . . . locked together science and technology, economic freedom, and competitive capitalist in what I am calling a 'culture of exploitation'" (Larson, *Laid Waste*, 1).
12. For a description of how the English turned abundance into scarcity, see Neal Salisbury, "The Colonizing of Indian New England," *Massachusetts Review* 26,

no. 2/3 (1985): 448–49. The article outlines the importance of emerging global markets and market capitalism during the first decades of Puritan colonization.
13. James F. Cooper, *Tenacious of their Liberties: The Congregationalists in Colonial Massachusetts* (Oxford, UK: Oxford University Press, 1999), 117.
14. Jean O'Brien, *Firsting and Lasting: Writing Indians Out of Existence in New England* (Minneapolis: University of Minnesota Press, 2010), 15, 166.
15. See Nicholas James Reo and Angela K. Parker, "Re-Thinking Colonialism to Prepare for the Impacts of Rapid Environmental Change," *Climatic Change* 120, no. 3 (2013): 674–78.
16. David J. Silverman, "Indians, Missionaries, and Religious Translation: Creating Wampanoag Christianity in Seventeenth-Century Martha's Vineyard," *William and Mary Quarterly*, 3rd ser., 62, no. 2 (2005): 149. Also see Marie Balsley Taylor, "Recovering Indigenous Kinship: Community, Conversion, and the Digital Turn," in *The Afterlives of Indigenous Archives*, ed. Gordon Henry Jr. and Ivy Schweitzer (Lebanon, NH: University Press of New England, 2019). She writes: "More than merely a means of organizing society, kinship was at the heart of an Indigenous person's identity. Kinship ties not only defined one's familial relationships, but they also determined one's place in society, one's relationship to land, and one's responsibility to his or her community" (3).
17. Lisa T. Brooks and Cassandra M. Brooks, "The Reciprocity Principle and Traditional Ecological Knowledge," *International Journal of Critical Indigenous Studies* 3, no. 2 (2010): 11, 13–14.
18. Quoted in John Frederick Martin, *Profits in the Wilderness* (Chapel Hill, NC: Omohundro Institute of Early American History and Culture, 1991), 116.
19. As William A. Farley writes, "[the] pressures [of] environmental degradation due to widespread deforestation" were felt as early as the third decade of colonization in the Massachusetts Bay Colony. His theme is that Indigenous adaptations to colonizer culture, or "European American norms," were not driven by a philosophical desire to assimilate but by a practical need to keep living in "a quickly changing environment." This sudden shift included "decades of the region being subject to intensive agricultural practice . . . that began to affect the environment negatively as early as the first half of the 17th century" ("Reservation Subsistence: A Comparative Paleoethnobotanical Analysis of a Mashantucket Pequot and Euro-American Household," *Northeast Historical Archaeology* 43–45 (2014): 93, 94, 102.
20. Philip J. Greven Jr., *Four Generations: Population, Land, and Family in Colonial Andover, Massachusetts* (Ithaca, NY: Cornell University Press, 1970), 24.
21. For details, see *History of the Town of Dorchester, Massachusetts* (Boston: Clapp, 1859), 35–37. For an in-depth description of colonizer farming and its demands on the land, see Brian Donahue, *The Great Meadow: Farmers and the Land in Colonial Concord* (New Haven, CT: Yale University Press, 2007).
22. Even a traditional scholar such as Virginia DeJohn Anderson includes a contemporary quotation about the irrationality of the demand for land without comment: "Haverhill's settlers negotiated with the colony government for a large tract for their town in order to satisfy their 'over-weaning desire . . . after Medow land'"

("King Philip's Herds: Indians, Colonists, and the Problem of Livestock in Early New England," *William and Mary Quarterly*, 3rd ser., 51, no. 4 (1994): 603.
23. Cooper, *Tenacious of their Liberties*, 117, 116.
24. Daniel R. Mandell, *Behind the Frontier: Indians in Eighteenth-Century Eastern Massachusetts* (Lincoln: University of Nebraska Press, 1996), 12. In this section Mandell talks about what I call English psychic distress (10–12).
25. McDermott makes a convincing argument against assigning a 100 percent victory to either religious or economic motivation (*The Puritan Ideology of Mobility*, 2–4).
26. Keith Pluymers, *No Wood, No Kingdom: Political Ecology in the English Atlantic* (Philadelphia: University of Pennsylvania Press, 2021), 9.
27. Katherine Grandjean makes yet another component of psychic distress clear when she details the obstacles to planting and harvesting that the Little Ice Age posed in Woodland New England ("New World Tempests: Environment, Scarcity, and the Coming of the Pequot War," *William and Mary Quarterly* 68, no. 1 [2011]: 75–80).
28. "Winthrop argued that a 'civil' right to the earth resulted when 'as men and cattell increased, they appropriated some parcells of ground by enclosing and peculiar maintenance'" (Anderson, "King Philip's Herds," 604).
29. Cooper tells the story of Philip Nelson's long harassment of Samuel Phillips in *Tenacious of their Liberties*, 118–19, 123–25.
30. William Cronon, *Changes in the Land: Indians, Colonists, and the Ecology of New England* (New York: Hill and Wang, 1983), 51–53.
31. John Keats, "On First Looking into Chapman's Homer" (1816), in *Poems* (Oxford, UK: Woodstock, 1989), 89.

CHAPTER THREE

1. Epigraphs cite Marie Balsley Taylor, *Indigenous Kinship, Colonial Texts, and the Contested Space of Early New England* (Amherst: University of Massachusetts Press, 2023), 78; Stephen A. Mrozowski, Holly Herbster, David Brown, and Katherine L. Priddy, "Magunkaquog Materiality, Federal Recognition, and the Search for a Deeper History," *International Journal of Historical Archaeology* 13 (2009): 430, 433; and John Eliot and Thomas Mayhew Jr., *Tears of Repentance*, quoted in Gregory Michna, "The Long Road to Sainthood: Indian Christians, the Doctrine of Preparation, and the Halfway Covenant of 1662," *Church History* 89, no. 1 (2020): 53.
2. Michael D. McNally, "The Practice of Native American Christianity," *Church History* 69, no. 4 (2000): 843.
3. Richard J. Boles, *Dividing the Faith: The Rise of Segregated Churches in the Early American North* (New York: New York University Press, 2020), 4.
4. Edward E. Andrews, *Native Apostles: Black and Indian Missionaries in the British Atlantic World* (Cambridge, MA: Harvard University Press, 2013), 11, 22.
5. The scholarly presumption of omniscience is evident even in well-meaning statements. For instance: "Of all the New England Indians, those on the

Vineyard—who were by no means the victims of coercion, as they outnumbered Europeans on the island for the entire seventeenth century—are considered to have accepted Christianity in the most wholehearted and committed way" (E. Jennifer Monaghan, "'She loved to read in good Books': Literacy and the Indians of Martha's Vineyard, 1643–1725," *History of Education Quarterly* 30, no. 4 [1990]: 496).

6. "Other signs are undeterminable: who can guess a worshiper's sincerity? . . . Qualitative discussions of religious devotion ultimately involved assessing actors' intensity, a concept difficult to define and measure" (Charles L. Cohen, "The Post-Puritan Paradigm of Early American Religious History," *William and Mary Quarterly* 54, no. 4 (1997): 718. See also Baird Tipson's definitive article, "Invisible Saints: The 'Judgment of Charity' in the Early New England Churches," which restores the original meaning of the judgment of charity as the Puritans practiced it (*Church History* 44, no. 4 [1975]: 465).

7. Richard A. Bailey, *Race and Redemption in Puritan New England* (Oxford, UK: Oxford University Press, 2011), 74.

8. Linford Fisher, "Native Americans, Conversion, and Christian Practice in Colonial New England, 1640–1730," *Harvard Theological Review* 102, no. 1 (2009): 106.

9. James P. Ronda, "Generations of Faith: The Christian Indians of Martha's Vineyard," *William and Mary Quarterly* 38, no. 3 (1981): 369.

10. Jean O'Brien, *Firsting and Lasting: Writing Indians out of Existence in New England* (Minneapolis: University of Minnesota Press, 2010), 107.

11. Harold W. Van Lonkhuyzen, "A Reappraisal of the Praying Indians: Acculturation, Conversion, and Identity at Natick, Massachusetts, 1646–1730," *New England Quarterly* 63, no. 3 (1990): 397. For an early and clear challenge to the purity test, see McNally, "The Practice of Native American Christianity." For a challenge to the purity test as it applies to the economics of the Atlantic triangle trade, see Paul Cohen, "Was There an Amerindian Atlantic? Reflections on the Limits of a Historiographical Concept," *History of European Ideas* 34, no. 4 (2008): 403. He argues that the colonial economy was not a "one-sided affair" but something offering many opportunities to bring "Amerindians and French together on the terrain of inter-cultural dialogue" and that "these relationships did not take shape as straightforward extensions of French imperial policy, commercial interests or missionary efforts, but rather as the constantly evolving outcome of negotiation and compromise" (401). His hypothesis could well be applied to Congregationalism in Woodland New England.

12. O'Brien, *Firsting and Lasting*, xvi, xx; Jean M. O'Brien, "Learning Together about Firsting and Lasting: Exploring Indigenous History with Professor Jean O'Brien," online forum, Facing History and Ourselves, April 14, 2022, http://facinghistory.org.

13. Russell G. Handsman, "Survivance Stories and Household Differences in Pequot Indian Country," May 15, 2013, revised version of a paper prepared for "Making the Invisible Visible in Plural Sites and Communities," session of a meeting of the Theoretical Archaeology Group, May 9–11, 2013, Chicago.

14. Elise M. Brenner, "To Pray or to Be Prey: That Is the Question. Strategies for Cultural Autonomy of Massachusetts Praying Town Indians," *Ethnohistory* 27,

no. 2 (1980): 146; J. Patrick Cesarini, "John Eliot's 'Breif History of the Mashepog Indians,' 1666," *William and Mary Quarterly*, 3rd ser., 65, no. 1 (2008): 105, 106; Charles L. Cohen, "The Post-Puritan Paradigm of Early American Religious History," *William and Mary Quarterly* 54, no. 4 (1997): 713.
15. Hilary E. Wyss, "'Things That Do Accompany Salvation'": Colonialism, Conversion, and Cultural Exchange in Experience Mayhew's 'Indian Converts,'" *Early American Literature* 33, no. 1 (1998): 40.
16. Glenda Goodman, "'But they differ from us in sound': Indian Psalmody and the Soundscape of Colonialism, 1651–75," *William and Mary Quarterly* 69, no. 4 (2012): 695.
17. Marie Balsley Taylor, "Recovering Indigenous Kinship: Community, Conversion, and the Digital Turn," in *The Afterlives of Indigenous Archives*, ed. Gordon Henry Jr. and Ivy Schweitzer (Lebanon, NH: University Press of New England, 2019), 7.
18. Laura Arnold Leibman, ed., *Experience Mayhew's Indian Converts: A Cultural Edition* (Amherst: University of Massachusetts Press, 2008), 233, 255, 256, 257. Wyss also describes Hannah Nohnosoo's blending of cultures, writing that her skill "is something that Nattootumau attributed entirely to God [as] any Puritan would have, [but] she did it in ways that are similar to the ways in which powwows relied on the spirit world to affect their cures." Wyss wonders if Wampanoag Christian women were "taking over the religious curing function of the powwow," citing the reports of Hannah Ahhunnut and Abiah Paaonit and a number of others who appear in "Mayhew's biographies of Native women" who saw visions at or on a deathbed. Her question about these visions as evolutions of powwowing is interesting ("Things That Do Accompany Salvation," 51–52). Kallie Kose has demonstrated how Stockbridge women would blend Christianity and Mohican identity. They "found ways to be Christian and Mohican and saw no conflict with these identities" ("Kauknausquoh as Mary Peters Doxtator: A Stockbridge Clan Mother, Attorney, and Stateswoman in Early America," 2, paper presented at the Organization of American Historians Conference on American History, April 6–9, 2017, New Orleans). See also Rachel Wheeler, "Woman and Christian Practice in a Mahican Village," *Religion and American Culture* 13, no. 1 (2003): 28, 34–46.
19. Van Lonkhuyzen, "A Reappraisal of the Praying Indians," 400.
20. Henry M. Knapp, "The Character of Puritan Missions: The Motivation, Methodology, and Effectiveness of the Puritan Evangelization of the Native Americans in New England," *Journal of Presbyterian History* 76, no. 2 (1998): 111. Gregory Michna echoes this: "How much more difficult was it to read the outward appearance and inward state of 'Praying Indians' (Indian Christians) whose cultural practices remained foreign and at times offensive to puritan colonists?" ("The Long Road to Sainthood: Indian Christians, the Doctrine of Preparation, and the Halfway Covenant of 1662," *Church History* 89, no. 1 [2020]: 44).
21. On scholarly contributions to the incompatibility test, see David J. Silverman, "Indians, Missionaries, and Religious Translation: Creating Wampanoag Christianity in Seventeenth-Century Martha's Vineyard," *William and Mary Quarterly*, 3rd ser., 62, no. 2 (2005), 145, n. 6, 158–59.
22. Alfred A. Cave, "New England Puritan Misconceptions of Native American

Shamanism," *International Social Science Review* 67, no. 1 (1992): 23. In short, the English believed that "Indians were considered the *objects*, the special instruments, of God's agency, but the English alone were God's *subjects*. God spoke *through* the Indians, but he never spoke *to* them" (J. Patrick Cesarini, "'What has become of your praying to God?' Daniel Gookin's Troubled History of King Philip's War," *Early American Literature* 44, no. 3 [2009]: 497). Cave's statements about the importance of the concepts of original sin and preordained damnation in Congregationalism are also evidence of the psychic distress inherent within the denomination specifically and within Christianity as a whole.

23. Neal Salisbury, "'I Loved the Place of my Dwelling': Puritan Missionaries and Native Americans in Seventeenth-Century Southern New England," in *Inequality in Early America*, ed. Carla Gardina Pestana and Sharon V. Salinger (Hanover, NH: University Press of New England, 1999), 112.

24. I'm using Richard W. Cogley's starting date of September 1646, when "John Eliot's first documented missionary lecture was delivered to . . . Cutshamekin and other Massachusett Indians then residing at Neponset (near Dorchester), about four miles from Roxbury" (*John Eliot's Mission to the Indians before King Philip's War* [Cambridge, MA: Harvard University Press, 1999], 40).

25. Robert James Naeher, "Dialogue in the Wilderness: John Eliot and the Indian Exploration of Puritanism as a Source of Meaning, Comfort, and Ethnic Survival," *New England Quarterly* 62, no. 3 (1989): 346. Naeher questions received wisdom about incompatibility; see esp. 351–55.

26. McNally, "The Practice of Native American Christianity," 837, 840.

27. Balsley Taylor, *Indigenous Kinship*, 141.

28. Salisbury, "I Loved the Place of My Dwelling," 113.

29. Stephen Silliman, "Indigenous Traces in Colonial Spaces: Archaeologies of Ambiguity, Origin, and Practice," *Journal of Social Archaeology* 10, no. 1 (2010), passim.

30. Christina J. Hodge, "Faith and Practice at an Early-Eighteenth-Century Wampanoag Burial Ground: The Waldo Farm Site in Dartmouth, Massachusetts," *Historical Archaeology* 39, no. 4 (2005): 65, 66.

31. Hodge, "Faith and Practice," 76.

32. Floris W. M. Keehnen, Corinne L. Hofman, and Andrzej T. Antczak, "Material Encounters and Indigenous Transformations in the Early Colonial Americas," in *Material Encounters and Indigenous Transformations in the Early Colonial Americas; Archaeological Case Studies*, ed. Corinne L. Hofman and Floris W. M. Keehnen (Leiden, NL: Brill, 2019), 2.

33. Stephen A. Mrozowski, D. Rae Gould, and Heather Law Pezzarossi, "Rethinking Colonialism: Indigenous Innovation and Colonial Inevitability," in *Rethinking Colonialism: Comparative Archaeological Approaches*, ed. Craig N. Cippola and Katherine Howlett Hayes (Gainesville: University Press of Florida, 2015), 121, 123.

34. Mrozowski et al., "Rethinking Colonialism," 123. Craig White writes, "Most analyses have approached the Indian speeches in the 'Eliot Tracts' as ex nihilo responses to European contact. Accordingly the Indians appear either to acquiesce to Christian theology by imitating Puritan genres or to challenge it in terms familiar to Western skepticism. . . . Though sympathetic to the Indians, these

studies restrict native expression to terms either of tractability or resistance to conversion" ("The Praying Indians' Speeches as Texts of Massachusett Oral Culture," *Early American Literature* 38, no. 3 [2003]: 439).
35. Balsley Taylor, *Indigenous Kinship*, 7.
36. Andrews, *Native Apostles*, esp. chaps 1 and 2.
37. Andrews, *Native Apostles*, 55, 56, 60, 116–17.
38. Charles Cohen, *God's Caress: The Psychology of Puritan Religious Experience* (New York: Oxford University Press, 1986), 713. See also Michael McGiffert, ed., *God's Plot: Puritan Spirituality in Thomas Shepard's Cambridge* (Amherst: University of Massachusetts Press, 1972); Patricia Caldwell, *The Puritan Conversion Narrative: The Beginnings of American Expression* (Cambridge, UK: Cambridge University Press, 1983); Meredith Neumann, *Jeremiah's Scribes: Creating Sermon Literature in Puritan New England* (Philadelphia: University of Pennsylvania Press, 2013); Sarah Rivett, *The Science of the Soul in Colonial New England* (Chapel Hill: University of North Carolina Press, 2011); and Andy Dorsey, "A Rhetoric of American Experience: Thomas Shepard's Cambridge Confessions and the Discourse of Spiritual Hypocrisy," *Early American Literature* 49, no. 3 (2014), passim. For many examples of persistent folk belief among English Christians in Woodland New England, see David D. Hall, *Worlds of Wonder, Days of Judgment: Popular Religious Belief in Early New England* (Cambridge, MA: Harvard University Press, 1990). See also Cohen, "The Post-Puritan Paradigm," 713.
39. For example, see Hall, *Worlds of Wonder, Days of Judgment*; and Mandell, *Behind the Frontier: Indians in Eighteenth-Century Eastern Massachusetts* (Lincoln: University of Nebraska Press, 1996).
40. "Church records, 1707–1871, First Congregational Church of Braintree, Mass.," viewer 69, NEHH, CLA.
41. "William Homes diary, 1715–1747," viewers 171, 173, NEHH, CLA.
42. "During a 1726 'General Visitation' of Wampanoag families who lived in scattered pockets throughout Plymouth County, [the minister Josiah] Cotton discovered deeply pious Native Christians who studied their Bibles assiduously, meditated in secret, prayed with their families, and joined Indian churches in full membership; others shied away from sabbath meetings and clung tenaciously to covert forms of ancestral religion. Thus, the majority of Indian families in southeastern Massachusetts remained, in the apt words of one local clergyman, 'half Christian.' . . . But in this respect the Native Christians of the Old Colony differed little from their equally eclectic English neighbors, who drew upon a broad spectrum of religious traditions ranging from the theological conventions of Reformed Protestantism to premodern folk wisdom. Inheritors of multiple, overlapping, and, at times, mutually incompatible religious traditions, provincials of both races inhabited a fluid spiritual world with few fixed boundaries" (Douglas L. Winiarski, "Native American Popular Religion in New England's Old Colony, 1670–1770," *Religion and American Culture* 15, no. 2 [2005]: 154–55).
43. For book-length analyses of the purity test in contemporary Indigenous life in the United States, see Kimberly Jenkins Marshall, *Upward, not Sunwise: Resonant Rupture in Navajo Neo-Pentecostalism* (Lincoln: University of Nebraska Press, 2016); and Clinton N. Westman, *Cree and Christian: Encounters and*

Transformations (Lincoln: University of Nebraska Press, 2022). Philip J. Deloria's *Indians in Unexpected Places* (Lawrence: University of Kansas Press, 2004) offers a thorough dissection of the notion of Indigenous purity.

44. Mandell, *Behind the Frontier*, 59.
45. The women were Elizabeth Cutter, Joanna Sill, and Jane Palfrey (Goodwife Willowes). See George Selement and Bruce C. Woolley, eds., *Thomas Shepard's Confessions* (Boston: Colonial Society of Massachusetts, 1981), 144–45, 50, 151.
46. Andrews, *Native Apostles*, 64–65.
47. Fisher, "Native Americans, Conversion, and Christian Practice," 112.
48. The first step in an English narration of spiritual preparation was "awakening to the fact that [one's] seemingly ordinary life was sinful" (Lori Rogers-Stokes, *Records of Trial from Thomas Shepard's Church in Cambridge, 1638–1649: Heroic Souls* [London: Palgrave Macmillan, 2020], 100 and passim).
49. Richard A. Bailey, *Race and Redemption in Puritan New England* (Oxford, UK: Oxford University Press, 2011), 16.
50. "Building these structures engaged the laity; gathering churches, challenging ministerial prerogatives, and nurturing their own hermeneutics, they played a significant—at times paramount—role in defining their faiths.... The paradigm is a work in progress, exhibiting gaps and discrepancies" (Cohen, "The Post-Puritan Paradigm," 700). This quotation doesn't refer to Indigenous Christians, but the description applies. Later in his discussion, Cohen promotes the purity test in his brief mention of Indigenous conversion, saying that "the preponderance of evidence suggest[s] that few individuals or bands in nations that retained their cultural and political integrity converted to Christianity and even those located within colonial borders or susceptible to Anglo-American authority and influence rarely gave themselves to Christ voluntarily.... Even the most notable missions, such as John Eliot's [and] the Mayhew family's ... cumulatively did not affect a numerically significant proportion of indigenous peoples, even supposing that all native converts were 'genuine'" (715). If *genuine* is so nebulous as to need scare quotes, why validate its use at all?
51. Mandell, *Behind the Frontier*, 15.
52. Fisher, "Native Americans, Conversion, and Christian Practice," 106–7. Ironically, Indigenous mastery of English norms is sometimes perceived as a deviation. Jacqueline M. Henkel's study of Indigenous conversion narratives provides a good example of the scholarly habit of veering into unconscious judgment even while trying to honor the gaps in English records of Indigenous speaking ("Represented Authenticity: Native Voices in Seventeenth-Century Conversion Narratives," *New England Quarterly* 67, no. 1 [2014]: 9).

CHAPTER FOUR

1. Epigraph cites Cotton Mather, sermon book 1, 1694–95, 154, viewer 98, NEHH, CLA. Thomas Miller emigrated from Birmingham, England, to New England in 1635 and by 1637 had married Isabel (last name unknown) in Agawam/Rowley

(*Torrey's New England Marriages Prior to 1700* [Boston: New England Historic Genealogical Society, 2015], 2:1039).
2. *Hartford County, Connecticut, County Court Minutes, Vols. 3 and 4, 1663–1687, 1697, transcribed and indexed by* Helen Schatvet Ullmann (Boston: New England Historical Genealogical Society, 2005), 47, 57–58, 59, 60–61.
3. *Hartford County*, 60.
4. *Hartford County*, 61.
5. *The Early Records of the Town of Rowley, Massachusetts, 1639–1673* (Rowley, MA, 1894), 1:v, viii.
6. George B. Blodgett, *Early Settlers of Rowley, Massachusetts: A Genealogical Record of the Families Who Settled in Rowley before 1700, with Several Generations of Their Descendants* (Salem, MA: Essex Institute, 1887), 242.
7. All citations of the church records are from "The Phillips Diary (church records), 1664–1784, First Congregational Church in Rowley, Mass.," NEHH, CLA. For simplicity's sake, I've included shortened references in the text. The page numbers refer to the number the minister wrote on the page of the actual record book (e.g., AR 249).
8. David D. Field, *Centennial Address* (Middletown, CT: Casey, 1853), 48.
9. "The leaving off, or forsaking of sin, is not sufficient to true Repentance; there must be a confessing of sin, and publick and particular confession of publick and scandalous sins" (James F. Cooper, *Tenacious of their Liberties: The Congregationalists in Colonial Massachusetts* [Oxford: Oxford University Press, 1999], 95).
10. Lisa Brooks, *The Common Pot: The Recovery of Native Space in the Northeast* (Minneapolis: University of Minnesota Press, 2008), 6.

CHAPTER FIVE

1. All citations from the N'ahteuk/Natick church record book are from "Church Records, 1721–1794, First Congregational Church in Natick, Mass.," NEHH, CLA. For simplicity's sake, I've included shortened references in the text. The page number listed may refer to either the number the minister wrote on the page of the actual record book (e.g., N 4) or to the page in the NEHH viewer (e.g., N v56).
2. *Vital Records of Natick, Massachusetts, to the Year 1849* (Worcester: Franklin Rice, 1906), 208–9. Margaret's civil birth record does identify her as Indian. Rachel's civil birth record does not, but her death record does. Jacob, alone of the children, is identified as Indian in both his civil birth and death records. The vital records also list a son named Benoni, born on October 31, 1737, who is not listed in the church records and therefore may be not the child of Jacob and Leah Chalcom
3. *Vital Records of Grafton, Massachusetts, to the end of the year 1849* (Worcester: Franklin Rice, 1906), 178; Jean O'Brien, *Firsting and Lasting: Writing Indians out of Existence in New England* (Minneapolis: University of Minnesota Press, 2010), xvi. See also Daniel R. Mandell, "The Saga of Sarah Muckamugg: Indian and African Intermarriage in Colonial New England," in *Sex, Love, Race: Crossing Boundaries in North American History*, ed. Martha Hodes (New York: New York

University Press, 1999), passim. The chapter is an in-depth recounting of Muckamugg's life, marriages, and children.

4. Philip J. Greven Jr., *Four Generations: Population, Land, and Family in Colonial Andover, Massachusetts* (Ithaca, NY: Cornell University Press, 1970), 6.

5. The English at this time used the Julian calendar, so their new year began on March 25. But they were aware, of course, of the Gregorian calendar, which was being used by more and more European kingdoms. Therefore, they often wrote two dates from January 1 through March 24 to show both calendar systems. Here, Jacob Chalcom's record was written on January 22, 1736, but recorded with the old calendar year of 1735 as well.

6. *Vital Records of Natick*, 194.

CHAPTER SIX

1. Experience Mayhew's concerns were shared by earlier missionaries, such as John Eliot, for whom "the matter of Wequash's dying was of particular concern to the English who had gathered. Each sought to capture Wequash's final words in order to make a particular claim about not only the state of Wequash's soul but the success or failure of their own mission" (Marie Balsley Taylor, *Indigenous Kinship, Colonial Texts, and the Contested Space of Early New England* [Amherst: University of Massachusetts Press, 2023], 48).

2. Douglas L. Winiarski, "Native American Popular Religion in New England's Old Colony, 1670–1770," *Religion and American Culture* 15, no. 2 (2005): 148. See also Jean O'Brien, *Firsting and Lasting: Writing Indians out of Existence in New England* (Minneapolis: University of Minnesota Press, 2010), 147. Neal Salisbury writes: "The Indians who responded to the missionaries, then, were not those who freely chose 'civilization' over traditional ways, for those ways were already disappearing under the impact of the English invasion. . . . The Indians were expected to repudiate their past" ("Red Puritans: The 'Praying Indians' of Massachusetts Bay and John Eliot," *William and Mary Quarterly* 31, no. 1 [1974]: 35, 41).

3. David J. Silverman, "Indians, Missionaries, and Religious Translation: Creating Wampanoag Christianity in Seventeenth-Century Martha's Vineyard," *William and Mary Quarterly*, 3rd ser., 62, no. 2 (2005): 146. Elsewhere, Silverman makes a strong case for "the important ways Christianity promoted native identity," even when he veers into assuming that adopting Christianity was sheer survivance on Indigenous people's part ("The Church in New England Indian Community Life: A View from the Islands and Cape Cod," in *Reinterpreting New England Indians and the Colonial Experience*, ed. Colin G. Calloway and Neal Salisbury [Boston: Colonial Society of Massachusetts, 2003], 266).

4. For those who converted, Congregational Christianity was so firmly a part of Indigenous identity that they were the first representatives of Christianity for at least some Indigenous people (Amy Den Ouden, *Beyond Conquest: Native Peoples and the Struggle for History in New England* [Lincoln: University of Nebraska Press, 2005], 59). Also see David J. Silverman, *Faith and Boundaries: Colonists, Christianity, and Community among the Wampanoag Indians of Martha's*

Vineyard, 1600–1871 (Cambridge, UK: Cambridge University Press, 2005), which is dedicated to posing questions about how Indigenous people could incorporate Christianity into their lives and remain Indigenous.

5. "Neil Salisbury has noted that 'What is so striking in accounts of praying Indian church services is not the theological proficiency of the converts but the enthusiastic participation of all—young and old, male and female—in catechizing, psalm-singing, praying, and other activities in which the members acted together or responded in predictable fashion'" (Robert James Naeher, "Dialogue in the Wilderness: John Eliot and the Indian Exploration of Puritanism as a Source of Meaning, Comfort, and Ethnic Survival," *New England Quarterly* 62, no. 3 [1989]: 363–64).

6. Laura Arnold Leibman, ed., *Experience Mayhew's Indian Converts: A Cultural Edition* (Amherst: University of Massachusetts Press, 2008), 143.

7. "While there are clear limits to using kinship as a methodology, when used cautiously, the reconstruction of Indigenous familial and social relationships allows us to imagine potentially new motivations for many of the Native people described in early American literature about whom we have little or no information" (Marie Balsley Taylor, "Recovering Indigenous Kinship: Community, Conversion, and the Digital Turn," in *The Afterlives of Indigenous Archives*, ed. Gordon Henry Jr. and Ivy Schweitzer [Lebanon, NH: University Press of New England, 2019], 207).

8. Linford D. Fisher, "Native Americans, Conversion, and Christian Practice in Colonial New England, 1640–1730," *Harvard Theological Review* 102, no. 1 (2009): 113–14.

9. Winiarski summarizes a message from the Congregational minister Josiah Cotton in Plimoth Colony: "Cotton's Indian sermons inadvertently may have reinforced traditional Wampanoag notions of the afterlife.... Cotton's description of a heavenly paradise of material sufficiency, robust health, and social union coincided with several key aspects of an ancestral Algonquian cosmology. Indeed, during the seventeenth century, Indians throughout southeastern New England believed that the souls of the dead traveled southwest to the house of Cautantowwit—the creator deity—where they dwelt amid sumptuous gardens in the company of relatives and ancestor" ("Native American Popular Religion," 165).

10. Leibman, *Indian Converts*, 237.

11. Leibman, *Indian Converts*, 237, 269, 344.

12. Leibman, *Indian Converts*, 212.

13. Leibman, *Indian Converts*, 212, 213.

14. As I have noted, many Wampanoag men acted as ministers in the eighteenth century and established a tradition of Indigenous ministers for Indigenous churches and congregations on Noepe/Martha's Vineyard. When the Harvard Corporation assigned the Mashpee Wampanoag Congregationalists a white minister named Phineas Fish in 1833, their protests led to the Mashpee Revolt, in which the people demanded that the English recognize and honor both their land and their religious rights. Reverend William Apess, a celebrated Pequot minister and liberator, described Fish's fate: "We also proceeded to discharge the missionary, telling him that he and the white people had occupied our meeting house long enough, and

that we now wanted it for our own use" (*Indian Nullification of the Unconstitutional Laws of Massachusetts Relative to the Marshpee Tribe, Or, The Pretended Riot Explained* [Boston: Howe, 1835], 29–30). Indigenous Congregationalists in N'ahteuk/Natick had made the same demand a century earlier, in 1729, when Oliver Peabody was ordained. See Daniel R. Mandell, "'To Live More Like My Christian English Neighbours': Natick Indians in the Eighteenth Century," *William and Mary Quarterly* 48, no. 4 (1991): 561, 562.

15. Leibman, *Indian Converts*, 312.
16. Leibman, *Indian Converts*, 238–39.
17. Leibman, *Indian Converts*, 241, 242.
18. Leibman, *Indian Converts*, 274, 276, 283, 286–87.
19. The Pequossette/Cambridge women's records were not relations but Shepard's personal notes on sessions of trial: private or semiprivate meetings with the minister in which seekers shared their experiences, progress, or setbacks on the path of preparation. See Lori Rogers-Stokes, *Records of Trial from Thomas Shepard's Church in Cambridge, 1638–1649: Heroic Souls* (London: Palgrave Macmillan, 2020), esp. intro. and chap 1.
20. Rogers-Stokes, *Records of Trial*, 91–94, chaps. 2 and 5 passim. For Alice Stedman's story, see George Selement and Bruce C. Woolley, eds., *Thomas Shepard's Confessions* (Boston: Colonial Society of Massachusetts, 1981), 102–5. All of the hesitation, confusion, self-reproach, fear, and despair that Jacqueline M. Henkel notes as typical of Indigenous relations characterize these Englishwomen's narratives ("Represented Authenticity: Native Voices in Seventeenth-Century Conversion Narratives," *New England Quarterly* 67, no. 1 [2014]: 9, 26–45).
21. Leibman, *Indian Converts*, 296, 297.
22. Leibman, *Indian Converts*, 300, 301.
23. Leibman, *Indian Converts*, 328, 334. Interestingly, one woman, Alanchchannum of Nunpaug/Edgartown, who did not claim to experience assurance, had it claimed for her by Mayhew, who admired how she had overcome the temptations of Satan: "But this Alanchchannum having, thro' Grace, been of so good Courage, (which, by the way, is the signification of her Name) as to have overcome, and become Conqueror in this her first and great Combat with her spiritual Enemies, we may henceforward consider her as a new Creature, interested in the new Covenant, and so united to Jesus Christ" (263).
24. Leibman, *Indian Converts*, 261, 266.
25. Harold W. Van Lonkhuyzen, "A Reappraisal of the Praying Indians: Acculturation, Conversion, and Identity at Natick, Massachusetts, 1646–1730," *New England Quarterly* 63, no. 3 (1990): 397, 417.

CHAPTER SEVEN

1. Frontispiece, "Hassanamisco church book, 1731–1774," records, 1731–74, Church of Christ in Grafton, Massachusetts, viewer 3, NEHH, CLA.
2. The first record in the church record book to use the name "Grafton" is dated April 22, 1735: "To the forgoing Letter we Recd an Answer 22 April 1735. to this

Effect that Brother Axtell is Under Suspension by the C^hh in Malbrough. . . . Whereupon Thos Axtell (as above) requested the C^hh in Grafton to Apply to the Revd Mr John Hancock of Lexington & the Revd Mr Baxter of Medfeild for their advice" ("Hassanamisco church book, 1731–1774"), 162, viewer 171).

3. Richard W. Cogley, *John Eliot's Mission to the Indians before King Philip's War* (Cambridge, MA: Harvard University Press, 1999), 143.

4. Richard W. Cogley, "A Seventeenth-Century Native American Family: William of Sudbury and His Four Sons," *New England Historical and Genealogical Register* 153, no. 610 (1999): 174.

5. In fact, the Nipmuc Congregational Church at Hassanamesit was strong and influential before the war: "Hassanamesit and Natick were the only praying towns reported to have had [Indigenous] churches; they served as centers for instruction for teachers who would later go to other villages" (Heather Law, Guido Pezzarossi, and Stephen Mrozowski, *Archaeological Intensive Excavation Hassanamesit Woods Property, The Sarah Boston Farmstead* [Boston: University of Massachusetts Boston, Andrew Fiske Memorial Center for Archaeological Research, 2008], 10).

6. See Lisa Brooks, "The Printer's Revolt: A Narrative of the Captivity of James the Printer," in *Our Beloved Kin: A New History of King Philip's War* (New Haven: Yale University Press, 2018), 169–200. The ransacking of Hassanamesit was publicized as a successful "emptying out" of the town, one that removed the threat of false praying Indians who continued to be dangerous to the English. The note writer probably inherited this view and believed that the town housed only a scattering of Nipmucs by 1731 as the rest had been forcibly removed or had voluntarily disappeared. "Although Hassanamesit persisted as a praying town on paper, it was supposedly emptied, along with all the other praying villages except Natick. Archaeological and documentary research concerning another of the seven original 'Praying Indian' communities, Magunkaquog, has demonstrated that it was not abandoned after King Philip's War. Hassanamesit is viewed as having been a larger and more cohesive community than Magunkaquog so it is not surprising that it survived the vagaries of the conflict" (Law et al., *Archaeological Intensive Excavation Hassanamesit Woods Property*, 12).

7. Daniel R. Mandell, *Behind the Frontier: Indians in Eighteenth-Century Eastern Massachusetts* (Lincoln: University of Nebraska Press, 1996), 26, 29. We know that there were many Indigenous people living in the praying towns after the war, in part because of the Better Rule and Government Act of November 8, 1693, which took effect in 1694 (see "An Act, for The Better Rule and Government of the Indians in their Several Places and Plantations," https://quod.lib.umich.edu). This assigned groups of three Englishmen as guardians of each Indigenous praying town, an indication that these were not the ghost towns that later writers made them out to be. Indeed, many Nipmuc people who fled Hassanamesit during the war or were taken prisoner by the English did not voluntarily disappear but began their return to the place to which they belonged to in the 1680s and 1690s. The Better Rule Act is often interpreted as a moral attempt by "the colonial government to prevent any penetration of white settlers into the reservations," one that was doomed by the greed of squatters: "On the whole, . . . it seems clear that

Massachusetts at least tried hard to protect the Indian land [from] encroachment [although] such policy was not always effective" (Yasu Kawashima, "Legal Origins of the Indian Reservation in Colonial Massachusetts," *American Journal of Legal History* 13, no. 1 [1969]: 51). For an example of the scholarly assumption that none of the Nipmucs who were driven out of their lands during and just after the war ever returned, see Thomas L. Doughton, "A People Who Had 'Vanished,'" in *Strangers in Our Land: The Invasion of Native New England*, n. 58, https://native newengland.wordpress.com).

8. Marie Balsley Taylor, *Indigenous Kinship, Colonial Texts, and the Contested Space of Early New England* (Amherst: University of Massachusetts Press, 2023), 6.

CHAPTER EIGHT

1. For a classic short description of the Halfway Covenant, see Ross W. Beales Jr., "The Halfway Covenant and Religious Scrupulosity: The First Church of Dorchester, Massachusetts, as a Test Case," *William and Mary Quarterly* 31, no. 3 (1974): passim. For a full and masterful and exploration of this opportunity or crisis in English Congregationalism, see also James F. Cooper, *Tenacious of their Liberties: The Congregationalists in Colonial Massachusetts* (Oxford, UK: Oxford University Press, 1999), chap. 5.

2. For a variety of reasons, it was common for people who were members of one church to have their child baptized in another church. For instance, if a person who was a member of a church in Town A moved to Town B and became a parent before they had gone through the process of having their membership transferred to the church in Town B, their infant would be baptized on their account with a note that the baptism was "on the mother's account, she a member at Town A." Congregational records were nothing if not thorough. All of these details were meticulously noted in the hundreds of pages of record books that I have read.

3. This story is well told in Robert G. Pope, *The Half-Way Covenant: Church Membership in Puritan New England* (Eugene, OR: Wipf and Stock, 1969).

4. For examples of people with "neither ancestral or spousal link to the church" who joined the church through the Halfway Covenant, see Katharine Gerbner, "Beyond the 'Halfway Covenant': Church Membership, Extended Baptism, and Outreach in Cambridge, Massachusetts, 1656–1667," *New England Quarterly* 85, no. 2 (2012): passim.

5. The church records offer many phrases to identify the status of Halfway Covenant members of the congregation. There was no standardization, and the same church—even the same minister—might record Halfway Covenant members as "joining the church," being "received into church communion" (meaning communion with the church body, not taking the sacrament of communion), "received into full communion" or "received into full communion with us," and other variations that use the word *full* in a misleading or unclear way. Of course, the meaning was clear to the minister when he wrote the record. For many instances of this in a single congregation, see Beales, "The Half-Way Covenant and Religious Scrupulosity."

6. Pope, *The Half-Way Covenant*, 186, 187.
7. Pope, *The Half-Way Covenant*, 246.
8. Cooper, *Tenacious of their Liberties*, 94, 95. Cooper also resolves the question of whether the Halfway Covenant was just evidence of Puritan declension (see esp. chap. 7).
9. Richard J. Boles, *Dividing the Faith: The Rise of Segregated Churches in the Early American North* (New York: New York University Press, 2020), 16.
10. Cooper, *Tenacious of their Liberties*, 110.
11. Richard A. Bailey, *Race and Redemption in Puritan New England* (Oxford, UK: Oxford University Press, 2011), 17, 18.
12. Quoted in Michna, "The Long Road to Sainthood: Indian Christians, the Doctrine of Preparation, and the Halfway Covenant of 1662," *Church History* (2020): 48.
13. Michna, "The Long Road to Sainthood," 45, 57.
14. See Lisa Brooks, *Our Beloved Kin: A New History of King Philip's War* (New Haven, CT: Yale University Press, 2018), passim, esp. chap. 5.
15. "According to Nipmuc chief Cheryl Holley, James probably did not have children of his own, but his lateral descendants took his name" (Brooks, *Our Beloved Kin*, 320).
16. Moses Printer and his wife Mary Pogenit died in 1729, when his daughter and nieces were nine and ten years old ("Printer, Moses,—1728," Native Northeast Portal, https://nativenortheastportal.com (hereafter cited as NNP). I have relied on two sources for the Printer dates: Donna Rae Gould, *Contested Places: The History and Meaning of Hassanamisco* (Ann Arbor, MI: Proquest UMI Dissertation Publishing, 2011), 211; and "Printer, Sarah" and "Printer, Sarah, 1717–1794," NNP. There is some disagreement between Gould and NNP, but there are no major discrepancies. NNP does not include an entry for George Muckamaug; I rely on the Hassanamesit/Grafton church records (cited in the text) and the Grafton vital records for him (*Vital Records of Grafton, Massachusetts to the end of the year 1849* (Worcester, MA: Franklin Rice, 1906), 94).
17. The record for Sarah Printer, daughter of Moses Printer and Mary Pogenit Printer, is unclear. NNP lists four daughters for the couple—Elizabeth, Bethia, Sarah, and Mary—and states that, after both parents died, "the children were bound out as apprentices" ("Printer, Moses,—1728"). The introductory timeline that begins box 1, folder 1 of the John Milton Earle Papers confirms that "an Indian girl daughter of Moses Printer called Betty or Elizabeth put as apprentice to John Hazelton" and that in 1738 "Zachariah Tom had married Mary Printer d of Moses." It does not specify what happened to Sarah Printer, so I have relied on both NNP and Gould's *Contested Places* (211) for the information she was the daughter who married Peter Lawrence. This means that the part of the Earle timeline that reads "Peter Lawrence m. d of Moses Printer" must refer to Sarah, not Bethia or Elizabeth. See Papers Related to Commissioners of the Indians Reports for Massachusetts, John Milton Earle Papers (manuscript), box 1, folder 1: 1715–1859, viewer 3–4.
18. All citations from the Hassanamesit/Grafton church record book are from "Church Records, 1731–1774, Grafton, Mass. Congregational Church," NEHH, CLA. For simplicity's sake, I've included shortened references in the text. The

page number refers to the number the minister wrote on the page of the actual record book (e.g., HG 4).
19. See Gerbner, "Beyond the 'Halfway Covenant,'" 291, 294; and Harry Stout and Catherine Brekus, "Declension, Gender, and the 'New Religious History,'" in *Belief and Behavior: Essays in the New Religious History*, ed. Philip R. Vandermeer and Robert P. Swierenga (New Brunswick, NJ: Rutgers University Press, 1991), 17.
20. In the Hassanamesit/Grafton church records between 1731 and 1774, sixty-two entries record children baptized on their mother's account, eighteen on their father's account.
21. Sarah Robins was born in about 1689 to Robin Petavit, a sachem. (For the full story, see Cheryll Toney Holley, "Unravelling Six Generations of Nipmuc Sarahs," April 22, 2104, https://cherylltoneyholley.com.) She would eventually have a daughter, a granddaughter, and a great-granddaughter named Sarah, which was fitting, given that the biblical Sarah, the wife of Abraham, was the mother of Isaac and of all Israel. Sarah Robins herself would become a Nipmuc matriarch whose descendants remained on the land she had inherited from her father into the mid-1800s. The English identified her as a landed proprietor in Hassanamesit and as the head of one of the seven families whom they had identified as deserving of a parcel of land after the 1728 sale (John Milton Earle Papers, box 1, viewer 56–57). When reading or discussing what was known as the Sarah Robins property in Hassanamesit, we must acknowledge the English reality that contemporary land records represent: "The name used to identify the parcel in English documents and maps reflects the male centered legal system that produced them. The Native reality was different. Land was passed down through the female line in Nipmuc society and that actuality is borne out by a history of female headed households on the property. Their story is one of accommodation, resistance and cultural continuity" (Heather Law, Guido Pezzarossi, Stephen Mrozowski, *Archaeological Intensive Excavation Hassanamesit Woods Property, The Sarah Boston Farmstead* (Boston: University of Massachusetts Boston, Andrew Fiske Memorial Center for Archaeological Research, 2008), 13–14). While it is confusing to read about Sarah Robins when one is searching for the Sarah Muckamaug who appears in the 1728 sale ("Peter Mukumuck & Sarah his wife"), the use of that name upheld Indigenous governance that allowed women to own land and pushed back on the English system that did not allow them to retain their own land after marriage, when female ownership was automatically transferred to the husband. A survey of property dated May 17, 1729, was "laid out for Peter Muckamaug Alias Sarah Robins." According to Holley, "though Native, Peter was not from Hassanamesit so the land could not be allotted to (or owned by) him. When Sarah Robins [Muckamaug] died, the land passed to her children" (Cheryll Toney Holley, "Hassanamisco Indians," *For All My Relations: New England's Communities of Color*, August 22, 2012, https://forallmyrelations.blogspot.com).
22. Linford D. Fisher, *The Indian Great Awakening: Religion and the Shaping of Native Cultures in Early America* (New York: Oxford University Press, 2012), 67.
23. This trend would continue through the Revolutionary War, putting another strain on Indigenous women who had been left behind temporarily or through widowhood, such as Abigail Printer Abraham, whose sons Fortune Burnee Jr.

and Joseph Anthony Jr. would fight in that war after her death. Neither returned: Joseph died, and Fortune was reported to have deserted and never reappeared in Hassanamesit/Grafton. See Heather Law Pezzarossi, "Assembling Indigeneity: Rethinking Innovation, Tradition and Indigenous Materiality in a 19th-Century Native Toolkit," *Journal of Social Anthropology* 14, no. 3 (2014): 342.

24. Marriage was transitioning in this period from the strictly civil ceremony it had always been for Congregationalists to a ceremony that ministers might conduct. Ministers made this difference clear when they were entering a marriage record to give to the town clerk: if they were recording marriages they had solemnized, they might title a page "Names of people married by me," or they might write "by me" at the end of a record. Samuel Prentice did not note he had married the Abrahams, so they were married civilly, in keeping with traditional Congregationalism.

25. Abigail Printer's acceptance of Andrew Abraham's Congregationalism was an extension of the idea that "some Christianized Indians followed family members into [the] new form of spirituality. Generational ties and kinship connections likely motivated many New England Indians who, at least partially in order to maintain harmony and attachment with blood relatives, accepted Christianization" (Jason Eden, "'Therefore ye Are no More Strangers and Foreigners': Indians, Christianity, and Political Engagement in Colonial Plimouth and on Martha's Vineyard," *American Indian Quarterly* 38, no. 1 [2014]: 41).

26. Neal Salisbury, "Embracing Ambiguity: Native Peoples and Christianity in Seventeenth-Century North America," *Ethnohistory* 50, no. 2 (2003): 250.

27. *Vital Records of Grafton, Massachusetts to the end of the year 1849* (Worcester, MA: Franklin Rice, 1906), 9. The value of Congregational church records is made clear by the fact that the John Milton Earle Papers record that the Abrahams had only one son, David: "[Abigail Printer was] married to one Abram, by whom she had one son, named David, who died without legal heirs some time in the year 1784" (box 1, viewer 92–93).

28. "Massachusetts, Worcester County, Probate Files, 1731–1925," http://familysearch.org.

29. "Worcester County, MA: Probate File Papers, 1731–1881," http://americanancestors.org.

30. "Worcester County, MA: Probate File Papers, 1731–1881."

31. "Worcester County, MA: Probate File Papers, 1731–1881."

32. "When the men died in the colonial wars or left the community, the women left behind were unable to handle the new crops and technologies or to renew older traditions. [Indigenous] households [that] contained only women [who] were unable to work the land, having successfully adopted colonial gender roles and lost their native agrarian skills . . . [were] asked to sell their combined holding [because] 'being brought up in Household business [they] are incapable of improving said lands.' The acculturation that was to have been their salvation became, in the end, their destruction" (Daniel Mandell, *Behind the Frontier: Indians in Eighteenth-Century Eastern Massachusetts* [Lincoln: University of Nebraska Press, 1996], 119).

33. Martha Printer was Abigail Printer Abraham's much younger sister, probably Sarah Printer Sr.'s last child.

34. Massachusetts Archives Collection, Colonial Period, 1622–1788, https://familysearch.org.
35. For an overview, see Stephen A. Mrozowski and D. Rae Gould, "Building Histories That Have Futures: The Benefits of Collaborative Research," *Journal of the World Archaeological Congress* 15, no. 1 (2019), passim.
36. Massachusetts Archives Collection, Colonial Period, 1622–1788.
37. *Vital Records of Grafton, Massachusetts*, 29.
38. *Vital Records of Grafton, Massachusetts*, 178.
39. Massachusetts Archives Collection, Colonial Period, 1622–1788. The English records are, as usual, confusing. The court record states that Temple paid £34 for his thirty acres, but the Worcester County deed signed seven months later on March 30, 1750, by Temple, Sarah Printer Burnee, and Fortune Burnee states that Temple paid "four Pounds Lawful Money" ("Massachusetts, Land Records, 1620–1986," https://familysearch.org). This may be a sum that Temple actually paid to the Burnees rather than to the trustees.
40. Charles Martyn, *The William Ward Genealogy: The History of the Descendants of William Ward of Sudbury, Mass., 1638–1925* (New York: Ward, 1925), 85–86.
41. Hezekiah Ward appeared in another court record related to Sarah Muckamaug Burnee, dated February 5, 1755, and regarding her estate. (She had died in June 1751.) Sarah had been ill for a long time, as demonstrated by a petition from three Englishmen—Charles Brigham, Joseph Merriam, and Deacon Abner Stow—asking for repayment of the money that Ward spent on caring for her: "[D]uring her sickness she was under the Care of Mr. Hezekiah Ward there placed by your petitioners as Selectmen aforesaid." Ward was supposed to have been paid with funds that the trustees held from "the sale of some of said Squaws Land, [but] upon her Death still Lies in their Hands unapplied" ("Petition of Charles Brigham, Joseph Merriam, and Abner Howe, Selectmen of the Town of Grafton, to the Massachusetts General Court," NNP).
42. For instance, on January 28, 1732, in Grafton, "Brother James Laland, & Hannah his Wife, first Signified to their Pastor and renewed before Several of the Brethren of our Chh, And A Considerable Many Witnesses" their desire to have their young daughter Prudence baptized in their home—"in the fathers house Because it was Apprehended by the Parents and others, to be very near its End" (HG 13).
43. Massachusetts Archives Collection, Colonial Period, 1622–1788.
44. The trustees inserted this note.
45. *Vital Records of Grafton, Massachusetts*, 362. The first book of extant Hassanamesit/Grafton church records ends on August 22, 1774, so doesn't record this death, but one would expect to find them in the second book, which ran from 1774 to 1828. Strangely, the only deaths recorded in the second book are dated 1827–28, with two outliers from 1788 and one from the 1800s. Baptisms and marriages were recorded as usual. Possibly there was another book for recording deaths, but that would have been an unorthodox choice for a minister, and the church would surely have opposed it.
46. "Massachusetts, Land Records, 1620–1986."
47. John Milton Earle Papers, box 2, viewer 46–47; Frederick Clifton Pierce, *History of Grafton, Worcester County, Massachusetts: From Its Early Settlement by the Indians in 1647 to the Present Time, 1879* ... (Worcester, MA: Hamilton, 1879), 61–62.

48. Pierce, *History of Grafton*, 61.
49. "Most noteworthy was the practice of English families helping elderly native neighbors and putting claims for this work after the individuals died. In many instance the children of these elderly residents did not have the means to pay these claims. The lone asset available was often land" (Stephen A. Mrozowski, "Violence and Dispossession at the Intersection of Colonialism and Capitalist Accumulation," *Society for Historical Archaeology* 53 [2019]: 502). "Effectively the court thus decided that the land was mortgaged for the debts, leaving no alternatives for renegotiating the debts if relatives or other heirs had wanted to do that" (Jeremy Dupertuis Bangs, *Indian Deeds: Land Transactions in Plymouth Colony, 1620–1691* [Boston: New England Historical and Genealogical Society, 2002], 191).
50. "Worcester County, MA: Probate File Papers, 1731–1881."
51. "Worcester County, MA: Probate File Papers, 1731–1881."
52. "Printer, Abigail,–1776," NNP.
53. John Milton Earle Papers, box 2, viewer 164–65.
54. John Milton Earle Papers, box 2, viewer 164–165.
55. *Vital Records of Grafton, Massachusetts*, 130.
56. *Vital Records of Grafton, Massachusetts*, 157, 130.
57. A case occurred in Agawam/Rowley in early 1705 that echoed the Thomas Miller case. A Black woman enslaved by Major Francis Wainwright named Samuel Ayres as the father of her child while she was in labor. This was a common time for unmarried women to be asked to name the unknown father as it was assumed that during their "time of travail" they would be unlikely to lie. The unnamed woman did not claim to have been raped, so the case fell into the category of fornication, and Ayres was banned from communion. On March 6, 1705, he went to the minister "of his own accord, and acknowledged the substance of what ye above S^d Negro charges him with, vizt carnal copulation with her." A church meeting was held on the matter on June 26, where Ayres read a statement admitting the fornication but denying his paternity. By this time, the still unnamed woman had apparently stated that her child might be either his or another man's. Ayres was banned from communion for another month while the church sorted out the issue. He appeared before the church again a year later, in October 1706, and "produced his confession for his great Sin of fowl uncleanness; wch was accepted, & he released from his Censure, & restored to communion." The minister Samuel Philips had died in 1696. Ayres's confession proves that Philips's successor, Edward Payson, and the church body he represented did not insist, as they had with Miller, that Ayres acknowledge the harm he had done to the Black woman and her (possibly his) child as well as to his own soul ("The Phillips Diary [church records], 1664–1784, First Congregational Church in Rowley, Mass.," 200, 207. NEHH, CLA).

CHAPTER NINE

1. For the overall story of Solomon Prentice, informed in part by the Hassanamesit/Grafton church records but omitting the sensational entries that tell the story of his deceit, see Douglas L. Winiarski, *Darkness Falls on the Land of Light:*

Experiencing Religious Awakenings in Eighteenth-Century New England (Chapel Hill: University of North Carolina Press, 2017), esp. 413-20.

2. The long probate file is found at "Worcester County, MA: Probate File Papers, 1731-1881," https://www.americanancestors.org.

3. Harold Field Worthley, *An Inventory of the Records of the Particular (Congregational) Churches of Massachusetts Gathered 1620-1805* (Cambridge, MA: Harvard University Press, 1970), 610.

4. Isaac Backus did not identify the English Ezekiel Cole as Indigenous: "There had been a great revival of religion in the Congregational society in Sutton, in the year 1741, and a separate church was formed among them, and Mr. Ezekiel Cole was ordained their pastor, January 31, 1751. But they were broken and scattered afterwards, and a Baptist church was gathered there" (*A History of New England, with Particular Reference to the Denomination of Christians called Baptists* [Newton, MA: Backus Historical Society, 1871], 176-77).

5. Frederick Clifton Pierce, *History of Grafton, Worcester County, Massachusetts: From Its Early Settlement by the Indians in 1647 to the Present Time, 1879 . . .* (Worcester, MA: Hamilton, 1879), 174.

6. All citations from the Hassanamesit/Grafton church record book are from "Hassanamisco church book, 1731-1774, Church of Christ in Grafton, Mass.," NEHH, CLA. For simplicity's sake, I've included shortened references in the text. The page number listed may refer to either the number the minister wrote on the page of the actual record book (e.g., HG 4, v21) or the page in the viewer (HG 21).

7. Pierce, *History of Grafton*, 174.

8. Ross W. Beales Jr., "The Ecstasy of Sarah Prentice: Death, Re-birth, and the Great Awakening in Grafton, Massachusetts" *Historical Journal of Massachusetts* 25, no. 2 (1997): 6; Douglas L. Winiarski, "New Perspectives on the Northampton Communion Controversy I: David Hall's Diary and Letter to Edward Billing," *Jonathan Edwards Studies* 3, no. 2 (2013): 282-94.

9. Stephen Mrozowski and Heather Law Pezzarossi, "The Archaeology of Hassanamesit Woods: The Sarah Burnee/Sarah Boston Farmstead," *University of Massachusetts Boston Cultural Resource Management Study* 69 (October 2015): 19. It is disheartening to see Pierce's history quoted here. The longevity of this type of nineteenth-century history is clearly correlated to the lack of access to church records.

10. Anthony Vaver, ed., *The Diary of Rev. Ebenezer Parkman* (Westborough, MA: Westborough Center for History and Culture, Ebenezer Parkman Project), 51.

11. Ross W. Beales Jr., "Solomon Prentice's Narrative of the Great Awakening," *Proceedings of the Massachusetts Historical Society*, 3rd ser., 83 (1971): 139. This outreach and Ezekiel Cole's response to it makes me reconsider Daniel Mandell's assertion that "Indian communities in Massachusetts were barely affected by the Great Awakening" (*Behind the Frontier: Indians in Eighteenth-Century Eastern Massachusetts* [Lincoln: University of Nebraska Press, 1996], 127).

12. "Records of the Court of General Sessions of the Peace from the County of Worcester, Massachusetts, 1731-1862," https://familysearch.org. Note that Ezekiel Cole's Indigenous identity was erased in the civil record as he was transformed into a Black man.

13. For painfully ironic examples, see Roger Thompson, "Pregnant Brides and Broken Promises" and "Family and Community," in *Sex in Middlesex: Popular Mores in a Massachusetts County, 1649–1699* (Amherst: University of Massachusetts Press, 1986), 54–70, 155–200.
14. Vaver, *The Diary of Rev. Ebenezer Parkman*, 22.
15. Vaver, *The Diary of Rev. Ebenezer Parkman*, n.p. Parkman's diaries from September 1728 to January 1740 have been lost. In September 2022, Ross Beales Jr. generously shared a transcription of the page containing the first entry, dated July 15, 1736.
16. Vaver, *The Diary of Rev. Ebenezer Parkman*, 39.
17. Beales, "Solomon Prentice's Narrative of the Great Awakening," 141, 143.
18. Vaver, *The Diary of Rev. Ebenezer Parkman*, 47.
19. David Hall, diary entry, October 22, 1752, n.p., David Hall diaries, 1740–69, MHS.
20. Vaver, *The Diary of Rev. Ebenezer Parkman*, 51.
21. This page and many others in the second church record book at Hassanamesit/Grafton, 1774–1828, are not numbered, so I've inserted the viewer page number from the NEHH digitization.

CHAPTER TEN

1. All citations from the N'ahteuk/Natick church record book are from "Church records, 1721–1794, First Congregational Church in Natick, Mass.," NEHH, CLA. For simplicity's sake, I've included shortened references in the text. The page numbers refer either to the number the minister wrote on the page of the actual record book (e.g., N 4), or to the viewer number (N v74).
2. Harold Field Worthley, *An Inventory of the Records of the Particular (Congregational) Churches of Massachusetts Gathered 1620–1805* (Cambridge, MA: Harvard University Press, 1970), 400. His statement that the second church in N'ahteuk/Natick "was gathered on Dec. 3, 1729 . . . in place of the extinct Indian church of 1660" is unusual in its inaccuracy.
3. "Report from the Committee of Honorable Commissioners for ye Indian Affairs, At a Meeting of ye President & Fellows of Harvard College at Cambridge. Oct. 28. 1729," Harvard College Records, vol. 16, part 2, book 4, 576–77, CSA.
4. Even the records at NEHH are titled "Church Records, 1721–1794, First Congregational Church in Natick, Mass.," although Oliver Peabody acknowledged them to be the records of the second church.
5. See Julius H. Rubin, *Tears of Repentance: Christian Indian Identity and Community in Colonial Southern New England* (Lincoln: University of Nebraska Press, 2013), 83.
6. "Church Records, 1721–1794, First Congregational Church in Natick, Mass.," NEHH, CLA.
7. Stephen A. Mrozowski and D. Rae Gould, "Building Histories That Have Futures: The Benefits of Collaborative Research," *Journal of the World Archaeological Congress* 15, no. 1 (2019): 407–8.

CHAPTER ELEVEN

1. Harold Field Worthley, *An Inventory of the Records of the Particular (Congregational) Churches of Massachusetts Gathered 1620–1805* (Cambridge, MA: Harvard University Press, 1970), 527. Those ministers were Samuel Phillips (1651–96), Edward Payson (1682–1732), Jedidiah Jewett (1729–74), Ebenezer Bradford (1782–1801), and David Tullar (1803–39).
2. Daniel R. Mandell, *Behind the Frontier: Indians in Eighteenth-Century Eastern Massachusetts* (Lincoln: University of Nebraska Press, 1996), 105.
3. Richard J. Boles, *Dividing the Faith: The Rise of Segregated Churches in the Early American North* (New York: New York University Press, 2020), 42.
4. Massachusetts Archives Collection, Colonial Period, 1622–1788, https://familysearch.org.
5. "Committee of Natick yr letter of 29th May 1722 to Mr. Leverett," May 29, 1722, Records of the Trustees of the Charity of Edward Hopkins, HUY 26, box 2, folder 18, Harvard University Archives.
6. "Petition of Benjamin Tray to the Massachusetts General Court," March 17, 1741, NNP.
7. Court of General Sessions of the Peace, Middlesex County, Massachusetts, https://familysearch.org.
8. "The Phillips Diary (church records), 1664–1784, First Congregational Church in Rowley, Mass.," NEHH, CLA. For simplicity's sake, I've included shortened references in the text. The page numbers refer to the number the minister wrote on the page of the actual record book (e.g., AR 249).
9. Minutes, "At a Meeting of ye Presidt & Fellows of Harvard College in the Library Novr 16: 1719," Harvard College Records, vol. 16, book 4, part 2, 446.
10. Harvard College Records, vol. 16, book 4, part 2, 455, emphasis added.
11. Harvard College Records, vol. 16, book 4, part 2, 476.
12. Harvard College Records, vol. 16, book 4, part 2, 483.
13. Harvard College Records, vol. 16, book 4, part 2, 513.
14. Harvard College Records, vol. 16, book 4, part 2, 515.
15. Harvard College Records, vol. 16, book 4, part 2, 540, 558, 598, 609, 645, 713.
16. Harvard College Records, vol. 16, book 4, part 2, 748, 758, 783, 789, 803.
17. Harvard College Records, vol. 16, book 4, part 2, 805.
18. Harvard College Records, vol. 16, book 4, part 2, 818.
19. Oliver Peabody Jr., letter to the Harvard Corporation, April 2, 1752, Harvard University. Corporation, Records of Grants for Work among the Indians, 1720–1812, UAI 20.720, box 1, folder 9, Harvard University Archives.
20. Oliver Peabody Jr., letter to the Harvard Corporation, April 2, 1752.
21. Boles *Dividing the Faith*, 77–78.
22. Boles, *Dividing the Faith*, 42.
23. "Church records, 1643–1805, in the First Church in Wenham, Mass.," viewer 156, NEHH, CLA.
24. "Church records, 1684–1800, Old North Church in Marblehead, Mass.," viewer 111, NEHH, CLA.

25. Oliver N. Bacon, *A History of Natick, from its First Settlement in 1651 to the Present Time; with Notices of the First White Families* (Boston: Damrell and Moore, 1856), 64.

CONCLUSION

1. Jill Lepore, *The Name of War: King Philip's War and the Origins of American Identity* (New York: Vintage, 1999), 74.
2. Samuel Symonds, report (April 1676), in Lepore, *The Name of War*, 77. Lepore also notes that English soldiers "could be punished for abandoning the protection of houses too soon" (78, 90).
3. Lepore, *The Name of War*, 76, 77.
4. Lepore, *The Name of War*, 79.
5. Lepore, *The Name of War*, 77.

Index

Abraham, Andrew Jr.: 133–34; Halfway membership, 110; marriage, 114; will 115–16

Abraham, David: Alstead, New Hampshire, 122, baptism, 115; civil record, 116; Revolutionary War, 122

Abraham, Elizabeth: disappearance from church records, 123–26; full membership, 114; Halfway membership, 111; land sales, 120

Abraham, John, 115–16, 118, 122

Abraham, Jonas, 115–16, 122

abundance, English perception of, 29, 31–36

admission: to full communion, 77, 92–97, 112, 114, 153

admonition, 81–85

adultery: in church records, 7; Jacob Chalcom, 76–85; Nathaniel Coochuck, 80; distinct from fornication, 124–25; Thomas Miller, 55–59, 61, 71–72, 74; Thomas Peegun, 79

Agawam/Rowley: 7, 16, 20, 22, 157; church records in Blodgett, 58–59, 68; enclosure case in, 36; and Mattabeseck/Middleboro church, 65, 66, 70–72; Thomas Miller case, 59–75; minister salary in, 160–61; ordination record in, 24; Wainwright adultery case in, 197n57

Anthony, Joseph, 122

assurance: concept of, 1, 42; and Pequossette/Cambridge women, 48–50, 95; role in church gathering, 13–15, 106; Wampanoag compared with English, 8, 48–49, 90–98, 190n23

authentic: conversion, 15–16, 20, 39–41, 43–49, 51, 103, 153; repentance, 17, 59, 64–65, 71–72

Badger, Rev. Stephen, 84, 114, 154–57, 167

Bailey, Richard A., 40, 49, 109

Balsley Taylor, Marie, 6, 10, 19, 22, 43, 104

baptism: infant, 119, 131–32, 134; purpose of, 8–9, 91, 106, 119; through the Halfway Covenant, 8, 107–8, 111–16, 124, 133; separatist, 148; transfer of, 192n2

Black Congregationalists, 5–6, 13, 39–40, 77, 108–9

Blodgett, George, 58–59

Boles, Richard, 5, 39, 158, 166

Bremer, Francis, 6

Brooks, Lisa, 18–20, 23, 26, 66, 110

Brooks, Noah, 146, 149

Burnee, Fortune, 118, 122

Burnee, Sarah Muckamaug: 171, 194n21; death, 122; disappearance from civil record, 118; land sales, 118, 120

Chalcom, Jacob: 7; admonition of, 81–85; adultery case, 76–81; church membership, 76

charity: church, 66, 77–80, 84, 136, 145; judgment of, 40

children: baptism of, 8–9, 76, 105–7, 111–12, 148–49; instruction of, 97, 134–35
church belonging, 9, 18, 76, 90, 105, 107–8, 112–14, 116, 122, 125, 149
church body: 4–5, 15–17, 23, 62; versus congregation, 13–15, 20, 60, 67; contrast with civil society, 6–7; and excommunication, 60, 83–85, 124–25; gathering of, 14, 91, 93; kinship between, 65, 72–75
church covenant, 15, 18, 35, 66, 91, 107, 151
church discipline: 4–5, 7, 50–51, 112; in Indigenous churches, 90–91; and rebuke-repent-restore, 16–17, 60, 65, 79, 82
church government, 6, 167
church membership: 14–15, 85; Indigenous, 8–9, 48–49, 96–97, 108–9, 152, 185n42
church meetings: 4, 6, 16, 21, 78, 157; minister's role in, 26, role in discipline cases, 80–81, 137–38, 140–42, 146–47
church record books, 2–4, 10, 106, 173; Agawam/Rowley entries, 56, 59, 64, 73–75; Hassanamesit/Grafton entries, 9, 99–104, 110, 114, 118, 124–25, 131, 133, 137, 149; loss of, 3–4, 10, 156–57; N'ahteuk/Natick entries, 78–79, 81, 84, 151; Rev. Edward Payson and, 160–62; Rev. Oliver Peabody and, 157–58, 167; Rev. Solomon Prentice and, 140–41, 143–45
civil courts: 5, 7, 25, 18; Chalcom case, 76–78; Cole case, 134–36; Miller case, 55–57, 61; ministers and, 159–60
civil government: 2, 13, 16, 20, 35, 113, 123, 154, 166; contrasted with church justice, 4–7, 10, 17–19, 22, 26–27, 72, 158
civil records: 28, 58, 84, 105; black removal from, 77, 118; unreliability of, 4, 105, 116, 118, 121–23, 129, 187n2
Cole, Ezekiel, Rev. (English), 130, 147–49
Cole, Ezekiel (Nipmuc): accusation against Solomon Prentice, 135–36; church membership, 133, 145, 149–50; lay exhorting, 131, 142–46; Pierce anecdote, 130; separatist claims against, 131–32, 147–48; and the Willard family, 133–36
Collins, Rev. Nathaniel, 67, 69–71
colonization: and conversion, 6–9, 42–44, 48, 51; economics of, 29–30, 35, 159–60; Indigenous identity and, 41, 45–46, 154: opposed to Congregationalism, 10, 18–20
communion: banning from, 79; full communion status, 76–77, 80, 91–97, 113–14, 119, 133–34, 148, 152; sacrament of, 8, 19, 145–46, 149; withdrawing from, 124, 137–38, 143–44
Congregational ideal, 4–5, 7, 9–10, 35, 171–73; and discipline cases, 74–75, 81, 85; and Indigenous society, 18–22, 26–27; and ministers, 18, 22–27, 90–91, 158–59, 165
Congregational kinship, 6–7, 10, 26–27, 138; and assurance, 8; and church health, 16–18; failure of, 19–20, 116–17, 125–26, 141; Indigenous parallels, 18–21; spiritual kinship model, 15–20
conversion: and Indigenous cultural abandonment, 39–40, 46–47, 49, 108, 112, 153–54
Coochuck, Nathaniel, 79–80, 152
Cooper, James F., 17, 32, 35, 108
creole religious practice: 44; English, 47–48; Indigenous, 51. See also syncretism

Eastern Woodlands, the, xv–xvi
ecclesiastical council: 21, 24, 138–40; alignment with Indigenous practice, 21; in Hassanamesit/Grafton, 138, 140–44, 147. See also synod
Eliot, Rev. John, 10, 21, 40, 42, 44, 110; and Indigenous churches, 99, 101–2, 152; missions, 22–23, 38, 91
enclosure, 30–31, 36
English-style house, 26, 47, 118, 120, 169–70, 172; historic, 170–71
Ephraim, Hannah Weekucks, 77–78
Ephraim, Joseph Sr., 78–79, 152

European: Christianity 19, 43–44, 51, 73, 94–95; society and colonization, 29, 36, 46
excommunication: 17, 26, 62; Jacob Chalcom, 81–82; Thomas Miller, 59, 67–74

First Great Awakening, the: 9, and Ezekiel Cole, 129–31; Halfway Covenant and, 107–8; Rev. Solomon Prentice and, 132–33; Abraham Temple and, 119–20; Elizabeth Abraham Tommack and, 124
Fisher, Linford, 7, 21, 40, 47, 112
fornication, 124–25
full communion, received to, 76–77, 95–97, 113–15, 133–34, 152, 192n5. *See also* full membership

Gould, Rae, 45–46, 156
grace: concept of, 8, 13–14, 39–40, 90, 97; and rebuke-repent-restore, 66–69, 84
Grosvenor, Rev. Daniel, 122, 125, 149

Halfway Covenant, the: Andrew Abraham, 110; Deborah Abraham, 110–12; controversy over, 105–6; definition of, 8–9, 192n5; Elizabeth Abraham, 111; Ezekiel Cole, 133–34; George Muckamaug, 112–13; Jacob Chalcom, 76; and King Philip's War, 99, 107–9; purpose of, 105–6, 126; Samuel John, 114; Synod of 1662 on, 105–6; Ephraim Sherman, 121; Hezekiah Ward Jr., 119
Hall, Rev. David: xiii; and Ezekiel Cole, 147–49; salary, 25
Hannit, Japheth, 43, 90–91
Hartford county court records, 55–57
Harvard College, 109, 158, 162–64
Harvard Corporation: 159–60; Rev. Oliver Peabody and, 153, 162–66
Hassanamesit/Grafton: xvi; alias Hassanamisco, 99–100; church records in, xii, 8–9, 105; destruction of first church in, 101–4; Indigenous education in, 121; King Philip's War, 102–3, 105, 110

heaven, 13, 66, 71, 173; Wampanoag concept of, 8, 90–94
Hutchinson, Rev. Aaron, 122, 125, 147

Indian Converts, 8, 89, 91–98
Indigenous belonging, 20, 113
Indigenous conversion: early missionary accounts of, 40; generational, 89–90; arguments against, 40–45; interrogating, 39, 42, 49–50; and survivance, 7, 41, 44–45
Indigenous disappearance: from civil records, 77, 116, 122, 187n2; and conversion, 40–42, 97–98; myth of, 77, 90; in N'ahteuk/Natick, 101–4, 152–56
Indigenous kinship, 42–43, 48–49, 90–97
Individuals, 8, 20, 90, 97, 106; relationship with church body, 14–17, 21, 26, 49, 73–75, 80, 93, 101–2, 108; and wealth, 30–35
infant baptism. *See* baptism

King George's War, 114–16
King Philip's War: 10, 45, 47, 102–4; 169–71; and the Halfway Covenant, 105–9, 112, 126; and Indigenous churches, 8, 152–54
kinship: Congregational, 2, 8, 16–18, 65, 138; failure of, 19–20, 26–27, 116–17, 121–22, 125–26, 141; contrast with civil law, 6, 58–59, 61, 63–64, 72, 75; and Indigenous belonging, 20, 22–23, 42–43, 47, 49, 91–97, 109, 180n16

land grabbing, 28, 35–37, 47, 116, 125
land sales, 28, 33–34, 117–18, 194n21
Lawrence, Esther, 124–5
Larson, John Lauritz, 28–30
lay people, 2, 35; and exhorting, 131, 142–45, 146, 148; preachers, 102, 131
Lepore, Jill, 169

Manchauge/Sutton, 25, 130, 139, 147–49
Mandell, Daniel, 19, 35, 49, 51, 158

markets: in England, 29–30, 165; global, 31–33; ministers and, 25, 165–70
Massachusett Congregationalists, 22, 78–79, 110, 152, 158–59, 163, 167
Mather, Cotton, 26, 44, 55
Mather, Increase, 171
Mattabeseck/Middletown: church gathering at, 60, 65–66, 69; Rev. Nathaniel Collins and, 67, 69–71; Thomas Miller 55–57, 59–75
Mayhew, Rev. Experience: 7, 43; *Indian Converts*, 8, 89; records of Wampanoag assurance, 90–97
Mayhew family, 38
meetinghouse, 4, 13–16, 130, 171–74; and baptism, 119, 125; split in N'ahteuk/Natick, 154–55, 166–67; repair, 122, 172
Miller, Isabel, 56–58, 60–61, 64–66, 69
Miller, Thomas: adultery, 55–58; civil trial, 55–57, 72; excommunication, 62, 67–71; guilt for wife's death, 60–61, 64–66, 70–72, 74–75; return to Agawam/Rowley, 73–75
ministers: Indigenous, 10, 39, 46–47, 90–91, 97, 102, 152; and church records, xi–xii, 2–4, 125, 145, 157; and ecclesiastical councils, 138–40; lack of civil standing, 24–27, 159–60; funerals of, 166–67; ordination of, 24, 27, 148, 152, 154; role, 16, 24, 26, 101; salary, 9, 25, 29, 47, 172, 159–64, 166, 178n28; compared with saunkskwa and sachem, 18–23; and the supernatural, 48, 94
missions: 39–41, 166–67, 178n32; Rev. John Eliot, 21–22, 101; Experience Mayhew, 7–8, 38, 43, 89, 96
mixed churches and congregations, 5, 7, 8–10, 105–8; in N'ahteuk/Natick, 152–53, 162, 167
Mrozowski, Stephen, 38, 45–46, 132, 156
Muckamaug, George, 41, 58, 112–15, 133
mutual watch, 8, 20, 34, 113, 115, 173–74

N'ahteuk/Natick: church division in, 155, 165–67; church records of, xii, 3, 10, 76–77, 157–58; first church in, 101, 151–54; early rebuke-repent-restore in, 22; second church in, 152–53
Nashouohkamuk/Chilmark: 43, 48, 95
Naumkeag/Stoneham, 2, 24
Nettleton, Sarah, 55–57, 68–69
Nipmucs: 99–100, 105, 109–10; churches, 10, 77, 101–4, 152, 158–59, 163, 191n5; Ezekiel Cole, 129–32, 147–49; Halfway Covenant membership, 8–9, 111–15, 124, 126, 133–34; land sales, 117–18; Noepe/Martha's Vineyard: 7, 10, 13, 14, 15, 26, 38–40, 42, 48–49, 189n14

O'Brien, Jean, xvi, 41, 77
orthodoxy, Congregational, 26, 51, 135, 137, 146; departures from, 48, 51, 89, 129, 143; and the Halfway Covenant, 108–9
owning the covenant, 8–9, 106, 108–9, 110–14, 119–20, 124, 133

Parkman, Rev. Ebenezer: accounts of councils, 139–40; and Ezekiel Cole, 132, 134, 146, 148–49
Payson, Rev. Edward, 24, 160–62
Peabody, Rev. Oliver: admonition to Jacob Chalcom, 81–85; commitment to mixed church body, 9, 152–53, 158, 162–67; death of, 164, 166–67; and the Harvard Corporation, 162–67; incomplete records of, 77, 157–58; invitation to ministry, 158; salary, 25, 164–65; search for records of, 3
Pequossette/Cambridge, 30–31, 49, 95, 105–6
Pezzarossi, Heather Law, 45–46, 132
Phillips, Rev. Samuel: 23, 24; enclosure case, 36; Thomas Miller, 59–62, 64, 67–69, 72–73; records of, 157; salary, 25, 161
Pierce, Frederick Clifton, 130–31
population growth, English, 30–31, 35, 106, 167

Praying Indians, 41–43, 103, 154, 189n5, 191n6
praying towns, 8–9, 101, 107, 191–92n7
preaching: 121, 178–79f (32); Indigenous, 39; orthodox, 25–26, 162–63; separatist, 131–36, 138; lay, 142–46
predestination, 13–14
Prentice, Rev. Solomon: 9, 110, 114, 129; aggravation of church conflict, 141–43, 146–47; bear shooting anecdote, 130; dismissal from Hassanamesit/Grafton, 147; encouraging lay exhorting, 131, 142–45; first church complaint against, 135, 137–38; neglect of church records, 142, 143, 145; preaching separatism to Nipmucs, 132–33; rejection of council result, 143–44
primary sources, xi–xii, 6, 10, 40, 46, 49, 169, 174
Printer, Abigail: birth, 110, 112, 122; death, 123; land sales, 117, 120; marriage, 114
Printer, Ami, 110, 112, 116
Printer, James the, 109–10
Printer, Sarah, 110, 113, 193n17
Printer, Sarah Jr., 110
privacy, spiritual, 8, 14, 90; in rebuke-repent-restore, 16, 77–79, 80, 82, 137, 141
psychic distress, 30–31, 36, 173

rebuke-repent-restore: alignment with Indigenous practice, 22; concept of, 16–17; Jacob Chalcom, 78–85; contrast with civil justice, 17–18, 72; Nathaniel Coochuck, 79–80; Joseph Ephraim Jr., 78; Thomas Miller, 59–75; Joseph Mills, 79; Thomas Peegun, 79; role of admonition in, 81–82
reciprocal relationships: alignment with Indigenous practice, 20–23, 90–91, 96; within church body, 72–74, 113; between church body and new members, 14–15, 108; between churches, 65, 138–40; between Indigenous and English, 10, 41; with natural resources, 33–34
relations of faith, 14–15, 190n20
Revolutionary War, 111, 122, 194n23

sachem, 18, 22–26, 38, 42, 165
sacrament. See communion
salary. See ministers, salary
Salisbury, Neal, 30–31, 44–45, 114, 189n5
salvation, 1, 4, 8, 13–14, 30–31, 82, 92, 96, 105–6. See also assurance
saunkskwa, 18, 22–23, 26
scarcity: in England, 28–30; and psychic distress, 31–37, 121, 173
secular courts. See civil justice
secular society, English, 6, 9–10, 25, 50, 159–60, 173
separatism, 9, 119–20, 124, 129–30, 143, 147–49
Shepard, Rev. Thomas, 10, 30–31, 95
Sherman, Ephraim, 118–20
Sherman, Nathaniel, 118, 120–21
Silliman, Stephen, 45
Silverman, David J., 34, 90
slavery (enslavement): xv, 135, 170; and church participation, 39; Indigenous, 6, 103, 108
spiritual preparation, 8, 14, 26, 49–50, 90, 95–96
spiritual seeking, 21, 35, 95, 49–50, 95, 106, 112–13
survivance, 7, 41–42, 44–45, 48, 110, 154, 188n3
Synod of 1662, 105–6
syncretism, 47, 51

Temple, Abraham, 118–21
testimony, spiritual, 39–40, 64, 78, 93
town: xvi, 169, 177n15; clerks, 4, 118, 125, 195f (24); and congregation, 2, 4–5, 13–16, 20–21, 106–7, 113, 116–17, 122, 154–55, 172; growth of, 9, 25, 35–36, 121, 123; histories, 33, 58–59, 99–100, 130–31, 151–53; and ministers, 25–26, 159–62, 166, 178n28
towns, Indigenous. See Praying Towns

Van Lonkhuyzen, Harold W., 41, 43, 97
vital records, 4, 77, 114, 116, 118, 123, 149

Wampanoag Congregationalism: concept of assurance, 8, 48–49, 90–98; converts, 39–40; deathbed visions, 94–95; generational, 89–90; Mayhew missions to, 38, 89; set prayers, 97
Ward, Hezekiah, 118–19, 121, 196n41

Whipsuppenicke/Marlborough: 2, 118
Wight, Rev. Daniel, 3, 151–56
Willard, Benjamin family, 133–36, 146
Winthrop, John, 17–18, 143
withdrawing from communion, 124, 137–38, 143–44, 146. *See also* communion
worship, role of, 4–5, 13, 16, 21, 50, 103, 120

www.ingramcontent.com/pod-product-compliance
Lightning Source LLC
Chambersburg PA
CBHW030650230426
43665CB00011B/1036